PRIDE AND GLORY

ABOUT THE AUTHOR

William Houston is an author and journalist who has written two books. The first was an unauthorized biography of the late Toronto Maple Leaf owner Harold Ballard, published in 1984. Five years later he wrote *Inside Maple Leaf Gardens: The Rise and Fall of the Toronto Maple Leafs,* which was an investigative look at the final years of the Ballard era. A revised form of that book, titled *Maple Leaf Blues,* came out in paperback a year later. Houston has covered hockey on and off for *The Globe and Mail* in Toronto in the past twelve years. He currently writes features and a daily sports column for the *Globe.*

PRIDE AND GLORY

100 Years of the Stanley Cup

William Houston

McGraw-Hill Ryerson
Toronto   Montreal

First published in 1992 by
McGraw-Hill Ryerson Limited
300 Water Street
Whitby, Ontario, Canada
L1N 9B6

Canadian Cataloguing in Publication Data

Houston, William, 1948 —
    Pride & glory: 100 years of the Stanley Cup

ISBN 0-07-551380-3

1. Stanley Cup (Hockey) — History. I. Title.

GV847.7.H78 1992 796.962'648 C92-095150-3

Photos: Harold Barkley and Bruce Bennett
Cover Design: Dave Hader, Studio Conceptions
Text Design: JAQ

This book was produced for McGraw-Hill Ryerson by Shaftesbury Books, a member of the Warwick Publishing Group, Toronto, Canada.

Printed and bound in Canada

CONTENTS

To Janet,
for a championship season.

ACKNOWLEDGEMENTS

I'm indebted to many. First, a thank you to the editors at McGraw-Hill Ryerson, who have considerate, thorough and supportive. Thanks also to Heather Somerville for promoting the book with her usual vigour, enthusiasm and creativity. And to Jim Williamson, who published my first book eight years ago, and designed and packaged this one.

Many helped in the research, with a name, a phone number, a suggestion or some information. They include Alan Adams, Greg Bouris, Neil Campbell, Jeff Davis, Benny Ercolani, John Halligan, Scott North, Phil Pritchard and Joe Romain. A special thanks to David Johnston, who sold the book idea to McGraw-Hill Ryerson.

And, finally, to my family. To my wife, Janet, for her editing skills and her love; to my mother, Ethel Houston, and sister, Mary Elizabeth, for their support and encouragement over so many years; to my brother-in-law, Richard Arnold, for the computer paper and to my nephew, Andrew, for his sense of humour.

INTRODUCTION

The Dreams That Come True

*H*is close friends call him Stanley. He sits in a plexi-glass showcase at the Hockey Hall of Fame in Toronto and is accorded the respect deserving of a famous sports icon. For 100 years, he has been coveted and pursued by the world's best hockey players. Stanley symbolizes winning and success. But he is also about dreams and aspirations. It could be a child's fantasy of skating triumphantly on the ice with the Stanley Cup in his arms. For those who play in the National Hockey League, it is the dream of climbing the mountain, of reaching the summit and grabbing professional hockey's greatest prize. It is the recognition of excellence. The confirmation that you are the best. That the pinnacle has been reached.

The Stanley Cup serves as a continuum in the history of game, a passing of the mantle from one era to another, from one team of hockey players to the next. It is a never-ending legacy, the experience of which is lived vicariously by every child who loves the game, but realized by very few.

In his youth Ted Kennedy, a star with the Toronto Maple Leafs during the team's glory years of the Forties, listened to Leaf games on the radio and dreamed of someday following in the footsteps of his heroes, Joe Primeau and Charlie Conacher. Jean Beliveau, the elegant captain of the Montreal Canadiens, cheered for Maurice (Rocket) Richard. Beliveau, in turn, was the idol of New York Islander captain Denis Potvin. Mark Messier was mesmerized by Bobby Orr and vividly remembers Orr's two Cup-winning goals in 1970 and 1972. Wayne Gretzky worshipped Gordie Howe, a man they called Mr. Hockey when Detroit was winning four Stanley Cups in the Fifties.

Gretzky once said, in comparing America's favourite pastime to Canada's national game, "Baseball players dream of getting into the Hall of Fame. Hockey players dream of winning the Stanley Cup."

Hockey, in many ways, defines the Canadian soul. If Americans champion freedom of the individual and entrepreneurship, Canadians, living in a cold and often harsh climate, deal in the collective, of working together for a common goal. That is what the Stanley Cup is all about. The pride and glory of winning as a team.

Howe, one of hockey's most honoured players, says that if it came to a choice, he would cash in all his personal awards for a Stanley Cup. Potvin concurs. "Any player I know would trade the Hall of Fame for a Stanley Cup," he says.

"What I remember most," says Craig Simpson, who played on two championship teams in Edmonton, "is not me winning the Cup. It is the memory of everybody on the team coming together. It's going to the wall for each other and coming through it."

In the hearts and minds of the players, the championship years hold a special place. Mario Tremblay, who was on four Cup winners in Montreal, says, "When I look back, they were the most enjoyable years of my life." Clark Gillies won four Stanley Cups with the New York Islanders, but he does not recall the playoffs with any great fondness. "It's six weeks of misery," he says. "It's just a wretched life. The rest of the world doesn't really exist because you're totally devoted to what you're doing. But when you get to the end, it's unbelievable. The payoff is more than worth it."

Gillies now works as a retail broker for an investment brokerage firm in New York. Whatever the rewards that come from his job, he knows that he will never again experience the thrill, the rush of adrenalin, the ecstasy of a Stanley Cup triumph. "I miss it," he says. "It was incredible."

"It was a fabulous feeling, like nothing else in the world," says Paul Coffey, a four-time Cup winner. When Coffey was growing up in Weston, Ontario, Paul and friends would fashion a Stanley Cup out of wood and award it to the winner of their road hockey game. Then they would carry it around, just that way the pros do. Denis Potvin recalls, "I grew up in a French Canadian family and my idol was Jean Beliveau. I don't know how many times in the Fifties and Sixties I watched Beliveau hoist the Stanley Cup and carry it over his head in the Forum. When I was handed the Cup in 1980 from Mr. Ziegler [the NHL president] I lifted it over my head and the flashbacks I had were incredible—seeing Beliveau and others carrying the Cup. It was an incredible feeling."

Howe calls the Stanley Cup the "unknown factor." He says, "You know when you have a great team. And you know when you've had a great year. But you never know about the Stanley Cup."

The Stanley Cup might be the most recognizable sports trophy in the world. The original cup that was awarded by Lord Stanley of Preston in 1893 is a conventional bowl made of a silver and nickel alloy, 7-1/2 inches deep and 11-1/4 inches across. It is the base that makes Stanley unique. The bowl sits atop a three-tiered collar which in turn rests on a large barrel that is 18 inches across at its base. In total, the silver trophy weighs 32 pounds and is 35-1/2 inches high.

The Stanley Cup has grown in size out of necessity. The practice of inscribing all the names of the team members on the trophy started in 1925, and in the ensuing years silver bands were attached to make room for the new champions. In the earliest years, the winners engraved the name of their teams right on the bowl.

Eventually, the silversmiths ran out of space. When that happened, a band was retired to the Hall of Fame and replaced by a blank panel ready to be filled with names of new champions. The old bands are in safe keeping, except for one. The ring that contains the names of the 1929-30 Boston Bruins has been missing for years. Archivists at the Hall of Fame suspect the Montreal Canadiens removed it and had it melted down into a small trophy for Toe Blake to commemorate his retirement as coach in 1968. In his book on the Canadiens, the club's long-time publicity director, Claude Mouton, wrote, "Blake was given a trophy made in part of silver from the very first Stanley Cup. Toe — Mister Stanley Cup— really deserved nothing less than that."

In addition to the winners' names, anomalies, spelling errors and corrections can be found. Only three women make the list: Marguerite Norris, who was president of the Detroit Red Wing championship teams of the Fifties, Sonia Scurfield, a part-owner of the 1989 Stanley Cup champion Calgary Flames, and Marie Denise DeBartolo York, the president of the 1991 champion Pittsburgh Penguins. The fathers of both Norris and deBartolo York were club owners: James Norris of the Red Wings and Edward J. DeBartolo Sr. of the Penguins.

Bob Gainey's name on the 1975-76 panel is spelled without an "e." Montreal Maroon general manager and coach Eddie Gerard is missing an "r" in his last name on the 1925-26 team. On the 1937-38 panel of Chicago Blackhawks, Pete Palangio shows up twice, once as himself and in another spot as simply "Palagio." The 1962-63 Leafs are spelled "Leaes." When the names of the 1983-84 Edmonton Oilers were inscribed, owner Peter Pocklington submitted the name of his father, Basil Pocklington. The league didn't allow this, so below Peter's name we now see 16 x's.

Stanley is the oldest trophy competed for in North American professional sport, although it should be noted the America's Cup for yachting was first awarded in 1851. In the beginning, the Stanley Cup was designated as a challenge trophy, to be awarded to the top amateur team in Canada. At the trustees' discretion, any team could challenge for the Cup, and in the early years, challengers came from some of the most remote regions of Canada. The most colourful quest involved a team from the Yukon that travelled in the dead of winter in 1905, at considerable risk, from Dawson City to Ottawa to play the Silver Seven.

In the early days, challenges could amount to one game, or a total-goal series or best-of-three or best-of-five series. The last challenge took place in 1926 when the Stanley Cup defending champions, the Victoria Cougars of the Western Hockey League played the Montreal Canadiens of the National Hockey League. Montreal won the series and from then on the Cup was competed for only by NHL teams. In 1946-47, responsibility for the Cup was officially transferred to the NHL.

However, a challenge was issued in 1953 by the Cleveland Barons of the American Hockey League. A year earlier, the Barons had applied for an NHL franchise but were turned down. Cleveland had a strong team that included on its roster Fred Shero, who would later gain fame as a coach of the Philadelphia Flyers. But when Cleveland submitted its Cup challenge, it was informed that the Stanley Cup was a closed competition, for major league clubs only. In other words, NHL clubs.

The Stanley Cup has produced more than its share of controversial, as well as tragic, events. In 1907, Owen McCourt, who played for a team from Cornwall, Ont., was killed in a stick fight during a playoff game between Ottawa and Cornwall. Charges were laid, but there was no conviction because witnesses couldn't be sure who wielded the death blow. Cornwall subsequently resigned from the league and Ottawa was awarded the series. Kenora went on to win the Cup that year.

In 1919, the Stanley Cup final between the Montreal Canadiens and Seattle was cancelled when an outbreak of influenza spread through the Montreal team. Thirty-seven-year-old Joe Hall, Montreal's star player, was sidelined with a high fever and died a few days later in a Seattle hospital. There is no official Stanley Cup champion for 1919. In 1925 the playoffs were disrupted again, this time by a threatened strike. When the Hamilton Tigers demanded $200 each to play in the two playoff games against Montreal, the NHL acted swiftly, suspending the players and awarding the series to Montreal, who headed West to play Victoria for the Cup.

Players in those days received nothing for competing in the playoffs. The honour of winning the Stanley Cup was expected to be enough. Indeed, over the years, pride has been the principal motivation for winning. Even today, players don't technically get paid for their work in the post-season. Their paycheques, considerable as they are, stop at the end of the regular season.

The bonus money for winning the Cup has always been small. Early in this century, each member of the Ottawa Silver Seven was awarded a silver nugget. By 1955, each player received a $1,000 bonus. By 1991, this amount had increased to $25,000 per winner. But it still wasn't much, considering that players had to perform in as many as 28 playoff games to win the championship. That is an average of about $1,000 per game, which is well below what the lowest paid player in the NHL makes per game during the 80-game regular season.

That was one of the reasons the NHL players went on strike in April, 1992. They wanted more of the playoff revenue. And they got it. In the new collective agreement, total prize money for the players was increased from $3.2 million to $7.5 million in 1992 with a further increase to $9 million for 1993. As a result, each member of the 1992 champions earned $40,000, which was a jump of $15,000 from the previous year.

In the beginning, the Stanley Cup was about pride, personal honour, and bragging rights. Today, the Cup, which originally cost less than $50, is about money. Ticket prices are hiked significantly for playoffs and a club that goes all the way could end up with as many as 16 extra home games. With a gross at the gate of more than $400,000 per game, a club stands to earn as much as or more than $6 million in ticket revenue alone. In terms of television money, the Canadian Broadcasting Corporation earns about $50 million in advertising revenue from the playoffs each year.

But for the fans, the Stanley Cup is not about the bottom line. It is about famous players, teams and achievements. It is the story of Mel (Sudden Death) Hill of the Boston Bruins scoring the overtime winner in three consecutive games, including the seventh game winner, against the New York Rangers in 1939. It's about Maple Leaf defenceman Bill Barilko knocking in the overtime winner against the Montreal Canadiens in 1951 to give the Leafs their sixth Stanley Cup in 10 seasons; he died tragically that summer in a airplane accident. We remember Guy Lafleur scoring the tying goal late in the third period of the seventh and deciding game of the 1979 Boston-Montreal series to keep the Canadiens' hopes alive for four straight Cups. Five years later, a young Mark Messier thrilled hockey fans in Edmonton by leading the Oilers to their first championship with a crucial goal in the third game of the final.

One of the early Stanley Cup heroes was Lester Patrick, the manager and coach of the New York Rangers. In 1928, the Rangers were in the final against the Montreal Maroons when Lorne Chabot, one of the best goaltenders of that era, was knocked unconscious by a shot from Nels Stewart of the Maroons. Chabot was rushed to Royal Victoria Hospital and found to have a severe concussion.

Teams carried only one goaltender in those days, but that night there were two sitting in the stands, Alex Connell of the Ottawa Senators and Hughie McCormick, a netminder with a London, Ontario, team of the Canadian Professional League. But to use either one, permission was needed from the manager of the Maroons, Eddie Gerard.

Gerard and Patrick went back six years to when Patrick was coaching the Vancouver Millionaires in a Cup series against the Toronto St. Pats. Vancouver won two of the first three games, partly because Toronto's defence was ravaged by injuries. When St. Pats' manager Charlie Querrie asked Patrick's permission to use Eddie Gerard, who played for another Ontario team, Patrick graciously agreed. With Gerard in the lineup, Toronto won the next two games and the Stanley Cup.

Six years later, Patrick might have expected Gerard to repay the earlier favour. But when he asked permission to use Connell, Gerard sent a note back saying, "Hell no, you can't use Connell."

Another note was sent by Patrick asking if McCormick could go in the net. "Forget it," replied Gerard. "Play goal yourself."

Patrick was furious. When he told his players, Frank Boucher, his star, said, mostly in jest, "Why *don't* you play goal."

Patrick was 45 years old, his hair was gray, he was out of shape and he hadn't played hockey in seven years. Furthermore, he had played goal only a few minutes in his entire life. Still, he strapped on Chabot's pads, put on his goaltender's skates which were too big for him, and took his place in the Ranger net. Newspaper reports would call him tough and courageous, but he said later he was just plain frightened. So awkward did Patrick appear that his players were afraid to take hard shots on him during the warmup.

When the puck dropped, the Rangers fought fiercely to protect their goaltender. Still, the Maroons had a fine team and Patrick was called upon to make some important saves. But Montreal couldn't beat him and the second period ended with New York clinging to a 1-0 lead.

However, early in the third, Nels Stewart, the man who had knocked Chabot out of the game, skated in alone on Patrick, faked a shot and then lifted the puck over him to tie the game. Into overtime they went. Stewart had four shots on Patrick during overtime but couldn't beat him. Then, in the eighth minute, Ching Johnson and Boucher took off down the ice and into the Montreal zone. As Maroons goaltender Clint Benedict came out to meet the attackers, Johnson slid the puck over to Boucher who slammed it into the net.

Triumphantly, the Rangers rushed to Patrick, and as they carried him off the ice, he wept. Moved by his remarkable performance, the Montreal fans stood up and cheered him. The Silver Fox, as he was called, was an inspiration to the Ranger players and they went on to defeat the Maroons with another goalie (Gerard, this time, gave his permission) and won the Cup. The Rangers would win the championship again in 1933 and 1940, but, today, they are remembered as one of the "original six" that has gone the longest without a championship. In the spring of 1992 it was 52 years and counting.

Winning the Stanley Cup, as the Rangers know, is not an easy task. Today, NHL teams must endure three gruelling best-of-seven series just to get to the final. By then they will have played at least 100 games, counting the regular season, in a rough, body contact sport. Players fortunate enough to win a Stanley Cup say it takes years to fully appreciate what they were able to accomplish. "You don't realize how hard it is, until later, when you look back," says Coffey.

For the players, the initial celebration is a hazy mixture of delirium and ecstasy. The buzzer sounds, the winners pour off the bench, the Cup is wheeled onto the ice and, in one of the most moving and spectacular celebrations in sport, the captain of the winning team hoists the huge trophy over his head and, with his teammates at his side, triumphantly circles the ice with his prize.

This isn't always the way the Cup was presented. Until the Fifties, the players stood around a table that held the trophy and sipped champagne in a manner not unlike guests at a cocktail party. But that changed with Ted Lindsay in 1950. Lindsay was a fierce competitor once described by *Look* magazine as a "a blood-red flash of cold fury." It took the Red Wings seven games, the deciding game of which lasted two overtime periods, to eliminate the New York Rangers. When Lindsay saw the trophy sitting on the table, he surprised everyone by picking it up and lifting it over his head.

"I was young, foolish and excited," Lindsay said. "It was an impulsive sort of thing. Everybody's emotions were running high and I guess mine were a little higher."

Lindsay didn't know it at the time, but he had started a tradition. After that, the champions hoisted the Cup, like warriors celebrating the spoils of battle, and skated for all to see with their prize.

Stanley may be loved and desired, but he's not always treated with respect. In addition to being toasted with champagne, hugged and kissed, and even slept with, he has been kicked, dunked at least twice, kidnapped, stolen, dented, battered, bounced and bruised, urinated on and defecated upon. So badly abused was the trophy in 1988 that it had to be taken to an Edmonton auto body shop by Oiler coach and general manager Glen Sather for repairs before it was returned to the league.

Some of the early Cup tales have become part of the game's lore, and although perhaps embellished over time, there is no evidence to suggest the stories are inaccurate. In 1905, for example, after a night of revelry the Cup was drop-kicked into the Rideau Canal by one of the members of Ottawa's Silver Seven, several of whom were accomplished football players. The next morning, one of the Seven returned to haul it out.

In a series played in 1907 between the Rat Portage (Kenora, Ontario) Thistles and the Montreal Wanderers, one of the officials on the Thistles became upset because he believed Montreal was using ineligible players. At one point, the official grabbed the Cup and threatened to throw it into Lake of the Woods.

A few weeks later, the Wanderers left the Cup at the home of a photographer whom they had hired to take the team picture. Apparently a young man stopped by, saw the Cup, and made off with it, hoping to extract ransom money for its return. However, nobody expressed any interest in retrieving Lord Stanley's gift, so the thief returned it to the photographer's home, where it served as a flower pot for next several months until it was reclaimed by the Wanderers.

It was almost lost again in 1924, after a night of celebration by the Canadiens at Montreal's Windsor Hotel. En route to the home of the club owner Leo Dandurand, they stopped to change a flat tire. It wasn't until several hours later that they realized they had left the Cup on the curb. Fortunately, it was still there when they returned.

In 1962, a Montreal Canadiens' fan attempted to steal the Cup from a display case in the Chicago Stadium. The Blackhawks, the defending champions, were leading the Canadiens in the semi-final, which was too much for the fan to accept. He broke the glass and attempted to make off with the trophy, but was quickly apprehended.

It should be known that the original bowl no longer sits atop the trophy barrel. In 1967 a replica was made from sterling silver to replace the original which was old and brittle. The NHL was concerned it would shatter, given the rough treatment it sometimes received. So Lord Stanley's original was retired permanently to the Hall of Fame. However, no one was aware of the switch until 1970 when the Cup was stolen and ransomed for $100,000. At that point, NHL president Clarence Campbell was forced to admit publicly the stolen Cup was not the real thing. Eventually, the Cup was returned without a ransom being paid.

Stanley was almost stolen one last time, in 1977, but the heist was thwarted when an employee at the Hockey Hall of Fame spotted seven men with a large tool bag near the trophy case. The police were called and the would-be thieves fled. Today, the Cup periodically is removed from the Hall of Fame and displayed in cities and towns in promotional excursions. When the Stanley Cup playoffs are over, the winning team keeps the Cup for several weeks. This is called the players' "time" with Stanley. Each player gets to take him home for a day or two, but most often, Stanley shows up in bars and restaurants, or is the featured guest at private parties. Sometimes players show surprising creativity it what they do with the trophy, and occasionally, disgusting vulgarity.

Players, in drunken stupors, have been known to urinate in the Cup. The late Dick Beddoes once wrote about Gordon Pettinger, an English-born centre with the Detroit Red Wings in the Thirties. When the Wings won their second consecutive Cup in 1937, Pettinger joined in the celebration in the club's dressing room by pulling down his pants and emptying his bowels in the bowl. When coach and manager Jack Adams discovered Pettinger's desecration of hockey's holy grail, he was shocked. "The gall of the son of a bitch," Adams told Beddoes years later. "Imagine: taking a shit in the Stanley Cup! First chance I got, I shipped the bastard to Boston."

The players, today, are less crude and more creative in their treatment of Stanley. Bryan Trottier, then with the New York Islanders, and his wife shared a bed with the trophy one night. Trottier said he just wanted to know what it would be like to sleep with the Stanley Cup.

When the Oilers won their fourth Cup, Messier and some of his teammates took the trophy onto the stage of an Edmonton strip club. It was probably the first time Stanley danced with naked women. Clark Gillies dished Kennel Ration into the Cup so his pet dog could join in the celebration. Guy Lafleur astonished his neighbours by sitting the Cup at the front of his house like an expensive lawn ornament. In the summer of 1991, Stanley ended up at the bottom of Mario Lemieux's swimming pool after a teammate took a dive with the Cup in his arms.

In addition to the antics, there are some moving human-interest stories. During the Islanders' winning years, Denis Potvin's father fought a losing battle with lung cancer. So when New York won the Cup, Potvin took it to his father's home in Ottawa. Armand Potvin had been a good hockey player himself and a member of the same junior team as Maurice Richard in the 1930s. When Denis arrived, he proudly presented the Cup to his father. "As weak as he was, he grabbed it and held it over his head," Denis says. "He looked at the names inscribed on the Cup, names of people he had played against in Junior A hockey. Those were my special moments."

Special moments, special memories, special dreams.

"The first Stanley Cup sticks in my memory," says Red Kelly, who starred with the Detroit Red Wings in the Forties and Fifties and the Leafs in the Sixties. "We had a young team in Detroit and we grew up together."

"Our fourth Cup was something special," Mike Bossy of the New York Islanders says. "We weren't supposed to win against Edmonton. But we played perfect hockey and defeated some great players. That was very special."

"Winning any Stanley Cup," says Gordie Howe, "is the ultimate."

One of the reasons the Stanley Cup is such a coveted prize is its domination by such a small number of teams. In a period of 100 years, six teams have held the Cup for 58 years. This concentration of power has only enhanced the mystique of the trophy and the glamour of the teams that have won it.

The six teams have produced eight dynasties. In this book, we take a look at these terrific Stanley Cup successions. We study their success and profile the talented and colourful people who made them great. From One-Eyed Frank McGee to Wayne Gretzky, it's been a wild 100 hundred years. Just ask Stanley.

1

Frank McGee
and the Silver Seven

*T*o find the soul of hockey, to identify a region that nurtured it, allowed it to grow, and played a significant role in making it great, we look to Ottawa. The nation's capital gave us hockey's first glamour team, the Silver Seven. It produced the game's first superstar, a remarkable young man named Frank McGee. And it bestowed upon hockey its most important and enduring symbol, the Stanley Cup.

Ottawa's relationship with hockey became important in the late 1880s, when the highest political office in the country took an interest in the new winter game. In Canada's early years, Governors General played important roles in developing a sports culture. The Marquis of Lansdowne encouraged rifle shooting competitions. The Earl of Minto donated the Minto Cup for a national lacrosse competition. Earl Grey offered the Grey Cup for rugby football. Hockey's patron was the Right Honourable Sir Frederick Arthur Stanley, Baron Stanley of Preston, in the county of Lancaster; in the Peerage of Great Britain, Knight Grand Cross of the Most Honourable Order of Bath, son of the Earl of Derby, Governor General of Canada from 1888 to 1893.

Before his Canadian appointment, Lord Stanley was a prominent English sportsman, actively involved in horse racing, cricket and soccer. After completing his term as Governor General, Stanley introduced hockey to England. Imagine, if you will, a scene in the winter of 1895 on a frozen pond on the grounds of Buckingham Palace in which five members of the Stanley family played the Palace team which included the Prince of Wales (later King Edward 7th) and the Duke of York (who became King George the 5th).

We can assume their match was of a genteel nature compared with the game Lord Stanley saw for the first time in 1888. Hockey then was violent and often brutal. In 1875, McGill University students participated in the first organized game played indoors, but it degenerated into a brawl in which "heads were bashed, benches smashed and lady spectators fled in confusion," according to Kingston, Ont., hockey historian William Fitsell.

In 1887, a reporter for the Toronto *Mail* covered a game played between the Ottawa Parliamentary and Vice-Regal team and the St. George's Granite Club of Toronto, and was appalled. He wrote: "Hockey is one of the most popular winter games in Ontario, Montreal and Quebec and other Eastern cities, while in Toronto the game has not been extensively played. There can be no doubt that the matches played on Saturday will have the effect of popularizing the game in the city so long as it is kept free from such objectionable features as took place in the afternoon game in the Granite rink. It is greatly to be regretted that in a game between amateur teams, some players should so forget themselves before such a number of spectators, a good proportion of whom on the occasion referred to being ladies, as to indulge in fisticuffs, and the actions of some of the spectators of rushing on the ice is also to be condemned...."

These elements obviously didn't dissuade Lord Stanley. He went ahead and built an outdoor rink and organized his own team, the Rideau Hall Rebels, which consisted of members of the Coldstream Guards as well as Stanley's two sons, Arthur and Algernon. Despite their high social position, the two boys weren't out of place on a rink. In Ottawa, hockey was a game played by wealthy sportsmen and sons of high-ranking civil servants, as well as ordinary folks.

Lord Stanley's decision to honour amateur hockey by donating a challenge cup was announced at a banquet in March, 1892, for Ottawa's top senior team, the Ottawa Hockey Club, which was usually referred to as the Ottawas, later to be known as the Silver Seven and then finally renamed the Senators. Lord Stanley's proposal was read to the assembled guests by his aide, Lord Kilcoursie.

"I have for some time been thinking it would be a good thing if there were a challenge cup which could be held from year to year by the leading hockey club in Canada. There doesn't appear to be any outward or visible sign of the championship at present. Considering the interest that hockey matches now elicit and the importance of having the games played under generally recognized rules, I am willing to give a cup that shall be annually held by the winning club.

"I am not quite certain that the present regulations governing the matches give entire satisfaction. It would be worth considering whether they could not be arranged so that each team would play once at home and once at the place where their opponents hail from."

His offer was readily accepted and Lord Stanley immediately commissioned a leading silversmith in London to craft a silver bowl with an interior finish of gold, sitting atop a cherrywood base. In the early years, it would be referred to as the Lord's "rose bowl." It cost 10 pounds sterling or the equivalent then of $48.67 Canadian dollars.

Two Ottawa trustees were named as Cup administrators, Philip D. Ross, a member of Stanley's Rideau Hall team and later the publisher of the Ottawa *Journal,* and John Sweetland, the Sheriff of Ottawa. They were responsible for the Cup rules set down by Lord Stanley and the trustees:

1. **The winners were to give bond for the return of the Cup in good order when required by the trustees for the purpose of being handed over to any other team who may in turn win.**
2. **Each winning team to have at their own charge engraved on a silver ring fitted on the Cup for the purpose of the name of the team and the year won.**
3. **The Cup shall remain a challenge cup and will not become the property of any team, even if won more than once.**

4. **In case of any doubt as to the title of any club to claim the position of champions, the Cup shall be held or awarded by the trustees as they might think right, their decision being absolute.**
5. **Should either trustee resign or otherwise drop out, the remaining trustee shall nominate a substitute.**

There was never any doubt that Stanley's wish was for Ottawa to be the first team to win the cup. In fact, it has been speculated that he donated the trophy with the explicit intent of rewarding his favourite senior team. For its part, the Ottawa club seemed to feel it had a right to be the first recipient of the trophy.

In the winter of 1893, Ottawa enjoyed a splendid season. It won the Ontario Hockey Association championship and finished second to the Montreal Amateur Athletic Association hockey club in the Amateur Hockey Association of Canada.

Ottawa, in fact, would have tied Montreal for top spot in the AHA but for a shocking loss to the Montreal Victorias in the first game of the season. It would turn out to be the Victorias' only win, but it was enough to keep Ottawa out of first place.

When it came time to determine who would compete for the Stanley Cup, the trustees found themselves in a quandary. They wanted the Ottawas to win the trophy. After all, it was Lord Stanley's wish. But they had to appear to be fair.

The trustees finally decided that the top two teams in the OHA would play for the championship. Ottawa would take on Toronto's Osgoode Hall team in a game played in Toronto. Ottawa was incensed. As the first-place finisher in the OHA, it felt it deserved home-ice advantage. Heated exchanges followed, and finally Ottawa decided not to play. And that's how the first year of Stanley Cup competition ended—in a stand-off, with no games played, no series to determine a winner. Several weeks later, the Cup was quietly awarded to the Montreal Amateur Athletic Association, the champions of the AHA of Canada and a team that should have been competing for the Cup anyway. It was a singularly shabby debut for Lord Stanley's prized trophy.

4

It would be 10 years before an Ottawa team would win the Cup. In the period between 1893 and 1903, the Ottawas experienced more than their share of disappointments. After losing to Montreal in the 1894 AHA final, they fell on hard times, failing to qualify for Cup competition in the next two years. The most embarrassing setback occurred in 1900 when Ottawa was scheduled to play the Montreal Shamrocks in a challenge, but failed to ice the required seven players and had to default and pay a $100 fine.

But despite this humiliation, Ottawa's future was bright. For starters, a star player was returning. Harvey Pulford had taken a year off to recover from a broken collarbone, suffered while playing rugby football. Pulford was a brilliant athlete, nationally renowned for competing in football, lacrosse, rowing, paddling, squash and boxing. In hockey, he was a defender who played almost seven years before scoring his first goal for Ottawa. He was neither a good skater nor stickhandler, but a strong checker and invaluable team leader, and was captain during Ottawa's glory years.

In 1901, with the help of Pulford, Ottawa dominated the new Canadian Amateur Hockey League with a perfect 7-0 record, but was unable to challenge for the Stanley Cup. Ottawa didn't clinch the CAHL championship until the final week of February and by then a team from Winnipeg, the Vics, had already defeated Montreal in a challenge series. Because of the lateness of the season and the questionable ice, it was decided there was not sufficient time to hold a series between Winnipeg and Ottawa, which, in those days, involved a considerable amount of planning and travel. The following year, the Ottawa club was foiled again when Montreal won the CAHL title and thus earned the right to challenge Winnipeg.

But in 1903, the Senators' fortunes changed radically with the arrival of a young man by the name of Frank McGee. McGee is usually referred to in historical terms as "One-Eyed Frank McGee," which might evoke an inaccurate image of a rough, grizzled, hard-bitten warrior. McGee was none of those things. He was 24 when he joined the team. He was tall, fair, good-looking, a smart dresser and known for always wearing a clean, pressed uniform.

He was also from one of Canada's most famous families. His uncle had been the Honourable Thomas D'Arcy McGee, a member of parliament and father of Confederation, an Irish Canadian from Montreal who was assassinated in 1868 by a terrorist from the radical separatist Feinian group. Frank's father, J.J. (John Joseph) McGee, was the Clerk of the Privy Council.

Frank's nephew, also with the name Frank McGee, is a former Progressive Conservative member of parliament who served in Prime Minister John Diefenbaker's cabinet as a minister without portfolio. In 1984, he was appointed to the Senate's intelligence review committee. Today, he's a citizenship court judge in Toronto.

McGee quite rightly refers to his uncle as "the Wayne Gretzky of his era." He notes that Frank was an all-round athlete who was involved in "rowing in the spring, lacrosse in the summer, football in the fall and hockey in the winter." In hockey, McGee's scoring exploits were legendary. He was also fearless, risking complete loss of eyesight by choosing a career with Ottawa in the senior league after being blinded in one eye by a stick in a pickup game against Cornwall several years earlier.

Frank played his first game with Ottawa in January, 1903, against Montreal, the Stanley Cup champions. Ottawa hammered Montreal 7-1, with McGee scoring two goals, all of which led to an Ottawa *Citizen* report: "It was McGee's first appearance as a senior hockeyist and he showed that he was qualified to stay with the finest in the land and finish strong. Frank was at centre and he invariably got the better of the face off. He followed up fast and was always in the vicinity of the puck."

In early February, Ottawa played the Montreal Victorias, and this time McGee amazed the crowd, which included the Governor General Lord Minto and a party from Government House, with an offensive display rarely seen in that era. In a 7-6 Ottawa victory, McGee scored five goals.

The *Citizen* noted that McGee had "worked like a beaver" and that Lord Minto had been "pleased." And so began, in the early months of 1903, the legend of Frank McGee and his scoring prowess. Some hockey historians will argue that Russell Bowie of the Montreal Victorias was the best player of this era. Indeed, Bowie's achievements were remarkable. He played 10 years in the Canadian Amateur Hockey League and led the league in scoring five times. In a total of

80 regular season games, he scored 234 goals, which, as historian Charles Coleman noted, "puts him in a class by himself." McGee, on the other hand, played only four years of senior hockey. He led the league in scoring once and finished with 71 goals in 23 games. The important difference between the two centre/rovers was that McGee led a team that held the Stanley Cup for three consecutive years and withstood eight challenges. Frank was at his best in the Cup challenges and without him there would have been no dynasty in Ottawa. Bowie, on the other hand, never won a Stanley Cup and wasn't a factor in the Victorias' three post-season series during his career, scoring only one goal in four games.

In the 1903 season, the Ottawas and the Montreal Victorias were the dominant teams of the Canadian Amateur Hockey League's regular season, both finishing with a record of six wins and two losses. Appropriately, the two met in the Stanley Cup two-game final, providing an opportunity for McGee and Bowie to go head to head. The first game was played in Montreal on bad ice and ended 1-1. Neither McGee nor Bowie scored, but Frank was effective, according to reports, while Bowie, a normally clean competitor, got in an altercation with one of the Ottawa players and didn't perform well. Back home, the Ottawa team took control early and crushed the Victorias 8-0. McGee was spectacular, leading the team with three goals.

Next up were the Thistles from Rat Portage, a small town in northwestern Ontario later to be renamed Kenora. According to the rules set down by Lord Stanley, any team in Canada could challenge for the Cup, providing it paid its way and was adjudged a suitable contender by the trustees. In those days, the Cup champion was required to defend the title two, perhaps three, and occasionally four times in a year. So it was that the Thistles travelled to Ottawa. The venture cost the visitors a total of $1,300, but the two games weren't well attended at Dey's Arena and Rat Portage not only departed without a win but also short $500.

With the convincing victory over Rat Portage, Canadian hockey not only had a new champion but, as it turned out, the finest collection of athletes ever to play on one team. Both the Victorias and Thistles were outstanding teams in their own right, but Ottawa had handled them quite easily. In the next two years, the Ottawas would continue to dominate and would become the most famous team in the country — a star-studded squad with a handful of players who would eventually be inducted into the Hockey Hall of Fame. In addition to McGee and Pulford, the 1903 Ottawa championship team included goaltender Bouse Hutton, who earned a 2.94 goals-against average despite playing in an era in which goalies wore narrow cricket pads and used a goalie's stick with a blade not much wider than that of an ordinary stick. After McGee, Ottawa's main offensive threat came from Hamilton Livingston (Billy) Gilmour, who scored five goals in Ottawa's four 1903 playoff games.

These were the four major Ottawa stars of 1903 — McGee, Pulford, Hutton and Gilmour — and all four are enshrined in the Hall of Fame. Teams played seven-a-side in those days, the rover being the seventh member. Rounding out the seven on Ottawa was the able defender Art Moore, who played seven seasons for Ottawa, and Billy Gilmour's two brothers Dave and Suddy.

To commemorate the first championship, a silver nugget was bestowed upon each of the seven players by the club's directors. Seven stars on the team, seven pieces of silver. The players on the Ottawa Hockey Club were henceforth called, most appropriately, the Silver Seven.

Regrettably during this period, petty feuds and controversies marred the competitiveness of the Canadian Amateur Hockey League. In 1904, Ottawa arrived late for a game in Montreal against the Victorias. With a delayed start, both teams agreed to call the game at midnight with Ottawa leading 4-1. A week later, the Montreal Shamrocks, slow in getting their baggage from the train, showed up an hour late for a game in Ottawa.

As a result of these incidents, the league fined the Ottawa and Shamrock hockey clubs $10 each, an amount that was later raised to $50. Ottawa was also told it would have to replay its game against the Victorias. This rankled the directors of the Ottawa team. Not only were they forced to pay the $50 fine, but they had to incur the additional cost of travelling to Montreal a second time. Ottawa flatly refused and threatened to resign from the league if forced to play the game. When the league governors stood firm, Ottawa made good its threat and quit with four games remaining in the eight-game season.

However, as Cup champion, Ottawa still had the right to defend its trophy, which it did a total of four of times in 1904. The first, and most determined, challenge came from the Winnipeg Rowing Club. This was a tough team led by Joe Hall, a forward and defender who would later be expelled from the Manitoba Hockey League for rough play. The first game took three hours to play, and when it was over the Winnipeg captain, bandaged and bleeding, told reporters it was dirtiest game he had ever been in. There had been fights, butt-ends, slashing, and, most important for the winners, nine goals for Ottawa to Winnipeg's one.

An overconfident Ottawa team lost the second game 6-2 to Winnipeg, which set up a third and deciding match that observers said later was the most brilliant game played in Ottawa. Others called it the roughest.

In the first 40 minutes, neither team could score; but then McGee, accepting the puck from Pulford, stickhandled through three Winnipeg players and beat the goaltender. That was enough for the win, with Suddy Gilmour getting an insurance goal. The next day, the Winnipeg *Free Press* reported the Rowing Club's casualty list. It began:

> Hospital cases of Rowing Club: P. Brown, lame; C. Richards, face swollen, leg hurt; C. Bennett, thumb broken, badly bruised; W. Breen, bruised and broken up; J. Hall, cut on head; D. Kirby, cut on head; W. Bawlf, cut and bruised. Seven out of nine injured; two forced to retire from game; three forced to remain in bed after game; one out of hockey for season.

The extent to which hockey was violent during this time should not be underestimated. In 1907, for example, a large Montreal crowd watched a game between Ottawa and the Montreal Wanderers, in which there were three major assaults. Ottawa's Baldy Spittal had apparently tried to split Cec Blachford's skull with a full, over-the-head swing of his stick. Blachford was carried off the ice with blood pouring from his head. Alf Smith of Ottawa skated over to the Wanderers' newest player, Hob Stuart, and laid him out with a wild

9

swing of his stick to the temple. Not to be outdone, Harry Smith, Alf's brother, levelled Ernie Johnson of the Wanderers with a stick to the face, breaking his nose. In a page one story, the Montreal *Star* said the guilty players should get six months in jail. "The professional butchers association of Ottawa organized an excursion to Montreal on Saturday," the *Star* reported, "and returned to Ottawa well satisfied with work done."

At a special meeting of the league, it was proposed by the Montreal Victorias and seconded by the Wanderers that Spittal and Alf Smith be suspended. Invoking, perhaps, the old "they were only doing their job" excuse, the proposal was voted down. Dismayed, the league president resigned.

The Montreal police, however, felt they had enough evidence for assault convictions. Two weeks later, when Ottawa returned to Montreal, the Smith brothers and Spittal were arrested. Alf and Spittal were eventually found guilty, fined $20 and told to stay out of trouble. Ernie Johnson's broken nose was not sufficient evidence to convict Harry Smith. He got off.

After their brutal series with Winnipeg, Ottawa quickly sent the Toronto Marlboroughs packing in two consecutive games. On the heels of the Marlies went the Wanderers. They lost a one-game challenge. Finally, a team from Brandon, Manitoba, fell in two games to the Silver Seven. During these 1904 playoffs, McGee wowed the fans with two five-goal games and two more in which he scored three goals. His total was 21 goals over eight Stanley Cup matches.

In the history of the Silver Seven, 1905 is the year best remembered, not only for McGee's magic on the ice, but also for the events that led up to Ottawa's defence of the Stanley Cup in January. The Cup trustees might have first suspected a hoax when in late 1904 they were informed that a team from Dawson City, Yukon Territory, had issued a challenge. As it turned out, promoter Joe Boyle was serious.

The Klondike Gold rush of 1898 had a attracted a boatload of dreamers and adventurers, among them Boyle, who was known as King of the Klondike and "Captain Boyle" because of his daring exploits of navigating prospectors through the dangerous Whitehorse River. Boyle, a native of Woodstock, Ont., worked as a promoter in Vancouver, mainly in boxing, and then headed north to make his fortune. In the Yukon, Boyle struck it rich by leasing 40 acres on the Klondike River from the Canadian government and building a saw mill, developing a hydraulic method of mining, and other facilities needed by the prospectors. During his colourful career, he would claim to almost have saved the Romanovs, the Russian royal family, from the Bolsheviks in 1917. He would later have a much publicized romance with Queen of Romania. In 1904, however, his passion was hockey.

While in Ottawa negotiating a government deal, Boyle convinced the Cup trustees to approve a best-of-three challenge series in January, 1905, between Ottawa and a team he was putting together in Dawson City. They were a youthful, inexperienced group, the youngest a 17-year-old goaltender named Albert Forrest of Trois-Rivières, Quebec. Boyle ran the team with an iron fist. No liquor consumption or tobacco were allowed, and the players were required to take with them on the trip light training apparatus—clubs and dumb-bells—to stay in shape. Indeed, the smoking car of the train that would take them from Vancouver to Ottawa was designated as an area where the players could skip rope and lift weights. As it turned out, their physical endurance was tested to its limit in simply getting to the Ottawa games.

Most of the players on Boyle's team were government workers, and because of local elections they couldn't leave the Yukon until December 19th. The first scheduled game in Ottawa was January 13, less than four weeks away, and ahead of the seven Yukoners who set out was a trip almost 6,000 kilometres in length. The first leg was a distance of 600 km to Whitehorse. From Whitehorse, a train would take them to a steamer in Skagway's harbour. From Skagway, they were to sail by steamer to Vancouver.

Initially, the trek to Whitehorse was seen by the players as a light outing, an opportunity to get in shape. Some took dog sleds, but others, reportedly, chose bicycles. They anticipated covering 80 km per day over hard-packed snow in good time. However, trouble started almost immediately. Shortly after leaving Dawson, there was a thaw that rendered both the dog teams and bicycles useless. So the men walked in slush, water and mud. But again the weather changed, turning bitterly cold. In freezing temperatures, the players' feet blistered and swelled from frostbite. Christmas was celebrated in a small shed 80 km from Whitehorse with the men huddling together to stay alive and warm. The next day they straggled into Whitehorse, exhausted, sore and cold but buoyed by the fact that the most difficult leg of the trip was over. Or so they thought.

The setbacks continued. Snow slides had closed the White Pass railway and delayed the trains leaving for Skagway by two days. As a result, the team missed its connecting steamer. At Skagway, the temperatures suddenly dropped to -48°F, which was enough to stop the steamer S.S. *Dolphin* from docking in the harbour. That caused a further three-day delay.

Time was starting to run out on the players from the Yukon and misfortune continued to plague them. Once aboard the ship, heavy seas and fog resulted in the voyage taking 13 hours longer than expected. Because of the fog, the *Dolphin* couldn't dock at Vancouver or Victoria. Seattle was the only alternative. More time was wasted.

By now, the challengers from the Yukon had caught the imagination of the country. Newspaper reporters were following their progress as their train made its way from Vancouver to Ottawa. At every stop, the players were met by crowds at the station cheering them on. After the train pulled into Winnipeg, the *Free Press* reported, "their efforts to win the greatest hockey trophy in Canada will be watched with interest as the great distances they have come and the hardship of a 450-mile trip over sub-arctic trails on foot cannot but fail to win the sympathy of all lovers of the sport."

It was now January 9 and the players' first scheduled game against Ottawa was only four days away. Finally, at 4:45 p.m., on January 11, they arrived. The *Citizen* described the players as "sturdy young Canadians, who, at an enormous sacrifice of money and a great display of pluck have travelled 4,000 miles from the frigid Yukon gold fields to do battle with the Ottawa hockey club representatives in an attempt to wrest from them the world's championship emblem, the Stanley Cup." They were greeted by a large crowd that included representatives of the Silver Seven, who apparently "looked after the players' wants in fatherly style," according to the *Citizen*.

The Silver Seven, it was often said, were rough players, but they had the curious custom of maiming opponents on the ice and killing them with kindness off the ice. Indeed, the Ottawa club always provided generous hospitality. After a series, they fêted the losers with food and drink and warm words. When the Dawson City boys arrived, Ottawa was magnanimous in its praise, but when it came to a genuine gesture of sportsmanship, the Silver Seven backed off quickly. Before the Dawson City team arrived in Ottawa, representatives had asked the Seven to delay the start of the games by a few days, just long enough to allow the players a rest and get in a few practices. But when they arrived, Ottawa turned them down flat. The first game went as scheduled on January 13.

Forrest, the youngest goaltender to play in Stanley Cup competition, was impressive, but he wasn't enough. The Ottawa players were big, rested, talented and playing at home. They won 9-2.

It was a game that was never in doubt and McGee had not exerted himself, although Forrest had made critical saves on several of his hard shots. For the game, McGee had one goal and had looked quite average, which prompted one Yukon player to say afterwards that the great McGee, the most famous player in Canada, hadn't "looked so hot." Such cheek, even from a team that had endured the hardship that the Dawson City boys had, was not to be taken lightly. Word got back to McGee and in the second game he accomplished something that is likely to forever remain a Stanley Cup record.

In the first half (teams played 30-minute halves in those days) McGee scored four goals. To open the second half, he got another. Then he scored three more in 90 seconds. And then four more in two minutes and 20 seconds. In a period of 8 minutes and 20 seconds he tallied eight consecutive goals. For the night he collected 14 goals in a 23-2 romp. And he had done it playing with an injury later diagnosed to be a broken wrist.

The Dawson City challengers left Ottawa is awe of the Silver Seven, but bitter over the team's unwillingness to adjust the schedule. Even well rested, the hockey players from the Yukon would have been no threat to Ottawa.

The same could not be said for the next challenging team, the Rat Portage Thistles. The Silver Seven had not faced a team as strong as the Thistles. They were led by a superstar of the period, Tom Phillips, who some thought might be a match for Frank McGee. There was no way of telling who was the best in the first game, because McGee was out of the lineup with his injured wrist. As well, the Thistles were using a new piece of equipment, the tube skate, which provided better balance and support and allowed skaters to take longer strides. The first game wasn't even close. Rat Portage skated away with a 9-3 victory.

The Silver Seven were shocked, but they were not without a plan, or so it was rumoured. Inexplicably, the ice for the next game at Dey's Arena was soft and almost slushy. In the bad ice, the tube skates were ineffective. The thin blades cut deeply into the surface and the skaters could barely move. It was widely rumoured that salt had been generously applied to the ice surface, if not by agents of the Silver Seven, at least staunch supporters. Enhancing Ottawa's prospects was the return to the lineup of McGee, who was wearing a protective cast on his wrist. It turned out to be a poorly played, dirty game with elbows, slashes and butt ends. But Ottawa stayed alive, defeating Rat Portage 4-2, which set up a third and deciding game.

Game three was watched by 3,500 spectators and they weren't disappointed. It was rough and exciting, and close right to the end, with each team's superstar dominating the game. Phillips scored twice and so did McGee. With the two teams locked at three and time running out, a numbing tension gripped the capacity crowd. With less than two minutes remaining, McGee had the puck in his own end. Skating with calm determination, he moved into the Thistles' zone; with 90 seconds remaining on the clock McGee lifted the puck past the Thistles' goaltender. The championship stayed in Ottawa.

In addition to his athletic achievements, McGee was a wit and sometimes quite inventive. He knew the series with Rat Portage would be rough and dirty, but also realized the Silver Seven needed him in the lineup. Concerned that the Thistles would attack his injured right wrist, he chose a diversionary tactic, attaching a large metal cast on his good wrist, the left, and supported his broken right wrist with a light cast that couldn't be seen.

The Silver Seven as a group played hard both on and off the ice. One of their better-known escapades was the drop-kicking of the Stanley Cup into the Rideau Canal after the 1905 Cup victory. This followed a night of drinking in a hotel and was probably due to the efforts of one of the football players on the team, perhaps McGee or Pulford.

Many of McGee's practical jokes were exacted at the expense of his teammates. One occurred when the Silver Seven were invited to Government House for a dinner with Lord Minto to commemorate a Cup championship. Few of the players on the Silver Seven had been exposed to the niceties of high society in Ottawa, except for McGee, who came from an distinguished family. So when it came to proper etiquette at the table the team looked to their star player. Before the dinner, McGee told his teammates to relax. "Watch me and do whatever I do. And don't worry about forks. Just use your fingers."

As the dinner progressed, McGee offered further assistance. When the finger bowls arrived, he immediately picked his up and started noisily slurping the water. His teammates dutifully followed course, lifting the bowls to their faces and drinking out of them. If the Governor General was shocked, he didn't show it. He, too, decided it was appropriate that evening to drink from his finger bowl.

These were heady times for the Ottawa hockey players. They were wined and dined and cheered on by the highest levels of Ottawa society. Never before had a Canadian sports team received such attention, and so much fame. They were the best at their sport and, despite an occasional lapse, they performed with class. When they finally lost, it was done with a certain style and courage. They succumbed not easily, but only after a terrible fight. And they fell hard, almost tragically, like a colossus crashing to the ground, or a great thoroughbred stumbling on the home stretch.

In 1906, Ottawa put together a fine record in the regular season and then defeated Queen's University, the representatives of the Ontario Hockey Association, and Smiths Falls of the Federal Amateur Hockey League, in Cup challenges. McGee made Ottawa's two wins against Smiths Falls possible, with five goals in a 6-5 series-opening victory and four more in an 8-2 triumph. To retain the Cup, Ottawa had to defeat the Montreal Wanderers, with whom they had tied in the regular season, but defeated in a tie-breaking Cup challenge in February.

But now it was March and the Ottawa club was tired after turning back earlier challenges by the Wanderers, Queen's and Smiths Falls.

Still, Ottawa was the defending champion and had the experience of playing under pressure, all of which made the result of the opening game unbelievable, impossible to fathom. The Wanderers stunned the Silver Seven, handing them a crushing 9-1 defeat.

The nation's capital was in shock. The players didn't know what to say, other than they would come back. But that didn't seem realistic. It was a two-game total goals series and Montreal already had an eight-goal lead.

Nevertheless, a record crowd of 5,000, including the Governor General and his wife, the Earl and Lady Grey, showed up at Dey's Arena to see their great team attempt a comeback. It started badly, with Montreal jumping into a quick 1-0 lead. But then McGee brought his team back with two goals, and the first half ended with Ottawa ahead 3-1. But in the second, Ottawa fought furiously, moving the count to 4-1, 5-1 and finally 8-1. Now they were only a goal behind in total goals for the series. Minutes later, Harry Smith picked up the puck, barrelled down the ice and drilled the puck into the Montreal net to make it 9-1. The series was even and Dey's Arena rocked in joyful pandemonium. Hats and scarves were thrown on the ice. Even the Governor General leaned over the boards to shake hands with Smith.

On another night in another year, McGee would have won the game for Ottawa, perhaps scoring four or five goals and stickhandling through the Wanderers almost at will. But on this night he did not. He didn't score any goals in the second half. Instead, the Wanderers came back with two goals of their own and the game ended 9-3 for Ottawa, a good showing but not enough for them to keep the Stanley Cup. So it was that the era of the Silver Seven ended. Ottawa would continue to be one of the dominant teams in hockey for years to come and would recapture the Cup, as the Senators, in 1909 and 1911 with new stars such as Fred (Cyclone) Taylor. In the 1909 series, the only holdover from the original 1903 team was Billy Gilmour, and he retired after the championship.

As the game changed, other great players came and went. Following the formation of the National Hockey League in 1917, the Ottawa Senators won Stanley Cups in 1920, 1921, 1923 and 1927, and were led by new stars such Frank Nighbor, Cy Denneny and Jack Darragh.

For his part, McGee retired after the 1906 loss. In the years following, there were consistent rumours that he would rejoin the team for a large amount of money, but he never did. There were probably a host of reasons for his decision to retire after only four seasons. He might have simply tired of the game. Certainly, in his final series against the Wanderers, he had not dominated the way he had in the past. He had accomplished just about everything a player could — league championships, Stanley Cups, personal records, fame — and he didn't need the money. He was a civil servant, employed by the department of Indian Affairs. One of advantages of playing for the Silver Seven was the availability of a government job, usually with Indian Affairs.

There was also the element of danger. The game was violent and, with only the sight of one eye, McGee may have decided not to push his luck. In 1905, for example, he scored three goals in a crucial game against the Wanderers that decided first place, but he also suffered a serious cut to the head. One Montreal newspaper called the game "a saturnalia of butchery."

McGee continued in sports and played football for several years. His final newspaper notice came in 1916. At the outbreak of the First World War, Frank enlisted in the army and served in as a lieutenant in the Canadian army. And in September, 1916, at the age of 37, he was killed in action in Courcelette, France, during the Somme offensive. Just how a man with sight in one eye passed the army's medical examination is anybody's guess. The story the family received from Frank was consistent with some of his other tricks. When he went for his eye examination, the doctor asked him to cover one eye with his hand and read the chart. McGee covered his blind eye. When he was asked to cover the other eye, he switched hands instead of eyes. He put his other hand over the same eye, all done smoothly in the graceful manner of a great athlete.

These are the stories that have been passed on from generation to generation in the McGee family. For the record, we are left with Frank's accomplishments and those of the Silver Seven. In addition to his 71 goals in 23 league games, he had 63 goals in 22 Cup games, which is a record for the pre-NHL period between 1893 and 1918. There was the memorable 14-goal performance, also a record, as well as seven five-goal games during his career. As for the Silver Seven, they did things never equalled before or since. In a period of four years, from 1903 to 1906, they had won 10 challenges, before losing in the eleventh to the Wanderers in March, 1906. During this time, they had outscored the best teams in Canada 161 to 86. In 22 playoff games they had lost only four times. These were the early years of hockey, but the achievements of McGee and Silver Seven were never forgotten. In 1945 Frank and Harvey Pulford were among the first group to be inducted into the Hockey Hall of Fame. In 1950, a poll of sports editors of Canadian newspapers selected McGee and the other members of the Silver Seven as Canada's outstanding team in the first half of the Twentieth Century.

2

The National Hockey League's First Dynasty

*T*oday, Toronto has more women, children and men playing hockey in recreational leagues than any other city in the world. Because of its large population base, Metro Toronto is also the hockey's leading marketplace for everything from NHL licenced products to ice-conditioning machines. It is accurately described as the leading hockey city in the world.

This wasn't always the case. In fact, in the early years, Toronto showed only marginal interest in the game. Ottawa and Montreal were the important hockey towns. Hockey was also popular in Quebec City and in the West. By 1910, when the top leagues — the Canadian Hockey Association and National Hockey Association — were purely professional, Toronto's leading senior team was still playing in a small Ontario league.

Upon completion of a new arena, Toronto was admitted to the NHA in 1913. When the National Hockey League was formed in November, 1917, Toronto was awarded a franchise, as were the Montreal Canadiens, Ottawa Senators and Montreal Wanderers. For the Toronto Arenas, 1917-18 turned out to be a memorable year. Given what would happen to the Toronto teams of the future, it was also appropriate that the first season be fraught with turmoil. The cast of characters would be familiar to followers of hockey in Toronto even 60 years later. Key roles were played by an interfering owner, a tyrannical coach and a group of free-spirited players.

The coach and manager in 1917 was Charlie Querrie, a disciplinarian who immediately laid down the law by posting rules in the dressing room:

---

1. **First and foremost do not forget that I am running this club.**
2. **You are being paid to give your best services to the club. Condition depends a lot on how you behave off the ice.**
3. **It does not require bravery to hit another man over the head with a stick. If you want to fight go over to France. [The First World War was still in progress.]**
4. **You will not be fined for doing the best you can. You will be punished for indifferent work or carelessness.**
5. **Do not think you are putting over something on the manager when you do anything you should not. You are being paid to play hockey, not to be a good fellow.**
6. **I am an easy boss if you do your share. If you do not want to be on the square and play hockey, turn in your uniform to Dick Carroll and go get some other work.**

As it turned out, it was Querrie who decided to seek another line of employment. He suddenly resigned, alleging interference from the team's former owner Eddie Livingstone, a fiery character who had so alienated his fellow owners in the old National Hockey Association, they had formed the new NHL just to get rid of him. "Don't get us wrong, Elmer," Sam Lichtenhein of the Montreal Wanderers told Montreal sportswriter Elmer Ferguson. "We didn't throw Livingstone out. He's still got his franchise in the old National Hockey Association. He has his team and we wish him well. The only problem is he's playing in a league by himself."

Once Querrie was assured that he had absolute control and Livingstone wasn't an owner, Querrie returned and led the team to a tie for first place with the Montreal Canadiens in the NHL's regular season. The Arenas were a solid team, led by three future Hockey Hall of Famers, forwards Cy Denneny and Reg Noble and defence-man Harry Cameron, as well as Jack Adams, who would go on to become the famous general manager of the NHL's Detroit franchise. But the players didn't like Querrie much and rebelled at least once during the season. On one occasion, Cameron and Noble were fined $100 each for walking off the team and refusing to play a game against Montreal.

The Canadiens of that season were a powerful squad led by goaltender Georges Vezina, scoring stars Joe Malone and Newsy Lalonde, as well as tough guy Joe Hall from the old Manitoba league. But in the playoffs they were upset by the Arenas, eliminated in two consecutive games. Toronto went on to win the Stanley Cup in that first year by knocking off the Vancouver Millionaires of the Pacific Coast Hockey League.

But, despite this initial success, the Arenas never really caught on in Toronto. The following year, Querrie continued to feud with his players. He fined Noble and Cameron for missing practices and finally traded Cameron to the Ottawa Senators, who finished first in the league. Toronto ended up last, which did little to kindle fan interest. In an attempt to draw from the city's considerable Irish constituency, the team was renamed the St. Patricks in 1919, but the results were only marginally encouraging. The St. Pats continued to struggle until 1926 when a group of businessmen expressed interest in buying the team and moving it to Philadelphia.

At that point, an extraordinary young man, Constantine (Conn) Smythe, entered the picture. Smythe was born in 1895 and grew up in Toronto. His father worked as a journalist for the Toronto *World,* performing tasks that included everything from writing editorials to covering horse racing at the Woodbine Race Track. When the elder Smythe went to the track, his son would tag along and courier his dispatches back to the *World* offices. These experiences nurtured in Conn a passion for horses, gambling and a love of most sports, particularly hockey.

Smythe played hockey as a youth and eventually moved into coaching. At the University of Toronto, where he earned a degree in engineering, he coached the varsity team, the Blues, and in 1926, took them to the Canadian collegiate championship. Because of his considerable accomplishments in the game, he got his first big break a few weeks later, when one of the new NHL expansion franchises in the United States, the New York Rangers, offered him the job of coach and manager. Smythe immediately went to work building a team that would go on to win the 1928 Stanley Cup. But by the time that happened, Smythe was long gone. He didn't get along with the club's owner, Colonel John Hammond, and was fired before the Rangers had played a single game.

Conn was short, about 5-feet 6-inches tall, and cocky, and he had a raspy voice that for many sounded a cautionary, if not menacing, note. He was intimidating and he was tough. But most of all, he was ambitious and determined to make his mark in the world. When he learned the St. Pats were up for sale and about to be moved to Philadelphia, he organized a group of investors and convinced them to join him in buying the team. Smythe's share of the $200,000 cost was $20,000. He said that had come from his Ranger severance pay of $10,000, which he doubled by betting on the horses.

Upon taking control in 1927, Smythe's first move was to rename the team the Toronto Maple Leafs, the maple leaf being the Canadian emblem. This wasn't a completely original idea. There happened to be an amateur hockey team in east Toronto during this time called the Maple Leaves. So it was that the Maple Leafs were born. They would become the most popular team in Canada and their success would be matched by only one team, the Montreal Canadiens.

Smythe wasted no time making the Leaf team competitive. With money made from gambling at the track, he bought the great defenceman, King Clancy, from the financially ailing Ottawa Senators for $35,000. In the depth of the Depression, he arranged the financing for the construction of Maple Leaf Gardens. He recruited brilliant young players such as Joe Primeau, Harvey (Busher) Jackson and Charlie Conacher.

His single-most important move may have been making Clarence (Happy) Day a key member of the organization. Hap Day had played for the Arenas and was one of the best defencemen of the day. When Smythe took over the team, he made Day captain of the Leafs and anointed him his unofficial advisor. In the summers, the loyal and hard-working Day ran Smythe's prospering Toronto sand and gravel business. Years later he would coach the Leaf teams of the Forties.

By the time Maple Leaf Gardens opened for business in November, 1931, Smythe's building job with the Leafs had concluded. They were a powerhouse, featuring Clancy and Day on defence, and Ace Bailey, one of the best goal scorers of that era, up front. Red Horner and Baldy Cotton were on hand if the play got rough. The show stoppers were the three young players who made up the flashy Kid Line — Conacher, Primeau and Jackson.

Reminiscing years later, Frank Selke, a hockey man who had worked in the amateur leagues until joining the Leafs as Smythe's assistant in the late Twenties, said: "The Maple Leafs were more than a good team, they were a grand team, and the fireworks were provided by the Kid Line, truly a sight to behold. When they stepped onto the ice, the fans teetered on the edge of their seats, and an electric tension seemed to permeate the entire auditorium. There have been other great forward lines in hockey, but none could match the frenzy that greeted the Kid Line in the mid-Thirties."

In the 1931-32 season, Dick Irvin was behind the Leaf bench, replacing Smythe who felt he couldn't devote enough time to coaching. Irvin had played in the NHL and, the year before joining the Leafs, had coached the Chicago Black Hawks to the Stanley Cup final. Then, for reasons unknown, he suddenly was fired. Irvin would become one of the most successful coaches of all time, but he, too, had his critics, one of whom was Smythe.

The Leafs were reasonably strong in the 1931-32 season, finishing second in the Canadian Division behind the Montreal Canadiens. Over in the American Division, the Rangers had finished first with a record superior to the Leafs. In the playoffs, the league's two leading teams ended up meeting in the semi-finals with the Rangers knocking off the Canadiens. Toronto enjoyed an easier post-season, eliminating Chicago first and then the Montreal Maroons. This, of course, set up the perfect grudge match — Smythe's Leafs against the Rangers, a team he had played a large hand in building, only to be fired. For Smythe, the series turned out to be sweet revenge. The Leafs swept the Rangers in three consecutive games to win the Cup. As Smythe phrased it in his memoirs, "three straight, 6-2, 6-4, 6-2. Like a tennis match."

By then, there was no doubt about the Leaf hockey team surviving in Toronto. The Gardens was selling out every game, partly because the team was winning, but also because Smythe was an outspoken, combative and colourful personality who feuded with other managers and coaches and who provided good copy for the sports pages. So popular were the Leafs that attending a game in Toronto became a significant social occasion. Men dressed in suits and women wore their furs. If a season's ticket holder wasn't properly dressed, a letter from the Gardens would be sent as a reminder of dress standards which must be met.

The Leafs epitomized class, and their success quickly made them the most popular hockey team in Canada, although there was little enthusiasm for them in Quebec where the Montreal Canadiens were *les glorieux*. The Leafs' immense popularity in English Canada could not have happened without Foster Hewitt and his almost-as-good-as-being-there radio broadcasts of the games. Hewitt became the country's first media star, and as Scott Young noted in his biography of Hewitt, the most famous Canadian of his time.

He was the son of William A. Hewitt, who in the Twenties was the sports editor of the Toronto *Daily Star* and secretary of the Ontario Hockey Association. When the *Star* started its own radio station in Toronto, Foster, a cub reporter at the newspaper, worked part-time as an announcer. The first hockey game he called was played at the Mutual Street Arena in 1923.

Smythe quickly saw that radio could be an effective marketing and promotional arm of his team. Soon Hewitt's play by play of the Leaf games was broadcast every Saturday night. When the Gardens was built, Hewitt advised the contractors where his broadcast booth, which became known as the gondola, should be situated. In the Gardens' second season, Hewitt's broadcasts were aired nationally.

One of the most famous Stanley Cup games called by Foster was played in the spring of 1933, a year after the Leafs' first Cup win. It was a bitterly fought semi-final between Toronto and the Boston Bruins. The best-of-five series was tied at two, and after three periods at the Gardens, the teams were locked 2-2 in the fifth game and going into overtime. Howie Meeker, who grew up in Kitchener, Ont., and who was to win the Calder Trophy as the league's top rookie in 1946-

47 with the Leafs, can remember sneaking downstairs late at night as a child, long after being sent to bed, to listen to that game in 1933. "I remember my mother had girls over to play bridge and I turned on the radio real, real low to hear the game," he said. "It was well past midnight, but I was transfixed."

The match stayed deadlocked after one period of overtime, then through two and three, four and five overtime periods. As the night wore on, some fans had left, but others flocked to the arena in the early morning to watch an historic event.

After the fifth overtime period, league president Frank Calder called Smythe and Boston Bruins president Art Ross together and asked them if they would agree on another means of deciding the game. An immediate resolution was necessary. The Cup final was set to start later the same day in New York. A coin toss and even playing without goaltenders were discussed.

The two teams opted for another overtime period, the sixth, and finally at about 1:55 a.m. Meeker and others heard the following description from Hewitt, as he called the play: "There's Eddie Shore going for the puck in the corner beside the Boston net. Andy Blair is on for the Leafs now. He hasn't played as much as the others and seems a little fresher than some. He's moving in on Shore in the corner. Shore is clearing the puck — Blair intercepts! Blair has the puck! Ken Doraty is dashing for the front of the net! Blair passes! Doraty takes it!

"He shoots! He scores!"

Hewitt's ringing announcement, "He shoots! He scores!" expressed in his sharp, crackling voice would thrill thousands of hockey fans for years. So would the Leafs, of whom great things were expected in the Thirties. But in the 1933 Cup final, after Doraty's goal had ended, up to that point, the longest overtime game in Cup history, the Leafs lost to the Rangers. As it turned out, the decade of the Thirties would be remembered for what might have happened, not for what did. The Leafs reached the Stanley Cup final seven times, more than any other team in the league, but after their initial championship in 1932, they were shut out.

As the years passed, the team went into decline. An illegal body check by Eddie Shore in late 1933 put Ace Bailey in the hospital with a fractured skull and ended his career. Day and Clancy grew old and were eventually traded. Conacher and Jackson were famous party-goers but weak leaders. They, too, were moved to other teams. In 1936, Joe Primeau retired at the relatively young age of 30.

Some felt Irvin was at least partly to blame for the lack of success. Although his winning record as a coach is second only to Scotty Bowman's, Irvin's teams often ended up losing important games. His critics complained that he made strange line decisions at crucial times, such as putting on a scorer, who was weak defensively, instead of playing his best checker in the final seconds of a game. "My father always felt that in the clutch, Irvin was not a good coach," Frank Selke Jr. said. "He would beat himself with his strange ways of doing things. It cost him his job in Toronto. When Smythe found out Montreal was looking for a coach, he forced Dick to go there."

With the retirement of Red Horner in 1940, the face of the Leaf team had changed completely from 1932. A new era was beginning and it would be the most successful in the club's history. There would be six Stanley Cups in 10 seasons and new heroes. But the mainstay was Hap Day who replaced Dick Irvin as coach in 1940.

Day is too often forgotten when discussions turn to the subject of all-time great coaches. Usually we hear the names of Irvin, Scotty Bowman, Punch Imlach, Al Arbour or Toe Blake. But Day's accomplishments in the Stanley Cup playoffs during the Forties outshone or at least matched any of the above.

Frank Selke Jr. says of Day: "He made a lot of ordinary and mediocre players into — if not superstars — certainly good journey-men guys who could more than carry their own weight. He did it by the sheer force of discipline. The Leafs of the Forties were the best-disciplined team probably in the history of the game."

Day was thorough and demanding without intimidating his players. Ted Kennedy, one of the stars of that era, likens him to a Tom Landry, the stalwart coach of the Dallas Cowboys in the National Football League for 27 years. "A lot of guys made him out to be a tyrant," Kennedy said. "But he wasn't. He was a good guy, a superb coach strategically and motivationally, and simply the best coach I've ever seen before or since."

The Leafs of the Forties were sometimes called "Hap Day's clutch and grabbers" because of their close checking. If they scored the first goal they were likely to protect it and win 1-0. Howie Meeker joined the Leafs in the late Forties and years later became a popular game analyst on CBC's Hockey Night in Canada. On television, Meeker would stress the importance of "finishing your check," which of course is what Day stressed to Meeker 30 years earlier.

"First of all, he demanded discipline and got it," Meeker said. "And he had a system, and it was very simple — you played to the system or you didn't play. Those were his rules and regulations, and he demanded hard work. And if you did those things he kept you there."

In practices Day was innovative. He sharpened his goaltenders' reflexes by prescribing hand ball as an exercise and or making them stop shots with without a goalstick—a routine the goalies saw as both effective and punitive. Day believed in repetition, sometimes making the team work on the same drill for an hour. The drill might have been faceoffs, or a checking system. Occasionally, he would run scrimmages in which one side used sticks and the other didn't. The Leafs were taught how to use their bodies, how to hold without getting caught, how to interfere without taking penalties.

In Day's defensive system, only one man, usually the centre, forechecked. The two wingers stayed back and picked up the advancing forwards. In those days the centre usually carried the puck through the middle and passed off to a winger. But with four Leafs — two defencemen and two forwards — protecting the blueline, this became impossible.

To counteract this strategy, the Detroit Red Wings became the first team to consistently shoot the puck into the attacking zone and chase it. Other teams copied them, and for better or worse, dump and chase, coupled with strong defensive play, became the trademark of the NHL style of hockey for years to come.

Day's conservative hockey, as well as the discipline and resolve of the Leafs in the Forties, very much reflected the personality of the country at that time. Canadians had endured the Depression and now the country was at war. Toronto was still conservative; "more British than the King," as the people were sometimes described. In this context, the Leafs embodied all that was pure, wholesome and good. Many of the teams' stars neither smoked nor drank. Day was strictly a "milkshake and ice cream man." Coupled with this image was Smythe's patriotism and the symbolism of his team wearing the Canadian emblem.

No one player epitomized Smythe's idealistic vision of the perfect Leaf more than Charles Joseph Sylvanus (Syl) Apps, a 6-foot centre from Paris, Ontario. Apps was not only an abstainer and non-smoker, but he played cleanly and never swore. He had considered going into the ministry of faith. He received his degree from McMaster University before joining the Leafs and, during his 10 years was considered the team's best player. He was an extraordinary talent who, some believe, has never been recognized as the superstar that he was. Kennedy, for example, says the two best players he has ever seen were Apps and Gordie Howe, in that order.

"He has never gotten the credit," Kennedy said. "People who played with him or against him knew how great he was. He could take the puck and roll with it. He was a great skater, he could score goals. He could make things happen and there weren't many players in the league who could do that."

Apps was an all-round athlete. He had been an outstanding half-back in football and had been wooed by the Hamilton Tigers. He had played third base for Paris in the Inter-county Baseball League. He golfed in the low 70s, although he had never taken a lesson, and had competed in track and field. Before joining the Leafs, in fact, he had represented Canada at the 1936 Summer Olympics in Berlin in the pole vault, finishing sixth with a vault of 13 feet and 1 inch.

The acquisition of Apps in 1936, and later defenceman Wally Stanowski from the New York Americans for Clancy and Day (who was still playing at the time), was the start of the rebuilding of the Leafs. Gordie Drillon, a big right winger, joined the team in 1937 and, a year later, won the scoring championship with 52 points in 40 games. Apps, his centre, picked up a league-leading 29 assists. Other key players were Billy Taylor, a slick little centre, and left winger Sweeney Schriner, an enormously talented veteran acquired from the New York Americans, who in 1944-45 streaked toward a 50 goals in 50 games season at a faster pace than the Canadiens' Maurice (Rocket) Richard before being injured. Most important, perhaps, was the goaltender, Walter (Turk) Broda, who was purchased from the

Detroit organization. Broda tended toward corpulence and some-times wasn't sharp in the regular season, but he was a money player and at his best in the big games.

By 1941-42, the NHL had shrunk from 10 to seven teams. The Depression killed off three — the Ottawa Senators, Montreal Maroons and Philadelphia — and one more, the Americans, would fold the next year. With Day behind the bench, the Leafs had fared well in the regular season, finishing second overall to the Rangers. Apps, who was the captain by this time, was a first-team all-star. Drillon, defence-man Wilfred (Bucko) McDonald and Broda made the second team. In the semi-finals, the Leafs eliminated the Rangers in six games. In the other series, Detroit defeated Boston.

This set up a Toronto-Detroit final. But any realistic hope of the Leafs winning the Cup seemed dashed in the first three games of the best-of-seven final. The Red Wings played a simple but effective game of dump and skate. They shot the puck into the Leaf zone and forechecked fiercely, and it worked brilliantly. Toronto lost the first three games and teetered on the brink of elimination.

At that point, Day shook up the roster. He sat out Gord Drillon who hadn't scored a goal in the series and benched veteran defenceman Bucko McDonald, who couldn't handle Detroit's intense forechecking. Day also suspected that he might have found another a way of motivating his dispirited team. Just before the fourth game, a letter arrived from a 14-year-old girl named Doris Klein, who lived in Detroit but cheered for the Leafs. She said she was heart-broken over the three losses. In an emotional appeal, she implored her team to fight their way back and win the Cup. The letter was given to Day and he read it to his players before they went on the ice. "Gentlemen," said Day. "Here's how a little 14-year-old girl feels about our situation tonight."

Day said later he had never sensed so much tension in the dressing room. Today, such a letter would evoke snickers and a few guffaws. But in a more innocent time, the Leafs went out with fire in their eyes, and backed by magnificent goaltending from Broda, fought back from a two-goal disadvantage, scoring twice in the third period to win the game 4-3.

One of the prominent performers in the game had been 26-year-old Don Metz, who had spent the season in the minor leagues and hadn't played in the first three games of the series. When Day benched Drillon, Don was suddenly put on a line with his older brother Nick, with Syl Apps in the middle. In the critical fourth game, Apps got the winning goal, with Don Metz setting him up.

So began the greatest comeback in the history of the Stanley Cup final. Back in Toronto, the Leafs hammered the Red Wings by a score of 9-3, with Don Metz getting three goals. Don would also score the winner in next the game, and would end up with a total of four goals in four playoff games. He wasn't normally a scorer, and in the seven years he played for the Leafs he never had more than four goals in an entire season. But for those few days, Metz was on a cloud, buoyed by euphoria of the moment and playing like an all-star.

"It was certainly the greatest experience I had in hockey," he said. "The fact that I was put into the lineup halfway through the series made it a little special, I guess. And the letter from the girl did have quite an effect on the players. It just hit home that we had a lot of fans out there, a lot of supporters from all over the place and they were with us all the way."

With the series tied 3-3 and Drillon still out of the lineup, the Leafs won the final game in Detroit in fine style. After Syd Howe gave the Wings a 1-0 lead, the Leafs came back with three straight, with Sweeny Schriner getting two. As Apps held the Cup high on the ice of the Olympia, he called to Smythe in the stands and said, "Come on out, Conn. Come on out and get it. You've waited long enough for this Cup." Indeed, it had been 10 long years. But not so long for the next one, although the Second World War was already having an significant impact on NHL teams.

When war was declared in 1939, Smythe, a veteran of the First World War, sent letters to his players urging them to enlist. They all took army training and belonged to militia units while they were still with the team. Not surprisingly, Smythe, despite being well into his forties, was determined to establish his own artillery battery and take it overseas. Finally, in September, 1941, he formed his 30th Battery, or Sportsmen's Battalion, as it was known. It included Don (Shanty) McKenzie, a former Argonaut football player who worked as superintendent of the Gardens after the war, and a couple of prominent sports writers, Ted Reeve of the Toronto *Telegram* and also an ex-Argo, and Ralph Allen of the *Globe and Mail*.

The Sportsmen's Battalion saw action in 1944 at Caen, where, in July, Smythe received an injury that would handicap him for the rest of his life. During a night attack by air, he was hit in the back by debris. The wound damaged his bowels and urinary tract. There was also nerve damage to one leg. He returned home in a wheel chair and for a while there was some question as to whether he would live longer than five years. But he was tough and he fought back, eventually walking with the aid of a cane, although he lived in pain for the rest of his life.

Early 1942 marked the dark days of the war. Pearl Harbour had been bombed December 7, the previous year. Germany and Italy controlled most of Europe as well as northern Africa. As a result, the heavy callups to military service started in Canada. After Toronto's 1942 Cup triumph, the team's best players—Apps, Broda, Drillon, Taylor and Gaye Stewart—marched off to war. The Leafs were decimated and failed to make the playoffs in 1943 and 1944.

But during the war years, Selke and Day, who ran the team in Smythe's absence, picked up two players, who, more than any others, would lead the team to an upset Stanley Cup victory in 1945. The first was Walter (Babe) Pratt, a strapping 6-foot-3, 210-pound defenceman from the Rangers and a free spirit who hated playing under Ranger coach Frank Boucher's conservative system. Pratt had great skills as an offensive defenceman, but Boucher refused to let him skate with the puck past the centre red line.

When Pratt was traded to Toronto, he said he felt as if a yoke had been lifted. Indeed, Day, despite his own disciplined system, respected Pratt's abilities and let him carry the puck into the offensive zone. In the 1943-44 season he produced an amazing 17 goals and 40 assists in 50 games, and became the first Leaf to win the Hart Trophy, awarded to the league's most valuable player. Day says he never attempted to stop Pratt from rushing the puck because, "it would have been like trying to tell Apps to play defensive hockey."

Day and Pratt had different personalities and attitudes, but Day liked Pratt immensely, as did the other players. Pratt was good natured, loved a joke and he was a team man, although he could be wild on his own time. In the year Pratt won the MVP, Day had him share his room during a road trip to Montreal for a particularly important game. Later, Pratt said he owed the Hart Trophy to Day for keeping him out of trouble. Said Day, "When he was on the ice, he was a hundred per cent team man. But when he was off the ice, you always felt a little dubious about what might be going on. To try to control any off-ice escapades, I had him registered in my room. It worked out well." It has been said that Day kept Pratt with him during the entire 1945 playoff, but Day says no. "I could only stand so much, too," he recalled with a laugh.

The other player acquired during the war would come to epitomize every fan's image of a Leaf. He was fearless, determined, hard working, and a great leader. Theodore (Ted, Teeder) Kennedy would become the heart and soul of the greatest of all the Leaf teams. Kennedy was from the village of Humberstone beside Port Colborne, Ontario. Two weeks before he was born, his father was killed in a hunting accident, leaving his mother, Margaret, to raise three boys and a girl. To make ends meet, she operated the hot-dog stand in the local arena and later had her own tea room.

Kennedy grew up to be a responsible young man, a non-smoker and non-drinker, and so talented that at the age of 16 he was playing senior hockey for the Port Colborne Sailors. In those days, an NHL team could put a player on its negotiation list without telling him, which was exactly what the Montreal Canadiens did, to the dismay of Kennedy, who had no interest in playing in Montreal. He had grown up listening to Hewitt and the Leafs were his team.

It happened that Nels Stewart coached the Port Colborne team at the time. He had played for the Maroons, the Bruins and the Americans, was from Toronto and was a good friend of Day. When Stewart tipped the Leafs about his young player, Day and Selke came down to have a look. They were impressed enough to contact the Canadiens about getting his rights and eventually a trade was worked out. Kennedy did not come cheaply. Montreal asked for and received defenceman Frankie Eddolls, one of the leading prospects in Canada at the time.

When Smythe, who was with his battalion, heard about the deal, he was furious about not being told and also over losing Eddolls.

Later, when he saw Kennedy play, all was forgiven. Selke, however, did have second thoughts—after he went to Montreal to run the Canadiens. "Kennedy always beat us," he said.

In the spring of 1945, the Leafs, still without most of their top players, finished third. That winter, the Canadiens dominated the league, winning 38 games and losing only eight. Rocket Richard scored 50 goals in 50 games and was on the big line with centre Elmer Lach, who was selected MVP that year, and Hector (Toe) Blake on left wing. The defence was led by 6-foot 2-inch, 205-pound Emile Bouchard who scored 11 goals and earned 23 assists in 50 games. And in goal was Bill Durnan, who would win the Vezina Trophy for six consecutive seasons.

They were a star-studded group. Before the semi-final series against Toronto, Irvin boasted that the Canadiens were "the greatest team in the history of hockey." This, of course, was a dig at Smythe who had been more than happy to see Irvin leave Toronto. However, the Leafs of 1945 would never forget Irvin's remarks, or what followed.

It has to be remembered that the most bitter rivalry in hockey existed between Montreal and Toronto, and in this era it played out on several levels. There was Irvin coaching against his old team. There was Lach, whom Smythe disliked and felt had been disloyal because he had left St. Michael's College in Toronto to play in the West before joining the Canadiens — which was Lach's circuitous way of avoiding the Leafs. And there were the two solitudes, French and English.

The tension between the two founding peoples was heightened during the war when it was widely reported in English Canada that Quebec had the highest percentage of callup deferments in the country, with some deferred individuals playing for the Canadiens. In that context, there were those who felt Richard's record of 50 goals in 50 games was worthless, or at best tarnished, because of the low calibre of competition during the war years. Smythe, himself, was certainly no paragon of tolerance and liberalism. He routinely referred to French Canadians as frogs and at least once began a speech with: "Ladies and gentlemen, and Frenchmen . . ."

In this context, the memorable 1945 semi-final series between the Canadiens and Leafs was played out. In the years that followed it would be described as Day's finest hour as a coach. He knew he couldn't match Montreal's three lines, so he used two lines, plus four defencemen. Up front, Gus Bodnar played between Schriner and Lorne Carr; Kennedy centred Mel (Sudden Death) Hill and Bob Davidson. Nick Metz, who had just been released from the armed forces, spelled off Kennedy and Bodnar at centre. The defensive pairings were Pratt with Elwin Morris, and Stanowski, who had recently been discharged from the army, with Reg Hamilton. The goaltender was 26-year-old Frank (Ulcers) McCool, who would win the rookie of the year award that season and was brilliant in the playoffs.

But the star of the series was Kennedy, a 19-year-old kid whose line was sent out against the Canadiens outstanding unit of Lach, Blake and Richard—the Punch Line. Davidson can remember Lach saying to Kennedy at the start of the series, "You come near me and I'll take your head off with my stick," and Kennedy sticking his nose in Lach's face and snarling, "You try it and I'll put you in the hospital."

Said Davidson, "Lach had been in the league quite a while and he would try to run most centremen. He was trying to give it to Teeder, but Teeder'd bring his stick up on Lach. You could not scare Teeder one iota."

Irvin's greatest team of all time was stunned by Day's clutch and grabbers in the first game, losing 1-0 in Montreal. The Leafs also won the second game, 3-2. In the Montreal camp, there was confusion and panic, but, finally, in Toronto, the Canadiens got a victory, 4-1. But a dramatic overtime victory at the Gardens gave the Leafs a 3-1 stranglehold in the series. They lost at the Montreal Forum, but back in Toronto they took the sixth game and the series. The Gardens exploded in jubilation. Hats, gloves and coats littered the ice. The Leafs vaulted over the boards to celebrate the victory. They mobbed McCool, whose ulcers had already started to kick up. The team hugged and they hugged some more. Against the best team in the league, indeed, the best team in the history of hockey, they had, with basically two lines and four defenceman, won. For Kennedy, this was his most memorable series, as it is for most of the players who were part of the Leaf organization in the Forties. "It was a tremendous effort, but more than anything it was a brilliant piece of coaching,"

Kennedy said. "Day had used his players so well. We were dead tired at the end, but it had been so satisfying."

The final against Detroit was a splendid seven-game series with Toronto winning the first three games, 1-0, 2-0, 3-0, but then losing the next three. In the seventh game, the teams were tied 1-1 in the third when a bouncing puck came out in front of the Detroit net. Davidson lunged at it, but couldn't get to it. Kennedy took a swipe but missed. Then, suddenly, in rushed Pratt from the blueline. In a second, the puck was on his stick. The big defenceman shot, and before goalie Harry Lumley could move, the puck was behind him to make the score 2-1. And that's how it ended.

Again, the Leafs were champions and the dynasty looked to be well on its way. The war was drawing to an end. Apps, Drillon and Broda would be back. That fall, at training camp in Owen Sound, Ontario, Kennedy told a reporter that the Leafs were a cinch to repeat as Cup champions. As it turned out, Kennedy was a better hockey player than prognosticator.

The Leafs fell apart in 1945-46, failing to make the playoffs and finishing in fifth place with a losing record. Age had caught up with some of the key players during the war years. Kennedy, who laboured as a skater, was further impeded by a groin injury for most of the season. Selke, however, received a large part of the blame from Smythe and left the organization in May, 1946.

In his memoirs, Smythe said he felt Selke had been disloyal and had plotted with other Gardens directors to remove him while he was away during the war. As Frank Selke Jr. remembers it, Smythe bullied his father. The last straw, apparently, was when the elder Selke returned from lunch to see a note from Smythe on his desk berating him for leaving the building without permission. Selke's response was to send a letter to Smythe saying: "Lincoln freed the slaves. Goodbye, I quit." Selke immediately joined the Canadiens as managing director and built the Montreal dynasty of the Fifties.

That summer, Smythe brooded over the state of his team and finally came to the conclusion that it had to be taken apart and reassembled. This was done with considerable expediency. Schriner, Carr and Davidson retired. Pratt, who had been suspended for allegedly betting on NHL games that season and then reinstated, was sold to Boston. Taylor went to Detroit for winger Harry Watson. Forward Vic Lynn was picked up from Montreal.

Most important, Smythe and Day rebuilt the defence. Of the six rookies who joined the team, four were rearguards who had been recruited at the age of 16 or younger during the war years by Selke. They were big and tough and they had talent. Jim Thomson, Garth Boesch, Bill Barilko and Gus Mortson would anchor the Leaf defence for years to come. That same season, Howie Meeker, a right winger and superb skater, played well enough to be selected the league's rookie of the year. Smythe's job was so thorough that there were only eight holdovers from the previous season — Apps, Kennedy, Stanowksi, Broda, Nick and Don Metz, Bill Ezinicki and Gaye Stewart.

Even Smythe could not anticipate the degree of success the changes would bring. Instead of developing into a contending team, the Leafs became champions overnight. In the next five years they would dominate the NHL, winning four Cups; three consecutively from 1947 to 1949. The Leafs were also a tougher team, largely because of their bruising young defencemen. Mortson wasn't big, but Meeker remembers him as mean. "If you went in the corner with Mortson and came out with the puck, he'd take your ankles off," Meeker said. Thomson was a good puck handler and tough. Barilko and Boesch were hitters. Meeker said, "If Barilko got a piece of you, you hurt for a week. He just tore the man apart."

The fiercest of all the Leafs was Bill (Wild Bill) Ezinicki, a right winger from Winnipeg who joined the team in the 1944 at the age of 21. He played in only eight games that year but went on to became a huge fan favourite at the Gardens. Wild Bill was 5-feet 10-inches tall, and weighed 170 pounds, and he was hard and sinewy from daily weight lifting; he hit like someone a lot heavier. If there was such a thing as an enforcer in those days, Ezinicki was it, and he was hated in the other NHL cities. In Detroit, he was accused of deliberately attempting to injure goaltender Harry Lumley. Boston *Globe* sports writer Herb Ralby said, "Toronto has the leading candidate for the most-hated opponent in Ezinicki." In New York, on one occasion, a woman sitting at ice level jammed a long hatpin in Ezinicki's rear end as he bent over to take a faceoff.

In his book, *Rivalry: Canadiens vs Leafs,* Stan Fischler notes that many of Ezinicki's linemates were Boy Scouts by comparison, particularly Syl Apps. "Apps is the cleanest player I've known," Day once said. "He doesn't smoke. He never bends an elbow except to twist his stick over an opponent's stick. The strongest language he ever used is 'By hum' and 'Jimminy Christmas.' " In one game, Boston Bruin defenceman Flash Hollett knocked out two of Apps' teeth with his stick, prompting Apps to say, "By Hum, this has gone on long enough," and promptly decked Hollett with a combination of punches.

If it wasn't Ezinicki, the opposition had to deal with Barilko or Boesch and their punishing body checks. In those days Rocket Richard, who had a vicious temper, would explode after being slammed by a Leaf check and usually would be ineffective for the remainder of the game. Kennedy said, "As long as you left him alone, he was anything but a dirty hockey player. He was just a good, clean hard-working competitor. But if he got hit, he got terribly upset. He couldn't take a hit, so we would hit him and hope that he'd do something to get ruled off the ice."

At no time was Smythe's famous dictum, "If you can't beat 'em in the alley, you can't beat 'em on the ice," more appropriate or applied more literally.

This rallying cry during this era at the Gardens came from John Arnott, a service station operator and season's ticket holder who would stand up and say in a loud voice, "Come o-o-o-n Teeder!" And indeed he would. Although Apps was the team's most skillful player, Kennedy usually led them in the playoffs. In 1947, for example, the Leafs won their first of three Cups in a row by defeating the Canadiens in six games. Kennedy led his team in scoring and had two of the winners. In the championship years of 1948 and 1949, he also led the Leafs in the post-season.

But despite the 1947 championship, and perhaps knowing that Apps planned to retire after one more season, Smythe decided to acquire another centre. The man he wanted was Max Bentley of the Chicago Black Hawks, a star player who had won the scoring championship in the two previous years and had been selected the league's most valuable player in 1946. The Black Hawks didn't want to give him up, but they needed players and were in some financial trouble. In 1945, the Black Hawks had finished second-last in the league, and in 1947 were at the bottom. Defensively they were the NHL's worst club and they lacked depth. So when Smythe offered the complete forward line of Bodnar, Bud Poile and Gaye Stewart, as well as defencemen Ernie Dickens and Bob Goldham — all for Bentley — the Black Hawks couldn't refuse.

Perhaps the easiest way to explain the significance of Bentley to the Leafs is to note that they now had three of the best six centres in the league, the other three being Lach, Milt Schmidt of Boston and Sid Abel of Detroit. Bentley, who was from a farm in Saskatchewan, was called a dipsy doodler, probably first by Hewitt on the radio, because he was slight (5-feet 8-inches, 159 pounds), elusive and clever with the puck. People of that era often compare Wayne Gretzky to him. The Leaf fan book from Bentley's first year in Toronto reported that, "Milking chores, Bentley claims, developed his wrists and is the reason for the snap that goes into his drives on goal . . . He's a chronic worrier, always imagining he has contracted some rare disease, but Max is at his best when he feels worst."

Most Leaf historians, as well as Conn Smythe in his memoirs, rate the 1947-48 team, with Bentley as the third centre, as the best ever. On the final weekend of the regular season, Apps scored three goals in a critical home-and-home series with Detroit to determine first place, which gave him the career total of 200 goals that he had been seeking. The Leafs finished first and lost only one game in the playoffs, sweeping Detroit 4-0 in the final.

Their dressing room in Detroit was pandemonium. Broda was held down and doused with Coca-Cola. Bentley sat in the corner, with a look of pure child-like delight. He had led the team in scoring during the season and was second to Kennedy in the playoffs. Together with Kennedy and Apps, he had given the Leafs not only the best centre-ice contingent in the league, but perhaps the top trio in the history of the game. Said Smythe in his raspy voice, "He's an even better player than I thought. He gave us the third centre we needed to give us the Murderers' Row of hockey."

The next day, the Leafs arrived back in Toronto by train and were met by tens of thousands of cheering fans. Led by the Queen's Own

Rifles band, a parade carried the players from Union Station to City Hall as thousands more lined the street and as clouds of ticker tape descended on the players in the open cars.

Apps made good on his decision to retire and accepted a job in marketing with the Simpson's department store chain. Two years later, when the Leafs failed in their attempt to make it four Cups in a row, Day decided to was time to step down, or more, specifically move up — to assistant general manager. Replacing him was Primeau, who had just taken the senior Marlboros to the Allan Cup championship. In Primeau's first year, 1950-51, the Leafs, no longer a young team and battle weary, still had enough in them for one more championship. It was another Montreal-Toronto confrontation in the Cup final, and it became a classic. Every game went into overtime. In the final game, the Leafs were behind 2-1 in the last minute of regulation time, when Primeau pulled Al Rollins, who shared the goaltending with Broda, for an extra player. With the seconds disappearing, Bentley passed to Sid Smith. The slick, skillful Smith sent it over to Todd Sloan and suddenly, with only 32 seconds left, the puck was behind Montreal goalie Gerry McNeil.

Bill Barilko's winning goal is probably the best remembered of all Toronto Cup winners. The teams were into overtime. The speedy Meeker had fired the puck into the Montreal zone and then had chased it down behind the net. He was able to work it out to Harry Watson who moved it to the left side. It was then that Barilko charged in from the blueline. From the faceoff circle, he took a swipe at the puck with such momentum that he fell forward as he shot.

At that instant, a photographer caught the big defenceman in the air as he was about to hit the ice. Ahead of him, McNeil had already tumbled back into the goal. The puck was behind him, high over his right shoulder, in the mesh.

That summer, Barilko embarked on a fishing trip from his hometown of Timmins, Ont. with a friend, Henry Hudson, who was a dentist and pilot, to the James Bay area. They never returned. The disappearance of the Fairchild 24, a single-engined pontooned craft, sparked widespread alarm as well as a massive manhunt. But Barilko and Hudson were not found. The Leafs' training camp began without their Cup hero and amid all kinds of rumour. Some still held out hope that Barilko was alive on a wilderness island after surviving a crash into a lake. The most far-fetched rumour had it that Barilko's plane had not gone down, but instead he had flown to the Soviet Union to secretly coach the Soviet national team. Barilko's parents, you see, were of Russian descent.

The famous photograph of Barilko's goal and the tragic disappearance came to signify the end of the Leafs' golden era — a 10-year period in which they dominated the NHL and won six Stanley Cups to become the NHL's first Cup dynasty. Eleven years would pass before they would win another championship. The crashed Fairchild and the bodies of the two men would eventually be found, but not until May, 1962, one month after the Leafs had won their next Stanley Cup and had begun their second dynasty.

3

Detroit's Tumultous Cup Years

*F*rom 1942 to 1960, three teams dominated the National Hockey League. They were Montreal, Toronto and Detroit. The have-nots — New York Rangers, Chicago and Boston — existed mainly to round out the six-team league and provide the occasional upset, although rarely in Stanley Cup play.

During this time, the Canadiens won eight Stanley Cups, Toronto, six and Detroit, five. The have-nots did not win any. Only once did a have-not finish first in the regular season — the Rangers in 1942. Although much has been written about the great Toronto and Montreal dynasties of the Forties and Fifties, little has been done on Detroit, even though the Red Wings, in some ways, dominated during their dynastic period like no team before.

The Wings have quite accurately been described as the Edmonton Oilers of their era — a flashy, exciting team led by a core of superstars, but lacking the depth and perhaps the discipline needed to claim possession of the Cup for more than two consecutive years. Still, the Wings were a major power. They finished first in the NHL's regular season seven straight years, from 1949 to 1955, which was a record for any major league team in North America. The closest to that mark were the New York Yankees who won five consecutive American League pennants and World Series from 1949 to 1953. In terms of NHL championships, the Red Wings won four Cups in a period of six seasons from 1950 to 1955. They were led by some of the great players of their time and all time, including Gordie Howe, Ted Lindsay, Red Kelly and Terry Sawchuk.

As famous as these men were, the front-office personalities in Detroit were every bit as colourful. In 1932, Jim Norris, a millionaire grain speculator from Chicago, bought the Detroit franchise and the Olympia Stadium for $100,000, for what he called "loose change." Big Jim Norris was among the wealthiest men in the United States, with investments in railroads, real estate and cattle, as well as grain. Also heavily into sports and entertainment, Norris was, not surprisingly, the most powerful governor in the NHL. He not only owned the Red Wings, but also the Chicago Black Hawks and New York Rangers. He also had a significant investment in the Boston Bruins, in the form of an unpaid loan to owner Weston Adams.

But Norris's first love was the Red Wings. He was an indulgent and patient owner. In 1933, when the Red Wings defeated the Rangers for the first time in 78 games, Norris paid the unheard-of bonus of $50 to each player. In the Thirties, he appointed as vice-president of the Wings his eldest son Jimmy, whose principal job was to call his father as soon as a game was over and provide a summary of what had happened.

During this time, Jack Adams was the general manager, a position he kept until his retirement in 1963. In the early days, the Detroit franchise was a loser and Adams was less than a top-level hockey man, until Norris gave him $100,000 to buy players and build a development system.

In the Thirties, the Toronto Maple Leafs and Montreal Canadiens had already established a network of amateur and minor-league teams, but the American teams had not. Even though Norris owned the Black Hawks and Rangers, he wasn't interested in how well they did, just so long as they made him money by putting people in Madison Square Garden and the Chicago Stadium. Jimmy Skinner, who worked for Adams for more than 20 years, said, "Toronto and Montreal were the dominant clubs and they dominated minor hockey in Canada for years. It wasn't easy for the American teams."

But the Red Wings took on the two powerful Canadian clubs and often beat them at their own game. The Wings, at one time, had more affiliated minor-league teams than either the Canadiens or Leafs. The key to the Red Wing farm system wasn't so much the genius of Adams. It was the organization's two top scouts, Carson Cooper in the East and Fred Pinckney in the West.

So successful were Cooper and Pinckney in finding talent that by the late Forties, the Red Wings had joined the power elite of the NHL. Not surprisingly, Adams tended to take most of the credit for the success.

Adams was a short, corpulent, cheerful character whose nickname was "Jolly Jack." His public image belied the personality of a man who was shrewd, temperamental and vindictive. But the media chose not to dwell on Jack's negative traits. After Adams finally retired in 1963, broadcaster and writer Ed Fitkin wrote, "Jack Adams was, in the parlance of the sports world, a great guy. To a young reporter, he was the perfect hockey foil. He would talk to you and tell you things about hockey that provided you with enough material to write endlessly about the game. He was never too busy to sit down and have a cup of coffee with you, or to talk about 'my kids' as he always referred to his Red Wings."

Adams' charm was lost on Conn Smythe, who, in his memoirs, wrote about sharing a Pullman with Adams during a trip to New York. "I thought there was no nicer guy to travel with," Smythe wrote. "He seemed content to take second place all the time to me, which was nice; nobody else tried to hog the limelight."

During the trip, Smythe pontificated about hockey, horse racing and the world in general, but Adams was more interested in what the Leafs were up to. As Adams pumped Smythe for information, Smythe casually mentioned that he had scouted a young defenceman by the name of Bucko McDonald, who was a weak skater, but had a good sense of the game and strong skills. As soon as Smythe returned to Toronto, he called NHL headquarters to list McDonald on the Leaf protected roster, only to learn Adams had claimed him just a few minutes earlier. McDonald would help the Wings win two Stanley Cups.

The Smythe-Adams feud was just one additional element to the bad blood between the Leafs and Red Wings. By the late Forties, they were not only the two best teams in the league, but they were also the biggest and toughest. Ted Kennedy, one of the Leaf stars of that era, says, "It was the Red Wings and us, and we had some awful battles." Games between Toronto and Detroit usually turned into bloody wars, anticipated with glee by sports writers and fans alike. "Detroit and Toronto are clashing again tomorrow night," wrote one reporter in 1947, "and lots of blood is sure to flow."

When there was blood on the ice, Ted Lindsay was usually near the scene of the crime. In addition to being a major star, Terrible Ted was also a wild competitor. When he turned pro with the Red Wings in 1944, *Look* magazine reported that there were widespread predictions that he would be "carried out on a board."

Lindsay wasn't big, only 5-foot-8 and 160 pounds, but he took on the biggest players in the league and carried on a long-time feud with Montreal's Rocket Richard. From the earliest days, Lindsay, with his cold sneer, went head to head against Richard — which, in Lindsay's case, meant poking him, elbowing him, slashing him until Richard would retaliate. To this day, the Rocket says he "bristles" whenever he sees Ted. They still don't speak.

One of Lindsay's most infamous battles occurred in 1952. Bill Ezinicki had been the Leafs' enforcer during the Forties and nothing changed when he was traded to Boston. On this particular night, Ezinicki attempted to remove Lindsay's eye with the end of stick. Lindsay response was to pole-axe Ezinicki with his stick. Since they were both still standing, they had a fist fight.

After it was broken up, Ezinicki circled behind Lindsay and attempted to jump him from behind. Ted, however, caught a glimpse of Bill from the corner of his eye and with perfect timing, turned around and dropped him with one punch. Then Lindsay, described by *Look* as a "picture of unmitigated villainy," pounced on Ezinicki and pummelled him, unaware, apparently, that the Bruin was out cold. "Then Ted got up and skated off the bloody ice to the screams of the hockey heathen," *Look* reported. In one of the most punitive measures taken by league president Clarence Campbell up to that point, both players were suspended for three games and fined $300.

44

Lindsay was a particular source of irritation for Conn Smythe, because Lindsay should have been playing for the Leafs. Tough, resourceful and immensely talented, he was just the kind of alley fighter who would have made Smythe proud. That Lindsay did not end up a Maple Leaf was one of the great blunders in the history of the organization.

Lindsay grew up in Kirkland Lake, Ont., and played on a fine juvenile team that won an Ontario championship. Also on that team was Gus Mortson, who would later be a standout defenceman on the Leafs. In those days, NHL scouts rarely made it up to Northern Ontario, so Lindsay, despite his considerable skill, remained a well-kept secret. Still, Ted was determined to make his way in the game, so at the age of 18, he packed up his equipment and took a train to Toronto for a tryout with the St. Michael's college junior team. St. Mike's, a Roman Catholic boys' school, was one of the two top junior affiliates of the Maple Leafs. The other was the Toronto Marlboros. In those days, Smythe would tell his assistant Frank Selke, "Put the dogans in the Micks' school and throw all the rest in with the Marlies."

Lindsay made St. Mike's on the strength of his performance at training camp, as did Gus Mortson. In their first game, the two rookies faced the Marlboros, a team that included Jim Thomson, another future Leaf. On one play that seemed harmless enough, Lindsay was checking Thomson when Mortson came up and caught Thomson with a check that sent him flying. But on the way down Thomson's skate dug into Lindsay's calf, cutting deeply into the tissue and muscle. Lindsay collapsed, writhing in pain as blood poured onto the ice. He was rushed to the Maple Leaf Gardens infirmary and then taken to hospital where he was told that he would miss two months.

This occurred in 1943. Smythe was with his Sportsmen's Battalion. Selke and Leaf coach Hap Day were busy with the Leafs and had not been at the game either. But one of the spectators, the father of one of the Leafs, Tom (Windy) O'Neill, had been there and had come away impressed with "the rookie forward" whose game he didn't know. O'Neill called Day the next day and suggested he check him out.

Day and Selke went to practice a few days later and, unaware that Lindsay was away recovering from an injury, picked out the other "rookie forward" on St. Mikes, Joe Sadler, and put him on the Leafs' protected list.

When Lindsay returned, he played poorly. By Christmas he had only one assist. During the Christmas break, however, he practiced incessantly, skating eight hours a day, backwards, forwards, sideways. In January, his career took off. "Everything fell into place," he says. "I was playing well, scoring goals, getting into trouble with the opposition and exerting my authority."

One night, after St. Mike's had played a game in Hamilton, Ont., against Detroit's junior farm team, a grey-haired gentleman walked up to Lindsay, and said, "Ted, my name is Carson Cooper. Have you ever thought of playing pro hockey?"

"My eyes lit up like I'd hit the jackpot," Lindsay says. "It was a dream come true."

The next day, Cooper, the Red Wings' hot-shot scout, added Lindsay to the Detroit protected list. Two weeks later, the Leafs realized they hadn't registered their young St. Mike's star. When they called the NHL head office in Montreal they were given the bad news. Over the years, the news got worse, because Lindsay became one of the greatest left wingers of all time, a leader who would captain the Red Wings during their glory years.

But Lindsay wasn't Cooper's only prize. Red Kelly was two years younger than Lindsay and had also played for St. Mike's, although initially, he wasn't good enough to play for the big team and was relegated to St. Mike's juvenile affiliate, the Buzzers.

The Leafs didn't think much of Kelly. They felt his skating was weak and didn't see him as an NHL prospect. Cooper did, and when he put him on the Wings' negotiation list, the Leaf brass laughed. Cooper, of course, laughed last, because Kelly went on to become a star in Detroit, an offensive defenceman second to none except Doug Harvey in Montreal. And Kelly turned out to be a terrific skater. He had a smooth, effortless stride.

In the West, Pinckney was most famous for discovering a young, slow-talking Floral, Saskatchewan, farm boy who would become simply the greatest player in the game, perhaps of all time. Gordie

Howe was such a gifted athlete that he could have excelled in baseball, lacrosse, boxing, or almost any sport. In hockey, he played all three positions: forward, defence and goal. The New York Rangers saw Howe in goal as a 16-year-old and invited him to their training camp in Winnipeg. The Rangers didn't have a spot for him and Howe wasn't sure how he fitted into their plans. So when Pinckney asked him if he would be interested in attending the Red Wing camp the following year, Howe readily agreed.

Adams saw immediately that he had an excellent prospect in Howe, and after training camp asked him to join the team's junior affiliate in Galt, Ont. Because Gordie was a transfer from the West, he couldn't play regular season games. So for one season, he practiced with Galt and then turned pro with the Wings at the age of 18.

In Ed Fitkin's profile of Adams, Jolly Jack tells the story of signing Gordie to his first contract: "He said to me one day, 'Mr. Adams, I'd like one of those windbreakers the Red Wings wear.' I said, 'Okay son. I'll get you one.' Then it promptly slipped my mind.

"Next fall at training camp, I decided I wanted him to turn pro and I offered him a contract. He looked at it but didn't sign it. So I asked him what was wrong, wasn't it enough money? He just looked at me and said 'I'm not sure I want to sign with your organization, Mr. Adams. You don't keep your word.'

"Naturally I was flabbergasted, and I asked him what he meant. 'Well,' he said, 'you promised me a windbreaker and you never gave it to me.' You can't imagine how quickly I got that windbreaker. But that's how close I came to losing him."

Before the arrival of Lindsay and Howe, the only standout on the Red Wings was Sid Abel, from Wilcox, Sask. Abel was a strong-skating centre, then in his mid-20s, who could score goals and set them up with equal proficiency. But without good linemates, he had not played up to his potential.

Lindsay hit the NHL at full speed in 1944-45, scoring 17 goals in 45 games. When Howe arrived two years later, Adams put his two young wingers with Abel and thus was born the "Production Line," so named for Detroit's booming automotive industry. Abel's skill level was high and on his wings he now had two of the most talented — and also toughest — players in the league. For 10 years, the

Production Line dominated NHL scoring, with Alex Delvecchio eventually replacing Abel at centre.

Perhaps most critical to the success of the Wings was Adams' decision, prompted by a Norris directive, to step down in 1947 as coach and hand the job over to Tommy Ivan, a smart young minor-league coach who had a good rapport with players. The result was immediate. In 1947-48, the Wings jumped from fourth place and a losing record to a strong second-place finish with 30 wins, 18 losses and 12 ties.

"Ivan was fair and honest," Kelly recalls. "He didn't say much but we had a disciplined team. Everything was hockey with us. We had a young team. A bunch of us came in together at the same time and we had a strong sense of friendship."

On the ice, Howe was the essential NHL scoring machine. At 6-foot-1, 205 pounds, he was one of the biggest players in the league. He was awesomely strong, couldn't be knocked off his feet and he was dirty, becoming almost as famous for his elbows as his wrist shot. Although he made devastating use of his size, he possessed the agility of a smaller man. He had speed, could turn on a dime and was the best stickhandler in the game. But what made him the greatest of them all was his anticipation, the way he could think the game and always be at the right place at the right time.

Off the ice, Gordie was something totally different, a warm, gentle easy-going man who, in the early days, followed Lindsay around like a puppy dog. "They were always together," Kelly said. "You wouldn't see one without the other." Ted was the leader. He was a bright but quiet man who didn't say much. When he did speak, he drew an audience. "It was all in the tone of his voice," Howe said. "It was very authoritative." Lindsay assumed a leadership role naturally and it wasn't long before he was the most influential man in the Red Wing dressing room, much to the chagrin of Adams who didn't like the idea of sharing his power with anyone, never mind a player.

In the early days, the four bachelors on the team — Lindsay, Howe, Kelly and Marty Pavelich — roomed at Minnie (Ma) Shaw's boarding house just three blocks away from the Olympia Stadium. Ma Shaw was an institution in the Detroit hockey community; she took in more than 175 Red Wing players, mostly rookies, from 1937 to 1959.

"Ma Shaw's was where the players would congregate," Howe said. "They'd drop by to see what was going on a particular night. Everything was done together. We had dinner parties and dances together. We had a team in the bowling league during the off-season."

The camaraderie only helped to make the Wings a stronger hockey team. Although blessed with a handful of remarkably talented players, Detroit, as Kelly recalls, "always played as a team. We were close friends. There were no egos."

The Red Wings advanced to the Stanley Cup final in 1948 and 1949, but were swept in both series by the Maple Leafs.

In 1949-50 season, the Red Wings won their second consecutive regular season title with a record of 37-19-14, 11 points ahead of second-place Montreal. The Production Line had enjoyed success unprecedented for a NHL forward line, with the three linemates grabbing the first three spots in league scoring. Lindsay was first with 23 goals and 55 assists for 78 points in 69 games, followed by Abel and Howe.

Still, the players approached the playoffs with trepidation. In the first round they would play Toronto, a team that had finished third, but had handled them easily in the two previous playoff years. The Leafs, by then, were known as a Jekyll and Hyde squad. The unremarkable Jekyll appeared during the regular season and then suddenly in the playoffs Hyde burst on the scene and laid waste the opposition. In 1950, the Leafs also were going for their fourth consecutive Cup.

Detroit's worst fears were confirmed early in the series. In the first game, the Leafs bombed the Wings at the Olympia 5-0. But that was the least of the bad news. The worst of it was an accident that almost ended Howe's career. It occurred as Leaf captain Ted Kennedy carried the puck and Howe swooped down on him from behind. "What I was trying to do," says Howe, "was ram him into the boards."

Kennedy, however, saw Howe from the corner of his eye and suddenly pulled up, which caused Howe to go flying past him into the boards. Howe, however, insists that Kennedy also "pitch-forked" him with his stick. "It was deliberate in that he was trying to protect himself," Gordie says. "It was not done deliberately to injure."

Kennedy disputes the allegation of his stickwork. Red Kelly, who watched the play develop, says Red Wing defenceman Jack (Black Jack) Stewart was the important element of the incident and ended doing most of the damage to Howe.

Stewart was lining up Kennedy for a hit when the Leaf centre suddenly stopped. So, instead of body checking Kennedy, Stewart went barrelling into Howe, who was already sliding into the boards head first.

For his part, Howe doesn't remember Stewart being involved at all. "By then," he says. "I was out cold." Howe was carried off the ice and taken to hospital where his injuries were diagnosed as a fractured nose and cheek bone, a concussion and possible brain damage. At about 1 a.m. doctors operated on Howe to relieve pressure on his brain. There was some doubt that he would live through the night.

Meanwhile, the fans, media and Adams were in an uproar. Adams accused Kennedy of something approaching premeditated murder and vowed the Leafs would be repaid. Sure enough, near the end of the second period of the second game, Kennedy was attacked by Leo Reise and sent to the ice. Both benches immediately emptied and an all-out donnybrook ensued. Just as it seemed to quell, Lindsay and Ezinicki, the enforcer who was still with the Leafs at this point, squared off and resumed their on-going war. There were two brawls but Detroit won the game, 3-1, to tie the series.

The series went back and forth. The Leafs won in Toronto. Then Detroit tied it. Back at the Olympia Toronto came through with a big 2-0 victory with Turk Broda getting the shutout. Toronto, with a 3-2 lead in the series, had two chances to put away the Wings. At Maple Leaf Gardens, the Red Wings turned the tables, beating Toronto 4-0 and setting up a seventh and deciding match in Detroit.

It was a gruelling confrontation. Toronto, with their string of three straight Stanley Cups on the line, played tightly, effectively checking the Production Line. There was no scoring in the first period, nor the second. The third, too, was blanked. Into overtime they went. Finally, in the ninth minute of overtime, Detroit defenceman Leo Reise moved deeply into the Leaf zone with the puck. As Leaf defenceman Bill Barilko moved to protect the net, Reise shot the puck. At 8:39 it bounced off Barilko's leg and behind

Broda. Barilko would make amends the following spring when he would win the Cup for the Leafs with an overtime goal of his own, but on this night, the Red Wings were triumphant.

As the crowd at the Olympia went wild, the Red Wing players called Howe in the hospital to give him the good news. Gordie told them he had seen the game on television. Big No. 9 was well on his way to recovery.

For Detroit, however, the battle was only half over. The Rangers stood between them and the Cup and they weren't going to be an easy out, having just eliminated the Montreal Canadiens in five games. But Detroit held one big advantage. Every spring, regardless of whether the Rangers were in the playoffs, the circus came to Madison Square Garden. That meant the hockey team had to vacate the building, Stanley Cup or no Stanley Cup.

The Canadiens offered the Rangers the use of the Forum in Montreal, but Frank Boucher, the Ranger manager, opted for Toronto. The first two games of the series would be played in Toronto and the remainder in Detroit. The teams split the games at the Gardens and then in Detroit, the Red Wings won two in a row, both in overtime. With a 3-1 series lead and home-ice advantage the rest of the way, the Wings seemed a cinch to win the Cup.

But the orphaned Rangers, as they were called, fought their way back, winning the fifth game of the series and the sixth to tie it 3-3. Suddenly the momentum had changed. The favoured Wings were now called "Ivan's fading Wings," and there was considerable doubt they had enough left to win the seventh game. Howe was still out and Lindsay was hurting. And Ranger coach Lynn Patrick was beginning to tell people that he liked playing on the road. "For a bunch of orphans," he said. "We're doing pretty well away from home."

The Ranger magic continued in the seventh game. In the first period they jumped into a quick 2-0 lead, but Detroit tied it in the second, scoring two goals in 21 seconds. New York took the lead again, but before the period was over, Detroit had deadlocked it at three.

In the third, the two exhausted teams fought to a goalless standstill. The first 20-minute overtime period failed to produce a winner, so into the second they went. On this night, the Detroit hero would be left winger Pete Babando, one of the few NHL players from the United States. The 24-year-old Babando had been born in Braeburn, Pennsylvania, and had played two years for Boston before joining the Red Wings in 1949. He played only one year in Detroit and could manage only two points in the 1950 playoff — but they were both goals and they both came in the seventh game. His first in the second period had knotted the game at two, and then in the overtime period, Pete got his second.

The Red Wings had carried the play to New York in overtime, but were consistently turned away by Ranger goaltender Chuck Rayner, who made 15 saves in the first overtime period. Into the second period they went, until the ninth minute when a faceoff was called in the New York zone. George Gee, a centre with Detroit, won the draw and was able to get the puck over to Babando, who took it on his backhand and fired from 15 feet out. Rayner lunged, but was too late. The puck was already behind him, in the left corner of the net.

The Olympia exploded in what Detroit *Free Press* hockey writer Marshall Dann called "the greatest celebration in Olympia history." Finally, after so many disappointments, the collapse of 1942 — when the Leafs had come back from a 3-0 deficit to win four in a row; the humiliating defeats in 1948 and 1949 when they were swept in four straight by the Leafs — the Cup belonged to Detroit. It had been a thrilling, exhausting, emotional rollercoaster ride that started with a defeat and the loss of Howe and ended, 14 games and seven overtime periods later, with a triumph. When the game was over, Jack Adams told the press, "This is certainly the gamest and one of the greatest of all NHL clubs."

His first observation was correct. Detroit's record in the playoffs showed it was a feisty, never-say-die team. But one of the greatest? That was in the future. In fact, further into the future than Adams and the Wings would have thought.

In 1950-51, the Red Wings appeared poised to dominate the league and win their second Stanley Cup. In the off-season, Adams had made a huge trade with Chicago. He sent goalie Harry Lumley and defenceman Jack Stewart, both well into their thirties by then, as well as Babando, the Cup hero, and a couple of lesser players to the Black Hawks. In return he got Bob Goldham, a fine, steady defenceman, winger Gaye Stewart, a 20-something player who had enjoyed some fine years in Toronto before joining the Black Hawks, and Metro Prystai, a talented centre.

The Detroit defence was further bolstered by the signing of 20-year-old Marcel Pronovost, a 6-foot, 190-pound defenceman with impressive skills and toughness. But the key roster move for Detroit was the promotion of Terry Sawchuk to first-string status in goal. As a 19-year-old the year before, Sawchuk had played seven games for Detroit. He was a big man at 6-feet tall and 195 pounds, but he had the quickness of a cat, with both hands, blocker and catcher, as well as the legs. He moved well, and had an easy, effortless style. Adams knew immediately he had something special and started thinking about moving Harry Lumley, a star in his own right, but now past his prime.

With a rebuilt defence, a rookie goalie and several new faces up front, the Red Wings enjoyed another marvellous regular season, winning 44 games, losing only 13 and tying 13. They finished first, but only six points ahead of a strong Toronto team. Howe had his first monster season, scoring 43 goals in 70 games and adding 43 assists, to lead the league in both categories.

Sawchuck, outstanding in goal, not only won the Calder Trophy as rookie of the year but was also a first team all-star. So was defenceman Red Kelly who was fourth in team scoring (ninth in the league) with 17 goals and 37 assist in 70 games. The addition of Howe and Ted Lindsay to the first all-star team brought the Detroit complement on the six-man squad to four. On the second team was Sid Abel and defenceman Leo Reise. Never had one club so dominated the all-stars.

But that spring, Detroit was upset in the first round of the playoffs, losing to Montreal in six games. It was a stunning collapse for a team that had finished 36 points ahead of the Canadiens in the regular season, but perhaps not all that surprising. Often teams that enjoyed excellent regular seasons fell short in the playoffs, possibly because of overconfidence or fatigue. Another factor in the Detroit-Montreal series was the rivalry between the two best right wingers in the game, Howe and Richard. Howe, at this point, was hailed as the league's new superstar, something that didn't sit well with the intensely proud Rocket.

A year older and wiser, the Wings took nothing for granted in the spring of 1952. They topped off another impressive regular season, with something that had never been done before or since — they swept the Stanley Cup playoffs, which in those days consisted of just the semi-finals and final. Toronto went in four straight and so did Montreal. But Detroit did something else quite remarkable. Not one goal was scored on Olympia ice in either playoff series. Sawchuk blanked the Leafs twice and then did the same against Montreal.

The young Sawchuk would help lead Detroit to two more Cup championships, and over a long career he would establish himself as arguably the best goaltender in the history of the game. When all-time all-star teams are picked, he's usually the man selected in goal. Over a 20-year career, he played on five Cup winners and won the Vezina Trophy as the league's best goaltender five times. A record likely never to be surpassed is Sawchuk's tally of 103 career shutouts. In an era that was remarkable for the number of splendid goalies that competed — Jacques Plante, Glenn Hall, Johnny Bower and Gump Worsley — Sawchuk was the best.

Despite his brilliance, or perhaps because of it, there was a distinctly dark side to Sawchuk's personality. He was quiet and moody, and had a short fuse. Jimmy Skinner, who coached him in 1955, calls him surly. Ted Lindsay says, "Uke [Sawchuk's nickname because he was of Ukrainian descent] was the greatest goaltender I've ever seen. You could throw him a handful of rice, and he'd catch every kernel. But he was also a miserable son of a bitch."

Lindsay remembers Marty Pavelich, an outgoing and well-liked member of the team, walking into the dressing room each day and saying, "Hi, Uke, how're you doing."

"For two weeks Marty would say hello and Sawchuk would say hello, and they'd talk," Lindsay recalls. "And then one day, Marty walked in and said hello, and Sawchuk ignored him and refused to speak to him. Every day, Marty would attempt to get a conversation going, but Sawchuk wouldn't speak. He never knew why."

Red Kelly says Sawchuk's health declined while he was in Detroit. He drank, whether or not what was part of the problem, and his weight eventually dropped from 205 to 165. He took on a gaunt look and Lindsay doesn't think he ever played as well afterwards.

Still, years later, in 1967, at the age of 37, Sawchuk played magnificently for the Leafs in their Cup upset win over Montreal.

After the Wings' thoroughly dominating 1952 championship, it seemed that they had finally arrived as a dynasty and would string together three or four Cup triumphs. But it didn't happen. In the 1953 semi-final, the Boston Bruins, a team Detroit had beaten 10 out of 14 times in the regular season, knocked them off in six games.

The Bruins, to their credit, had been shrewd in taking advantage of all the Detroit flaws. To begin with, the Red Wings lacked depth. After Howe, Lindsay, Abel and a young centre named Alex Delvecchio, there wasn't much up front. If the Production Line was checked, the Detroit offence stalled. The line of Milt Schmidt, Joe Klukay and Woody Dumart threw a blanket over the Red Wings' big line and the three, Howe particularly, couldn't get going.

Defensively, Detroit broke down against Boston. Red Kelly was an offensive star, and Bob Goldham and Marcel Provonost were solid blueliners, but that wasn't enough over a seven-game series. The Bruins were able to penetrate the attacking zone and Sawchuk couldn't hold them off.

A lack of depth was the main reason that during the Fifties Detroit was unable to win three Cups in a row — arguably the true test of a great dynasty. But there were other reasons for the Red Wings' inconsistency. Lindsay notes that Jack Adams, year after year, would tinker with the lineup during the playoffs.

Indeed, in the newspaper reports of the day, Adams was consistently telling the press during the playoffs that reinforcements from the minor leagues were being called up and that new players would be inserted into the lineup — this, for a team that had just dominated the NHL in the regular season.

"We used to hope like hell that the Omaha and Edmonton teams (Detroit affiliates) went all the way in the playoffs," Lindsay says. "That way, Adams wouldn't be able to bring them up. Adams, because of his ego, thought that anybody he put in a uniform would perform. But, what it did was destroy the morale and chemistry of the team. If he hadn't jerked around with the roster, I'm convinced we would have won six or seven Stanley Cups instead of four."

One indisputable factor working against Detroit was simply the era in which the Red Wing team excelled. No other NHL dynasty faced such daunting competition. First it was the great Leaf teams of the late Forties, and then, the emerging powerhouse in Montreal in the Fifties.

With Detroit eliminated in 1953, the Canadiens defeated the Bruins to win the Cup. But the following season, Red Wings were back and this time they advanced to the final, setting up a showdown with Montreal. With the infusion of young players such as Bernie Geoffrion and Jean Beliveau, the Canadiens were on the verge of establishing their own dynasty. But Detroit still had its lineup of stars. Howe had won his fourth consecutive scoring title. The team as a whole had matured and had a good deal of playoff experience.

The final was a tug of war. The Wings took the first game. The Canadiens tied the series. Detroit went ahead, Montreal tied it. And so it went until they were facing a seventh and deciding game. At the Olympia, the largest crowd to see a hockey game in Detroit — 15,791 — were treated to a thriller. Montreal took the lead on a goal by Floyd Curry, but then Red Kelly made it even in the second. A scoreless third meant overtime once again for the Wings, who by now, were used to playing extra periods, even in seventh game of finals.

But this one didn't last long. In the fifth minute, the puck came to Tony Leswick, who was standing at the faceoff circle 30 feet from Canadiens' goaltender Gerry McNeil. Leswick took a swat at the puck and as it rose over defenceman Doug Harvey's shoulder Harvey swatted at it, tipping it with the end of his glove. The puck lost momentum and dropped in over McNeil's shoulder.

As the Detroit players mobbed Leswick, the Canadien players quickly left the ice without the traditional handshake. Gaye Stewart, a former Red Wing, who was now with Montreal said, "The players wanted to come out on the ice and shake hands, but we were restrained from higher up."

Dick Irvin, the temperamental Montreal coach, had held them back. "If I had shaken hands," he said. "I wouldn't have meant it, and I refuse to be hypocritical."

Irvin's short temper and dubious sportsmanship would become a more important factor in the 1955 playoffs. Again Montreal and Detroit met in the final, but not before one of the most controversial incidents in league history. Late in the season, with Detroit and Montreal neck and neck for first place, Rocket Richard punched a linesman in Boston during an attempt to get at the Bruins' Hal Laycoe. NHL president Clarence Campbell acted quickly and punitively, suspending Richard not only for the remainder of the season, but also the playoffs.

Montreal fans vented their outrage a few days later when the Red Wings played the Canadiens in Montreal. Despite death threats, Campbell chose to attend the game at the Forum. Initially the fans booed, then they threw debris at Campbell, and finally one fan walked up to him and attempted to hit him. The police moved in, a tear gas bomb went off and a riot inside and outside the arena ensued. The important result for the Canadiens was they were forced to forfeit the game to Detroit. Then in the final game of the season, with Detroit and Montreal tied in points, the Red Wings pounded the Canadiens, 6-0, to win their sixth consecutive regular season title.

Montreal's chances in the playoffs would have been best served if Irvin had downplayed the Richard incident, especially in the context of the Red Wings' fine season. Instead, Irvin complained incessantly about the unfairness of the suspension and said several times the Red Wings hadn't deserved to finish first.

Says Jimmy Skinner, who coached the Red Wings that year, "He never quit harping about it. He kept saying Montreal had been shafted by Campbell and that Campbell was trying to make sure they didn't win the Stanley Cup. He never gave us credit for anything. Every time he said something in the newspapers, I'd bring it in and show to the players."

In one widely reported incident during the playoffs, Irvin cornered a linesman in a hotel lobby and loudly berated him, accusing him of lying during the Richard hearing. When Campbell was told about Irvin's accusations, he said he would overlook his remarks.

Fittingly, the Canadiens and Red Wings met in the Stanley Cup final. It was a match made in heaven. The Detroit team was at its peak. Howe, Lindsay and Delvecchio were enjoying a strong playoff. The Canadiens, a year away from their glory years, were led by a young star, Bernie Geoffrion, who had just won the regular-season scoring title. But the most interesting matchup was in goal. By then,

Sawchuk was generally recognized as the best goaltender in the game. Others, however, felt Jacques Plante, who had played his first full season with Montreal, would soon supplant Sawchuk.

The first two games of the series were played in Detroit and Sawchuk was almost unbeatable, allowing two goals in Game One and only one goal in the second. Detroit won both and carried a two-game lead into Montreal for the third and fourth games. Montreal made it a home series by winning its two games at the Forum and tying the best-of-seven at 2-2. After two more games, it came down to a seventh game in Detroit.

By the spring of 1955, Detroit's three best players were Howe, Sawchuk and Delvecchio. In the seventh game, they made the difference. Delvecchio scored twice, Howe got the other, Sawchuk let only one in, and Detroit had won its second consecutive Cup — its fourth in six years. It would be their last, but as Lindsay said that night in Detroit, "This was the greatest of them all."

It was the greatest because the Detroit team had finally established itself as one of the best ever — perhaps the finest in terms of pure talent, up to that point. But on the horizon the Montreal era was about to begin, and though the Wings could come close in the Sixties, they would never again win the Cup.

For this, Lindsay blames Adams. But if bad management led to the downfall of the Red Wings, Adams was ably assisted by a weak Detroit ownership. It started in 1952, with the death of Big Jim Norris. By then, his son, Jimmy, was president of the Chicago Black Hawks. Norris had two other children, a daughter Marguerite and second son, Bruce. Jimmy Norris had little use for his half-brother Bruce, who was unreliable and a heavy drinker, so he supported Marguerite as president of the Red Wings, a position she held for three years, from 1952 to 1955. At that point, Bruce, supported by his mother, was able to wrest control from Marguerite.

During Marguerite's presidency, the Red Wings had enjoyed their most prosperous years. She had held Adams in check and had even planned to replace him with Tommy Ivan, who eventually grew impatient waiting for Adams to leave and moved to Chicago where he coached and managed the Black Hawks.

With the dissolute Bruce Norris ensconced as president, Adams' power increased. Ill-tempered and vindictive, he made decisions based more on personal animosity than the good of the team. His first questionable deal came right after the Wings' 1955 Cup triumph, when he sent Sawchuk and a package of players to Boston for five players, none of whom were well-known, or had any impact on the Wings. Adams said at the time he made the trade to make room for Detroit goaltending prospect Glenn Hall. If that was the case, he paid a heavy price and received little in return. Sawchuk was difficult and surly, and was disliked in the Red Wing organization, but he was also the best goaltender in the game.

Two years later, Adams traded with Boston to get Sawchuk back. This time he gave up John Bucyk, who would go on to become one of the best left wingers in the game. Lindsay, for one, thinks Skinner should have done more to convince Adams of Bucyk's worth.

Tommy Ivan, when he coached the team, would stand up to Adams and was respected by the players for doing so. But as Red Kelly says, Skinner was an "Adams man," so when Jack came to the conclusion that Bucyk couldn't check, Skinner readily agreed.

Lindsay says, "Skinner was just a door opener, not a coach. When Adams would say 'Bucyk can't check,' Skinner would parrot him and say, 'Yeah, when's he going to learn to check.' "

Lindsay notes that in a period of two years, Adams sent the Bruins three players who would compose one of the best lines in the NHL during the Fifties — Vic Stasiuk, Bronco Horvath and Johnny Bucyk, but received basically nothing in return, except Sawchuk, who had originally belonged to Detroit anyway.

The most shocking deal, however, occurred in 1957 when Adams traded Lindsay, his star left winger and captain, and Glenn Hall to Chicago. In return, Detroit received only marginal players. Three years later, Red Kelly went to Toronto. Again the Wings got little in return. In Lindsay's case, Adams moved him because he was attempting to establish a players' union. Hall was described by Adams as "a young pest." And Kelly was traded because of a contract dispute.

Howe stayed on, of course, and established himself as Mr. Hockey, the greatest of them all. But the great years never returned. And eventually, even Howe left the organization to play in the rival World Hockey Association.

4

The Tradition of Excellence

*T*he Montreal Canadiens were founded in 1909 during hockey's early days of professionalism. In the beginning, the Canadiens were little more than a marketing strategy for a new league — an ethnic curiosity in a sport that, at its highest level, had been controlled by English-speaking Canadians. There were no French Canadian owners in senior hockey and only a few French Canadian players.

By 1906, near the end of the Silver Seven dynasty, senior teams were paying their best players top money. Many clubs, especially those in the remote, resource-rich communities of Canada, were openly professional — pay-for-play teams, as they were called.

In 1908, for example, a star player of the period, Tom Phillips, signed for $1,800 per season with his hometown Kenora Thistles, which was a hefty amount in those days. In the West, Joseph Patrick, the father of Lester and Frank, was a millionaire timber king who financed the Pacific Coast Hockey League. That league, which was run by his two sons, wooed such eastern stars as Cyclone Taylor and Newsy Lalonde and soon became a force in Canadian hockey. In 1915, the Vancouver Maroons, later to be called the Millionaires, whipped the Ottawa Senators to become the first Western team to win the Stanley Cup.

In Northern Ontario, wealthy mine owners used riches from cobalt and silver deposits to pay for their recruits. Teams in Haileybury and Cobalt played a violent brand of hockey to packed houses that often had fans literally hanging from the rafters. Mike Rodden, a player and coach, and later sports editor of *The Globe* newspaper in Toronto, once said the arena in Cobalt resembled an airplane hangar that was built to seat 1,200, but regularly squeezed in 2,000. "The rafters were black with people," he told writer-broadcaster Brian McFarlane.

Still, the financial success of these teams didn't depend so much on gate receipts as on the huge amounts wagered on the games by the owners. Rodden recounted a time when the wealthy mine speculator Noah Timmins bet $50,000 on his Haileybury team only to see the team fall behind 5-0 in the first period. At intermission, he made a dash to the dressing room and screamed at his players, accusing them of laziness and saying that he was being "taken for a ride."

Led by the legendary Art Ross, Haileybury came back to tie the game 5-5 in the second period. Again, Timmins stormed into the dressing room, this time to announce that he would pay $1,000 to the man who would score the winning goal. This, of course, was a huge amount. The best players of that time were making no more than $2,000 for the entire season.

So, in the third period, Art Ross guaranteed Timmins' investment and made Horace Gaul, an import from Ottawa, $1,000 richer by setting up Gaul for the winning goal. Haileybury won the game and the little arena shook from top to bottom from the celebration until a railing gave way and fans fell 15 feet to the ice. Some were seriously injured and had to be taken to hospital on sleighs.

Railroad and mining multi-millionaire Michael John O'Brien had money invested in the Cobalt and Haileybury teams, but what O'Brien and his son John Ambrose O'Brien really wanted was a third team, this one situated in the family's hometown of Renfrew, in the Ottawa Valley. Indeed, it was their quest for a Renfrew franchise in the Eastern Canada Hockey Association that led to the birth of the Montreal Canadiens.

The power brokers of senior hockey in those days were the

Ottawa Senators, formerly known as the Silver Seven, plus the three Montreal teams — the Wanderers, Shamrocks and Nationals. Ottawa, for its part, had no interest in allowing a Renfrew team in the ECHA, well aware that O'Brien would go to any extreme to build a team that would defeat Ottawa. Besides, Renfrew was small time compared with the big cities of Ottawa and Montreal. When J. Ambrose O'Brien approached two Ottawa directors about supporting a franchise application for Renfrew, they sneeringly turned him down.

In Montreal, there was trouble of a different type. The famous Wanderers, who had dominated hockey after the downfall of the Silver Seven in 1906, had a new owner, P.J. Doran, who was the proprietor of a small arena in the east end of Montreal called the Jubilee. Doran intended to move the Wanderers to his arena, but the other clubs in the league were strongly opposed to playing in the Jubilee rink where, at 40 per cent, their cut of the gate would be smaller than for the games played in the large Wood Avenue arena.

Everything came to head in November, 1909, during an ECHA governors meeting in Montreal. In a slick finesse, the ECHA owners rid themselves of their two problems, the Wanderers and Renfrew, by folding the ECHA and starting a new league, the Canadian Hockey Association. It included Ottawa, Quebec, the Montreal Shamrocks, the Montreal Nationals and a new team called all-Montreal.

In his 1967 biography of M.J. O'Brien, author Scott Young interviewed J. Ambrose O'Brien about those tumultuous times. Ambrose's story began with the Wanderers' general manager, Jimmy Gardner, storming out of the ECHA meeting upon learning that his team had been excluded from the new league.

"Gardner came out and sat down in a chair beside me," Ambrose told Young. "He was so mad he could hardly do anything but swear — and then he turned to me and said, 'Say, you O'Briens have other hockey teams in the north, don't you? In Haileybury and Cobalt?' I said we had, at least we helped support the hockey teams up there.

"And he said, 'Ambrose, why don't you and I form a league? You've got Haileybury, Cobalt and Renfrew. We have the Wanderers. And I think if a team of all Frenchmen was formed in Montreal it would be a real draw. We could give it a French-Canadian name.' "

According to Ambrose, they kicked some names around and came up with Les Canadiens. There are other versions of how the Canadiens got their name. In 1964, Montreal sports journalist Elmer Ferguson wrote that the idea came from James Strachan, one of Doran's partners, who, in turn, suggested it to Ambrose. That same account was given by Ottawa promoter Tommy Gorman in memoirs of his in 1957. Ambrose, however, in his conversation with Young, was firm in his contention it was Jimmy Gardner.

Whatever the origin of the name, the important point is that the Montreal Canadiens franchise officially came into being on December 3, 1909, as part of the new National Hockey Association that included Haileybury, Cobalt, Renfrew and the Wanderers. Immediate success ensued for the Canadiens at the gate, if not on the ice. (They finished last in the NHA in the first season.) Boosting the league's draw was the considerable reputation of the Wanderers, not to mention the star-studded lineup in Renfrew, which included Lester and Frank Patrick, Newsy Lalonde and Fred (Cyclone) Taylor, all of which meant the league became an instant success.

Just as quickly, the CHA, the hybrid of the old ECHA, declined. Before the 1910 season was over, Ottawa and the Montreal Shamrocks had applied, caps in hand, for admission to the NHA and were accepted.

The NHA quickly became the dominant Canadian league and was the forerunner to the National Hockey League. In the early years, the owners in the NHA felt so secure in their new league that in 1912 they designated their own trophy, the O'Brien Cup. The Stanley Cup was never meant to be the championship trophy for one league, anyway. It was a challenge trophy, presumably awarded to the best team in Canada.

In J. Ambrose O'Brien, the Montreal Canadiens had an Irish Canadian owner who didn't have a great deal of interest in the team. The Canadiens were added to the new NHA for the sole purpose of adding ethnic flavour to the league and selling tickets in Montreal. Ambrose had financed the team with the explicit understanding that it would be sold to French Canadian owners when the opportunity arose.

George Kendall wasn't French Canadian, but he had a high

profile in Montreal as a professional wrestler with the stage or ring name of George Kennedy. He was also the owner of the Club Athletique Canadien, a popular French-speaking sports club in the city. At the start of the 1910-11 season, he informed the NHA that the Canadiens team was an infringement on his club's trademark and threatened legal action if the hockey team wasn't sold to him. The NHA, seeing the economic advantages of its hockey team associated with the popular Club Athletique Canadien, readily agreed. Ambrose sold him the team for $7,500.

With French-Canadian stars of the early days, such as goaltender Georges Vezina, Didier Pitre and Jack Laviolette, the Canadiens won their first Stanley Cup in 1916. Right from the beginning, they brought a flare to the game with ethnic pride and a wide-open, full-speed-ahead style of playing — "fire wagon hockey," it was called. The Montreal club always had the best French-Canadian players. But the Flying Frenchmen also included some of the top hockey players from English Canada. In the early Twenties, there was the great Joe Malone who in one season scored an amazing 44 goals in 20 games. Howie Morenz was the best player of his era and according to some, the greatest of all time. He was from Stratford, Ont., and called the Stratford Streak, or Mitchell Meteor.

By the end of the Thirties, the Canadiens had won four Stanley Cups. But there had been no dynasties in Montreal. In the decade of the Forties, the opportunity existed for Montreal to dominate the NHL and win a string of Cups. The club had not been touched by callups to the Second World War, and with a team that included the famous Punch Line of Maurice (Rocket) Richard, Elmer Lach and Toe Blake, as well as goaltender Bill Durnan, a six-time Vezina Trophy winner, the Canadiens' coach Dick Irvin was confident enough to utter his famous boast in 1945 that his was the best team.

The Canadiens ended up winning two Cups in the Forties, but were perceived, more than anything else, as a talented team that should have done better. The club was also suffering financially. Tickets were under-priced and the Montreal Forum was rundown, an ugly spectacle that needed plumbing and major renovations. "It was like walking into a cave," grimaced Frank Selke Jr., who added that in the mid-Forties there was even serious talk at the league board of governors' level of folding the franchise because it was poorly managed and losing money.

So, when Frank Selke Sr., who had assisted Conn Smythe in building the first Maple Leaf dynasty, took over the Canadiens as general manager in July, 1946, he had his work cut out for him.

In the Thirties, during the Depression, the Canadiens had designated 4,000 seats in the north end of the 9,600-seat Forum as the high-priced $1 seats — 'the millionaires' section," it was called. Over the years, this never changed. When Selke took over, the seats in the north end were still selling for $1, one reason why the Canadiens had the lowest ticket revenue in the league. Selke immediately did away with the millionaire's section and raised prices across the board. The interior of the arena, which was coloured a drab brown, was smartly painted red, white and blue.

Selke also reorganized the club's minor hockey system, which was in disrepair. Junior hockey in the Montreal area was inferior to the same level in Ontario and Western Canada. The teams played only 24 games in a season and were able to have game dates at the Forum only late on Saturday nights after the Canadiens' games. Nobody watched the juniors, so players with talent lost interest. In the mid-Forties, for example, there had been only five or six French Canadians on the Montreal team, not because the best were playing elsewhere, but because there was a sum total of only five or six French Canadians available to the team.

Early on, Selke met the junior operators in Quebec and together they worked to upgrade the system. The Junior Canadiens and other city teams, such as the Montreal Royals and Verdun Maple Leafs, were given the opportunity to play at the Forum on Saturday afternoons and other evenings. Fan interest grew, player participation increased and soon the junior league was playing 40 and 50 games a season. Selke, with the help of his righthand man Ken Reardon, developed a Montreal farm system with teams across Canada. The Canadiens, for example, sponsored junior clubs in Regina and Fort William-Port Arthur (now called Thunder Bay). Selke once said the club spent $300,000 developing a junior hockey system in Edmonton alone. In the Montreal area, Sam Pollock, a young man from Montreal's West End, started running the Canadiens' junior organization.

By the early Fifties, these development systems were paying big dividends. As the old warriors of the Forties — Emile Bouchard, Elmer Lach, Toe Blake and others — retired, talented young players took their places. Still, when Canadiens finally set about establishing their first dynasty, they were led by two important holdovers from the old days — Maurice Richard, the team's explosive right winger, and Doug Harvey, a defenceman without equal in the NHL.

Richard had grown up in Montreal and as a teenager had been a skilled boxer. He played baseball in the summer but wisely chose to channel his intense competitiveness into hockey. He joined the Canadiens in 1942 as a 21-year-old but didn't excel until his second season when he scored 32 goals in 46 games. The following season, he became the first man to score 50 goals in 50 games, thus securing himself a prominent spot in the history of the game. He also became the Canadiens' first French-Canadian superstar, a magnetic figure with a fiery determination. The stories of the Rocket scoring "with two men draped on his shoulders" became legendary. His dark eyes would blaze as he drove for the net. He quickly became the most popular sports figure in French Canada.

The Rocket also had a wild temper. He earned notoriety not just for his goal scoring, but for his stick fights and his fists. Many blamed Irvin for the Rocket's almost uncontrollable temper. Irvin felt Richard was most effective when he was enraged, so he would needle him and egg him on. Teammates can remember Irvin teasing Richard in the dressing room, by saying, "You're not going to let Bill Ezinicki do that to you, are you? They'll think you're a coward." So, the Rocket would go back out, almost crazy with rage, and attack Ezinicki.

Frank Selke and Irvin were close friends, but Selke intensely disliked the way Irvin handled Richard. Selke also had problems with the fact that Montreal had won only three Stanley Cups in the 15 years Irvin had coached the team. Two incidents in the 1954-55 season, both involving Richard, resulted in a coaching change and led, indirectly, to the beginning of one of hockey's greatest Stanley Cup dynasties.

The first incident occurred at Maple Leaf Gardens. After a stick fight with Bob Bailey, a Leaf fringe player, Richard, who was encouraged by Irvin, confronted referee Red Storey and hurled epithets at him. That resulted in a meeting with NHL president Clarence Campbell and a warning. Then, with a week remaining in the season, Richard punched a linesman in a game by Boston, while attempting to get at Hal Laycoe. Campbell moved swiftly and punitively. Not only was Richard suspended for the remainder of the season, but he also had to sit out the entire playoffs.

It was a devastating blow. Richard was leading the league in scoring at the time and would have won his only scoring title. But with Maurice sitting out his suspension, teammate Bernie Geoffrion beat him out by one point on the final day of the season. Also, in Richard's absence, the Red Wings moved past the Canadiens and grabbed first place. Without their inspirational leader, Montreal lost the Stanley Cup final to Detroit. Frank Selke wrote in his memoirs, "Without Richard, the team had lost its soul. Our boys were certain that, in one fell stroke, they had lost both the league championship and in the Stanley Cup."

If that wasn't bad enough, the Richard suspension also sparked the infamous riot in Montreal. After his ruling, Campbell received death threats and warnings to stay away from the Forum. Defiantly, he attended the Montreal-Detroit game as placard-carrying protesters marched outside the Forum. Inside the arena, Campbell was pelted with rotten fruit and vegetables. At one point, an enraged fan attempted to get at Campbell at his seat, but was turned away. When a tear-gas bomb went off, Campbell made a quick exit.

The sight of distressed fans leaving the Forum incensed an unruly gang outside that pelted the arena and passing cars with stones and bricks. The chaos spread quickly though the streets and alleyways near the Forum and soon store windows were smashed and newsstands overturned. When the rampage ended, the total damage was estimated at more than $100,000.

When the season ended, Selke made his move to replace Irvin, who had already expressed an interest in leaving Montreal to coach the Chicago Black Hawks. His replacement would be Toe Blake, who had remained in the Montreal organization after retirement. With Blake behind the bench, the glory years of Montreal would begin. The Rocket, who was past his prime by the time Blake took over, would remain an effective player and team leader. The Rocket's temper-tantrums stopped and, despite his advanced age, he played some of the most effective hockey of his career.

Although Richard was the team captain during this period, the real leader was Harvey, the smooth defenceman who made the game look so easy with an effortless style of play. He won the Norris Trophy seven times as the league's best defenceman and today would make most lists of all-time all-star teams.

Harvey also was invaluable in the dressing room. Richard's introverted personality, combined with his exalted status, made him just about unapproachable, especially to the new players. The affable Harvey, on the other hand, loved to talk hockey with anybody and was a great help to young men who had just joined the team. Bernie Geoffrion remembers that his first piece of advice came from Harvey, who would tell all the rookies that they had to keep their sticks on the ice. "If you did what he said, he'd hit your stick with a pass every time," Geoffrion said. "If you didn't, he'd ignore you. We soon learned."

Harvey's devotion to the Canadiens and hockey affected his personal life. Time that should have been spent with his family was spent with his teammates. Although he had a long, remarkably productive career, his drinking eventually became problem, particularly after he retired. Frank Selke Jr. said, "Away from the game, he was a totally undisciplined human being. He was a lost soul. He didn't care about anything else outside of hockey."

Harvey would become a tragic figure later in life, but in the Fifties he was at his peak. Along with Richard, he represented the foundation on which Selke built the Canadiens teams of that decade. When Bernie Geoffrion joined the Canadiens in 1950, he quickly established himself as one of the best right wingers in the game. Dickie Moore, another Montrealer and an all-star who could play either wing, arrived one year later. A skilled left winger, Donny Marshall, from Verdun, also made the team in 1951. In 1950-51, Selke acquired winger Bert Olmstead, a tough, demanding veteran, from Chicago. Olmstead's irascible and exacting nature brought a whole new meaning to peer pressure in the Montreal dressing room.

For a while, Irvin used Olmstead on Richard's line, but eventually the Rocket asked to play on another line. Olmstead would berate anybody if he felt he wasn't doing his best and that included Richard. Teammates can remember Olmstead giving it to the Rocket after coming off from a shift. "He'd chew Richard out right on the bench," said a teammate. "To this day, I'm amazed Rocket didn't punch him out. Olmstead would scream at him, 'You stupid son of a bitch, pass the goddamn puck when I'm open!' Rocket would just glare at him. Finally he went to Dick and said he didn't want to play with him anymore."

The additions of Olmstead, Geoffrion and the others were important to the success of the Canadiens in the Fifties. But key to making them the best team in hockey was Jean Beliveau, a tall, elegant centre, who would follow in Richard's footsteps to become the second French-Canadian superstar on the Montreal team.

Beliveau was from a small town in Quebec called Victoriaville. He played junior hockey there and then in Quebec City for the Citadelles. Jean rejected offers to play for the Junior Canadiens, perhaps because Quebec City was closer to home and had more of a small-town atmosphere. "I had a better feeling about Quebec," Beliveau said. "I was impressed by Frank Byrne, who was an important figure in pulp and paper in Quebec City. He owned the team. It wasn't that I had anything against Montreal at all, it was just that Quebec and Byrne offered more of a family environment."

Time after time, Selke tried to get Beliveau to play for the Junior Canadiens. But on each occasion, Beliveau, the best junior in Quebec, turned him down. It became an embarrassment to the Montreal organization. Then, when Beliveau rejected the Canadiens for semi-pro hockey with the Quebec Aces, the Montreal brass was at wits' end. "Why?" they asked him. The answer was money and familiarity. The Aces were owned by the Anglo-Canadian Pulp and Paper company and Beliveau had received a generous contract. As sports writer Andy O'Brien noted in an article, Beliveau, only 21, had already been given two cars by the club, the most recent a cream-coloured convertible, the licence plate of which read "2 B." The Quebec Premier Maurice Duplessis had "1 B."

O'Brien wrote: "Jean parked his convertible directly in front of the main entrance of the famed Château Frontenac Hotel and we went up to my room. He poured himself a beer and was in the act of lighting up a cigar when there came a knock on the door. I opened it and in walked a Quebec City policeman. Taking off his fur cap, the cop said in French, 'If you let me have your key, Jean, I'll park your car.' Without interrupting his discussion, Jean threw the cop his keys. The cop backed out of the room apologetically."

Punch Imlach, who would run the Maple Leaf organization of the Sixties, coached and managed the Quebec Aces and Beliveau for two years. In Punch's memoirs, he called Beliveau the finest player he had ever coached. For starters, there was his size. He was 6-foot-3, 200 pounds, which made him very large indeed by the standards of those days. He towered over defencemen and, with his long reach, he was a gifted stickhandler and playmaker. In Beliveau's second season with the Aces, the boastful Imlach told the newspapers, "The NHL certainly must know by now that my boy rates only with Gordie Howe and Rocket Richard in the league."

Under league rules, the Canadiens, who still owned Beliveau's NHL rights, were allowed to call him up on a three-game trial. Beliveau accepted the offer and in three games scored five goals, getting a hat trick against the New York Rangers. After his stint with the Canadiens, Selke offered him a huge contract by the standards of those days. It included a $20,000 signing bonus and an annual salary of $10,000, $11,000 and $12,000 over three years for a total package of $53,000. Only one player was making that kind of money on the Canadiens: Rocket Richard. But it wasn't enough for Beliveau. He turned it down.

In the summer of 1953, two developments finally led to Jean joining the Canadiens. First, there was a directive sent to Selke from the team's owner, Senator Donat Raymond: Sign Beliveau at any cost. Second, Beliveau was married in Quebec City. "I met my future wife during the 1952-53 season and we married in the summer," Beliveau said. "When that happened I said to myself, 'Now is the time to move to Montreal.' "

Beliveau ended up signing the largest contract in the history of the Montreal club. It amounted to $110,000 over five years, guaranteed. At a glitzy news conference in October of 1953, Beliveau posed for pictures. Behind him, Dick Irvin put up a V for victory sign. Frank Selke smiled and when asked how he had managed to sign the

Aces' star, said, "It was really simple. All I did was open the Forum vault and say, 'Help yourself, Jean.' "

Beliveau matured slowly in his first two years with the Canadiens, as did the club itself. Montreal advanced to the Stanley Cup final in 1954 and 1955, only to be knocked off both times by Detroit in seven games.

But by the 1955-56 season, several things changed. After two average seasons, Beliveau was about to blossom into a superstar. Playing between Geoffrion and Olmstead, he led the league in scoring with 47 goals and 41 assists. He won the Hart Trophy as the league's most valuable player and established himself as the Canadiens' best player. For a young star such as Beliveau, the cantankerous Olmstead was an irritant, but looking back, Beliveau says Olmstead was an important factor in the success of his line. "Some nights he would make us mad all the time, but he also made us play our best," Beliveau said.

Joining the Canadiens that same season was the Rocket's younger brother by 15 years, Henri, who was so quiet that Toe Blake said for years he didn't even know the younger Richard could speak French because he never said anything. But Henri proved himself to be a top player. Although not tall, he could stand up for himself and gave the team great speed and agility down the middle.

In goal, Jacques Plante had become the Canadiens' first stringer. Unlike the others, Plante was a loner who had little to do with his teammates. He had a reputation for being cheap and was thought to be slightly eccentric. For a hobby, he knitted, and to save money, would knit his underwear.

But Plante was shrewd, bright, a dedicated student of the game and a fine goaltender. He was the first of his era to wear a mask (he started practicing with one in 1955-56 and began wearing the mask in games in 1959-60). In later life, he became a respected hockey analyst on television. As Beliveau noted, "Jacques didn't talk to us very much, but he loved to talk on television. Just like many goaltenders, he was a different type. He was a private person and wouldn't hang around with the players."

The 1955-56 campaign turned into one of those wonderful seasons that great teams have perhaps once in a player's career. The

Canadiens started with a 2-0 shutout of Toronto and then got better. Beliveau was dazzling. In an early 4-1 win over the Rangers, he scored all four Montreal goals. The Rocket was still a force and ended the season with 38 goals, the same as the younger Gordie Howe in Detroit. In goal, Plante was a rock. He played in all but six of Montreal's games that year. Of his 64 games, he won 42, which was tops in the league. And he recorded an amazing 1.86 goals-against average, which also was the league's best.

Plante won the Vezina Trophy as the league's top goaltender, Doug Harvey was voted best defenceman and Beliveau had the scoring title and MVP. Richard, Beliveau, Harvey and Plante took four of the six all-star team spots. Tom Johnson and Bert Olmstead were on the second team.

Unlike the two previous years, there were no disappointments in the playoffs. In the first game of the Canadiens' semi-final, they pounded the Rangers 7-1 and eliminated them in five games. It took them five more to sweep aside Detroit, the team that had been their nemesis for the past two years.

During the Red Wing series, the Detroit sportswriters made fun of the mask Plante used in practices and suggested that Jacques was less than masculine for resorting to such paraphernalia. In the third game of the series at the Olympia, a 3-1 Detroit win, the Montreal players got into an altercation with the Detroit fans behind the bench. After the game, the Wings' general manager Jack Adams gloated and told the media the Canadiens couldn't take the pressure. "You know the Canadiens are choking when they start fighting our fans," he said. In the fourth game, also at the Olympia, Montreal blanked Detroit 3-0 and then knocked the Red Wings off back at the Forum.

"It was very satisfying," said Bernie Geoffrion, "after losing the two previous years to Detroit and after listening to some of things Jack Adams was saying. We also knew that we were going to win it a few more times before it was all over." In fact, the Canadiens would win the Stanley Cup for five consecutive years, something that had never been done before or since.

The Habs of the Fifties were a team of stars, but they were kept in tight rein by Toe Blake. The leaders such as Beliveau and Geoffrion had grown up listening to Canadiens' games on the radio in the

Forties when Blake was a member of the legendary Punch Line with Richard and Elmer Lach. They idolized Blake and accepted his strict rules and tough standards, because they remembered how he had played and what he had demanded of himself. "We all respected him," Beliveau said. "On the Punch Line, Toe was the digger, the guy who worked. If you worked, Toe was behind you one hundred per cent. He was tough, but honestly tough."

The team as a group got along well, according to those who were part of it. There were rumours that Richard was upset over Beliveau's rookie contract, but that would have been understandable considering that the Rocket was a veteran and the team's star player, who happened to be making less than a rookie. That problem, apparently, was corrected in the years that followed, although it is not known if Richard retired as the team's highest paid player.

Geoffrion, who would become the second player to score 50 goals in one NHL season, in 1960-61, often said that he felt overlooked — never more so than in 1960 when Beliveau was appointed captain despite Geoffrion's seniority. Geoffrion was a genuine star of that era and is usually credited for being the man who developed the slapshot. By drawing the stick well over his shoulder, he shot the puck probably harder than anybody before him. His nickname "Boom Boom," was well earned.

Boom Boom was talkative, good natured and a media favourite, but those close to him sensed a deeper insecurity. "Boom Boom felt he didn't get the adulation he deserved," said Frank Selke Jr., who served as the team's public relations director during the Fifties. "He was loud, lots of fun, had a big voice, but underneath he was an insecure and sensitive kid."

There were consistent rumours of a feud between the aging Rocket and the up-and-coming Geoffrion. But Bernie, today, says there was no animosity. "The Rocket was always my idol. I don't care what other people said. I had no problem with him at all. I never got all the credit I was supposed to. But that's the way it was. To get it, you were fighting an idol."

The remarkable success of the Canadiens was a testament to Frank Selke's scouting and farm systems. In addition to the stars, Selke developed a strong second tier of players who would have been

Ottawa's Silver Seven team, led by Frank McGee, was hockey's first dynasty, holding the Stanley Cup from 1903 to 1906.

Captain Ted (Teeder) Kennedy was often called the heart and soul of the Toronto Maple Leafs of the 1940's.

Assembling at Toronto's City Hall became a rite of spring for the Leafs of the 1940's and early 1950's. In 10 seasons, they won six Stanley Cups.

A team picture of the 1955 Detroit Red Wings. That spring the Detroit dynasty won it's fourth Stanley Cup in six years.

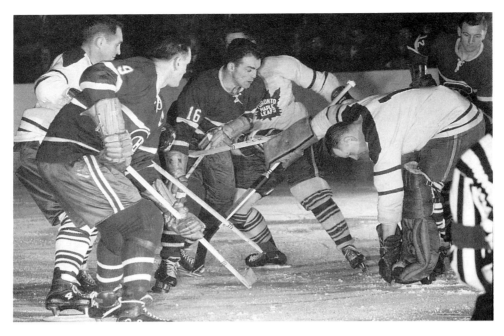

In the 1950's, the most illustrious brother act in hockey was Maurice (Rocket) Richard and younger brother Henri. Here, the Richards lead a rush to the Leaf goalmouth.

Some would rank the Canadiens of the 1950's the greatest dynasty in the history of the game.

The Maple Leafs pour over the boards after winning another Stanley Cup. In the 1960's they won four in six years.

Goaltender Johnny Bower was a big part of the Maple Leaf's defence in the 1960's. Here, Bower holds off the New York Rangers.

Guy Lafleur was the Canadiens' third French Canadian superstar, after Rocket Richard and Jean Beliveau. In the 1970's, he was the Hab's dominant offensive player.

The key members of the Montreal defense during the team's four successive Stanley Cups of the 1970's were Larry Robinson and goaltender Ken Dryden.

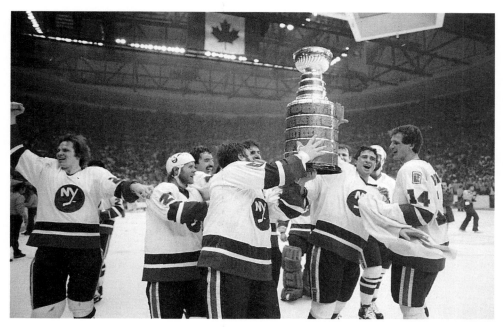

The New York Islanders did not begin their domination of the Stanley Cup in the 1980's until the trade for Butch Goring (left, with beard).

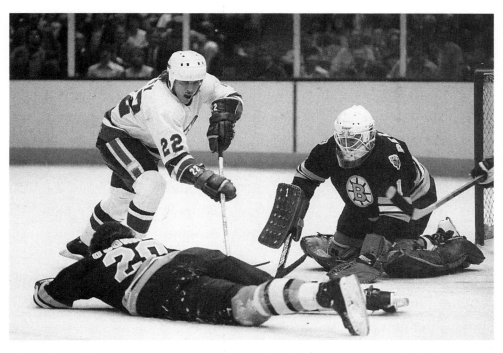

Right winger Mike Bossy was not only the Islanders' leading goal scorer of the 1980's, but the first man after Rocket Richard to score 50 goals in 50 games.

Wayne Gretzky, also known as The Great One, celebrates one of the four Stanley Cups won by the Edmonton Oilers while he was with the team.

The Oilers weren't always a happy group, but in the 1980's smiling faces surrounded the Stanley Cup on four occasions. They won the Cup again in 1990.

first-liners on other teams. Defenceman Tom Johnson was a significant talent who played in the shadow of Harvey, but was regarded highly enough to be awarded the Norris Trophy in 1959. Also on defence were capable young players such as Bob Turner and Jean-Guy Talbot. Up front, the stars were ably supported by Floyd Curry, Claude Pronovost, Ralph Backstrom and Phil Goyette, among others.

In the Rocket's final years he was overweight, but still a scorer and still a charismatic figure on and off the ice. For Toe Blake and Frank Selke, the need wasn't to motivate Richard, but to smooth the troubled waters — to do everything they could to keep the lid on his temper. Author Josh Greenfeld once said, "Blake and Selke were trying to give the Rocket all they had by way of a tranquilizing program. They started giving him de-pep talks long before the season began. They pointed out to him that he was 35 years old, that he did not have to carry the emotional burden of victory alone, that he still would be treated with sufficient respect by the other players around the league even if he went a little easy on the roughhouse, and the important thing was not one game, not one fight, but to lead the team to a Stanley Cup victory."

In Blake's coaching system, the focus was always the Stanley Cup. At the end of each regular season, he would sit down with the team and outline his "eight steps to the Stanley Cup." In an era in which there were only four teams in the playoffs and only two series, the semi-finals and final, each step represented a playoff victory. Eight of them meant another championship. Beliveau can remember Blake telling the younger players on the team after each win, "We're getting closer, we're getting closer."

It's worth noting that during the Canadiens' Fifties dynasty, the team was never pushed to a seventh game in any series, and only once in the Cup final did the Habs have to play a sixth game. In addition to dominating Stanley Cup play, the team finished first in the regular four of those five years. Never in the history of the league had one team so overwhelmed the competition.

It was because of the Canadiens' daunting superiority that the NHL system of penalizing a team was changed. The Montreal power play was dazzling. On the point was Harvey, the best play-making defenceman in the league and the team's quarterback. Geoffrion, with his booming slapshot, was on the other point. Up front were Beliveau, Rocket Richard and Dickie Moore, an all-star in his own right, and twice the league scoring champion.

In those days, the penalized player in a two-minute minor did not return once a goal was scored. He stayed off until his two minutes were up. The problem was that the Montreal power play was so strong that the game was often out of reach once the penalized player did get back. Beliveau, for example, can remember scoring three goals in one power play by himself. Because of this, the five other teams insisted on a rule change that allowed the penalized player to return to play after one power-play goal had been scored.

During Montreal's winning years, the league entered a transitional period. For most of the Forties and Fifties, the NHL was divided equally between have and have-not teams. But by the mid-Fifties, the old order had disappeared. The Maple Leafs declined significantly in the Fifties and, after 1957, so did Detroit. The Canadiens, arguably, did not face the stiff Stanley Cup tests in their dynasty that the Leafs of the Forties and Red Wings of the early Fifties did.

In 1957, for example, Montreal downed the Rangers in the semi-finals and then met the Boston Bruins in the final. With Milt Schmidt behind the bench, the Bruins had enjoyed a fine regular season, third over all, and had actually bettered the Canadiens with seven wins and three ties in 14 meetings. However, Boston couldn't match the Canadiens' lineup in talent or experience when the games really counted, and Montreal defeated them in five games in the final. Montreal met Boston again in 1958 and this time the series went six games, but with the same result.

But 1959, the Maple Leafs had been partially rebuilt by Punch Imlach and had improved to become a reasonably strong challenger. Before the playoff started, Imlach confidently predicted that his team would eliminate Boston in six games and then defeat the Canadiens in seven. Actually, it took the Leafs seven games to get past Boston. He was completely wrong about Montreal, even though both Richard and Beliveau hardly played in the series. Beliveau had suffered an injury in Montreal's semi-final and Richard, hampered by age and some nagging ailments, spent most of the series on the bench. Asked at one point if he would play, he said no. Pointing to his teammates, he said, "Those guys are winning the games."

Even without their two stars, Montreal bounced the Leafs in five games in 1959 to win their fourth consecutive championship. After the final game, Toe Blake said, "They say we've getting old, but we won this one without Beliveau most of the way and with Richard very little of the way. They'll be back next season and so will we. I don't see why we can't win a fifth in a row."

By 1959-60, age had become a factor. Richard was 38, Harvey was 35. The young lions — Beliveau, Geoffrion and Moore — were now in their late 20s. So was Plante. Nevertheless, the Canadiens were a proud and dedicated group. They finished first again in the regular season, losing only 18 of 70 games. And in the playoffs, it was a sweep. Four games to get past a new power in hockey, the Chicago Black Hawks, and four more to knock off the Maple Leafs. Said Henri Richard, "That 1960 team was the best I ever played on. We had a well-balanced team — Plante in goal, Doug Harvey and Tom Johnson on defence, Beliveau, my brother, Geoffrion, Backstrom. We won in eight straight games and that was the last time it was ever done." (The New York Islanders accomplished this feat in 1982.)

The Canadiens' dynastic era ended in the spring of 1961 when the Chicago Black Hawks eliminated them four games to two in the Stanley Cup semi-final. Rocket Richard was gone by then, retiring at the start of the season. The Black Hawks were bigger and tougher than the Canadiens and with Bobby Hull, Stan Mikita, Pierre Pilote and Glenn Hall, could match the aging Montreal stars in talent. The Black Hawks went on to win the Cup that spring, defeating Detroit in the final. Just over the horizon was the Maple Leaf dynasty and three consecutive Cups for Toronto.

In the period of the early Sixties, Montreal could only look to the past and the glory of the Montreal dynasty that had just ended. Not only had the Montreal team won five straight championships, but it had set a standard of hockey excellence.

5

The Leafs of Autumn

*F*or the Toronto Maple Leafs, the dynasty of the Sixties grew out of lean years and hard times.

After the team's 1951 Cup victory, the Maple Leafs declined quickly. In 1951-1952, they slipped to third place in the regular-season standing and were swept in the first round of the playoffs. In 1953, they failed to make the playoffs. From being the best and the brightest in the Forties, the Leaf organization had grown tired and old. King Clancy, who had returned to the Leaf organization, took over as coach from Joe Primeau in 1953, but the Leafs continued their downward path. Howie Meeker replaced Clancy in 1956, but stayed only a year. The next man behind the bench was Billy Reay, who guided the team to last place in 1957-58.

In the front office, Hap Day, the team's general manager, was forced to retire by Conn Smythe in the spring of 1957. Smythe, who was in poor health and spending most of the winter months in Palm Beach, Florida, called a news conference in New York to announce that Day would be asked if he was "available" for the following the season. This was Smythe's curious and somewhat cowardly way of telling Day, the most loyal of all his employees, that he was no longer needed or wanted. Day immediately resigned and was replaced by Smythe's eldest son, Stafford, who had been working in the Leaf minor-hockey system, mostly with the Junior A team, the Marlboros.

Stafford was a competent and hard-working hockey man, but not popular. He attempted to emulate his father, but instead of being seen as a tough self-made man, he was perceived to be arrogant — the boss's son whose behaviour was a caricature of the old man. Still, in the years to come, Stafford would prove his worth as a hockey man. The youngsters Stafford and his scouts recruited for the Leaf-sponsored minor hockey teams in the Fifties would become the nucleus of the great Toronto teams of the Sixties. These players included Bob Pulford, Bob Baun, Carl Brewer, Bob Nevin and Billy Harris, as well as Dave Keon and Frank Mahovlich, the latter two having been discovered in Noranda, Quebec, and Kirkland Lake, Ontario, respectively.

One of Stafford's first decisions as Leaf boss turned out to be his most important. In June, 1958, he hired 40-year-old George (Punch) Imlach, as assistant general manager. Punch was from Toronto and had coached and managed in the minor leagues. Since the club had not no official general manager, Imlach was pretty much in control. Imlach was a bald, unremarkable man in appearance, but he was a fire-brand who got his nickname during his playing days from skating around throwing punches at people after absorbing a bump on the head.

Punch was determined to make the Leafs a winner, and by the end of November he had convinced Smythe's hockey committee to give him official control and make him general manager. A week later, Imlach fired Reay and took over as coach. With Imlach behind the bench, the Leafs played .500 hockey and moved from sixth place to fourth at season's end.

In addition to intense optimism, Imlach provided stability and leadership to the organization. Good or bad, he was the boss — the "Big I" as he was called, in part because of his liberal use of the first-person singular. Frank Mahovlich says, "All of a sudden there was somebody in charge. Nobody had been able to do that before, and he did instill confidence in a lot of players."

As a coach, Imlach's greatest skill might have been making adjustments in the heat of a battle. He had excellent instincts and could tell immediately when a certain player wasn't performing up to potential, and then make the necessary change on the line.

When Day was coaching, Conn Smythe would view the game from his seat in the Gardens green seating section, called *"Berchtesgaden"* (Hitler's wartime retreat) by the sportswriters, a reference that was both ironical, given Smythe's war record, and appropriate, given his managerial skills. During a game he would send a messenger to the bench to tell Day that a certain player wasn't performing and should be benched. But with Imlach, Smythe experienced something almost like telepathy. Imlach would make the necessary adjustment just as Smythe was about to dispatch one of his missives. Of Imlach, Smythe would write in his memoirs: "He was the best coach I ever saw. It was like he was a mind reader."

As well as a mind reader, it appeared the Leafs would need a magician to get into the 1959 playoffs. By March 14, they trailed seven points behind the Rangers for the fourth and last playoff spot with only five games remaining. On the eve of a weekend home-and-home series against the Rangers, the league had issued to the media various playoff combinations and dates of games. Among the different matchups no mention was made of the Leafs. Imlach used this to motivate the players for the two critical games against the Rangers, and the Leafs responded by winning both.

The two victories moved Toronto out of last place, ahead of Detroit and three points behind New York. What worried Imlach was that his team had not won more than two consecutive games all season, and to get into the playoffs they had to keep winning, beginning with a game in Montreal against the first-place Canadiens. It was the Leafs' most important match of the season, and they responded with a victory, pulling to within one point of New York. But a few days later, the Rangers turned up the heat with a win over the Red Wings. The New York win was followed by another Toronto triumph, this time over the Black Hawks.

An element of the Leaf-Ranger battle was a feud between Imlach and Ranger coach Harry Watson. More than once Imlach brazenly predicted his team would finish ahead of New York. Watson responded by saying, "All the time Imlach is saying 'I did this and I did that, and I've won so many games since I took over.' Before that it was always 'we' and 'these guys.' Wasn't Imlach with the club at that time? Always he's predicting what the Leafs are going to do. The only crystal ball he's got is on his shoulders. What a beautiful head of skin."

The race came down to the final day of the season. Montreal was in New York, the Leafs in Detroit. The game at Madison Square Garden started an hour earlier than the one in Detroit, so by the end of the second period Imlach and the Leafs knew that the Canadiens had defeated the Rangers 4-2. Now all Toronto had to do was defeat Detroit, which didn't seem likely after one period of play and with the Red Wings ahead 2-0. According to Imlach in his first book, *Hockey Is a Battle,* Stafford Smythe came along between periods, talked to Imlach in the hall and said, "Well, at least you had a good try. You have nothing to be ashamed of."

"What the hell are you talking about?" Imlach yelled. "We've come too far to lose now. Don't be stupid."

On the way out for the second period, George Armstrong told Imlach, "We'll get it for you." And they did, fighting back twice to tie the game and then taking the lead in the third period. It ended 6-4 with right winger Larry Regan scoring twice as well as setting up Dick Duff's game winner.

In the semi-finals, the Leafs lost the first two games to Boston, but then bounced back to defeat them in seven games. Toronto fell to the Canadiens in the Stanley Cup final in five games, but the team had been competitive and every game was close.

For the players, the events in the spring of 1959 are among their fondest memories. Billy Harris says the season-end surge was deliciously satisfying after enduring the difficult years. They were finally seeing progress and they knew it would get better. "We got slapped around pretty good for a few seasons before it happened. Henri Richard played on five Stanley Cup teams in his first five years in the league. I don't think it would have been as thrilling for him to come into the league and it's automatic for five years. We missed the playoffs twice and had a lot of frustrations, but after 1959, there was a feeling it was just a matter of time before we won everything."

In the following season, 1959-60, Imlach made probably the most important trade of his 11 years in Toronto, in acquiring Red Kelly.

Kelly had been a star with the Detroit Red Wings, but by 1959-60, he was into his 30s and the Wings were looking for younger players after finishing last the year before. That summer Imlach attempted to make a deal for Kelly who was having contract problems with Jack Adams. Nothing came of it and Kelly eventually signed again with Detroit.

In February, 1960, Adams finally did trade Kelly, to the New York Rangers, but the deal was vetoed when Kelly refused to report. Imlach again made a bid for him, this time offering defenceman Marc Reaume. Adams agreed.

But instead of putting Kelly on the blueline, Imlach decided to use him as a centre. It was an inspired move because Kelly made the transition easily and became the team's top centre on the big line between Mahovlich and Bob Nevin.

Of all the Leafs in those days, Mahovlich had the most natural talent. He was a big man (6-foot-1, 194 pounds), a wonderful skater with a blistering slapshot. But he had only one great year in Toronto, in 1960-61, when he scored 48 goals. He was never the fan favourite he should have been and his inconsistency was a frustration not only for the fans, but also Imlach. Over the years their relationship deteriorated.

The second line was made up of Dave Keon at centre between Dick Duff and George Armstrong. Both wingers usually had seasons in the 20-goal range and Duff was known as a money player, at his best in a big game. Armstrong, the captain, was part Ojibwa and nicknamed "the Chief." Over the years, he was among the steadiest of all the Leaf players.

The third line consisted of the checkers, with Bob Pulford in the middle between Eddie Shack, a flamboyant crowd pleaser, and Bert Olmstead, the former Montreal Canadien veteran who had been claimed by Toronto in the 1958 waiver draft. The goaltending was handled by Johnny Bower, with Don Simmons as his backup. Bower had spent 15 years in the minors, except for the 1953-54 season when he played a season with the Rangers. A gentle and likeable man, Bower was intensely competitive and in the early Sixties there was no better goaltender in the league.

In 1960-61, Bower suffered a leg injury that kept him out of the lineup for 12 games. The Leafs were battling the Canadiens for first place at the time, and Imlach said later that Bower's injury had not only cost them the top spot but felt it had left them tired for the playoffs. Indeed, the Leafs were upset in the first round, which was a bitterly disappointing way to end a good season.

Still, there was much to be enthusiastic about. Mahovlich had developed into a superstar, falling just short of Richard's 50-goal mark. Keon had won the Calder Trophy as the league's top rookie. Bower had won the Vezina Trophy, as the best goaltender. Bower and Mahovlich were first-team all-stars. Allan Stanley was a second-team all-star. At centre, on defence and in goal, the Leafs were as good as any team in the league.

As it turned out, the 1961-62 season marked the beginning of the second Leaf dynasty. In the Sixties they would win three consecutive Stanley Cups and a total of four in six years. Except for a handful of young players, this was a mature group often called the Leafs of Autumn. The only major change for the 1961-62 season was strategic — less emphasis on first place and more on winning the Stanley Cup. When the playoffs arrived, the team was rested and healthy. In the first round, they eliminated the Rangers in six games, which set up a final against the defending Stanley Cup champions — the Black Hawks.

In those days, the Leafs and Black Hawks were the league's two toughest squads. Chicago could not match the Leafs in depth, but their front-line talent was remarkable. At left wing, Bobby Hull was already a superstar and had scored 50 goals that season. Stan Mikita, along with Jean Beliveau, were the most skillful centres in the league. In Mikita's case, he was also probably the dirtiest. Kenny Wharram was among the best right wingers. On defence, Pierre Pilot was the NHL's best blueliner. Glenn Hall was an all-star.

But before the series started, most of the talk was about which team was going to intimidate the other. Tommy Ivan, the Black Hawks' general manager, said, "No Leaf is going to push us around." Imlach was quoted as saying, "The Hawks should know by now that they can't run us out of any rink." It was a rough series and the Leafs more than held their own. After the fifth game, with the Leafs leading the series 3-2, Reggie Fleming, a muscular Chicago winger, sounded quite demoralized and bitter over the way some of the Leafs were playing. "They're crude, just crude," he said. "You know who they are. They're always waving their sticks in somebody's direction."

Led by Frank Mahovlich and George Armstrong, the Leafs eliminated Chicago in six games. Johnny Bower had been almost unbeatable in goal, with one shutout and two one-goal games.

The next season, 1962-63, marked the high point of the Imlach era. The team finished first overall — something it hadn't done since 1947-48 — and in the playoffs eliminated the Canadiens in five games and then knocked off Detroit in the final, again in five games.

In ranking the top Leaf teams of all time, authorities on these matters place the 1962-63 team close to the 1947-48 squad. There were several similarities. Both were strong at centre, the best of their particular era. Both had great defences and were quite content to sit on a one-goal lead. The Leafs of the Sixties probably had a better defence, but the centres on the 1947-48 team were superior. Both teams had veteran goalies who played their best under pressure.

One significant difference was that Day's team won three Cups in a row without a great deal of difficulty, and would have won five consecutively, except for an upset in the first round by Detroit in 1950.

Imlach's team, on the other hand, struggled to win three straight and would not have been able to do it without a key trade made in February of the 1963-64 season. The Leafs did not look anything like defending champions that winter. It was clear Mahovlich could no longer play for Imlach. Duff wasn't scoring, nor was Nevin. In one game, the Leafs were humiliated 11-0 by the lowly Bruins.

For most of the season Imlach had tried to make a deal for Andy Bathgate, a smooth playmaking right winger who could also score goals. In 1958, Bathgate had won the league MVP with the Rangers, but by 1964 he was 31 and a step or two slower. Finally it was agreed the Leafs would send the Rangers a package made up of veterans and young players for Bathgate and Don McKenney, a centre and left winger. The Rangers received Duff and Nevin, minor-league right winger Bill Collins, and two young defencemen in the Leaf organization, Arnie Brown and Rod Seiling.

McKenney took Duff's spot on the line with Keon and Armstrong, and Bathgate played with Kelly and Mahovlich. The addition of Bathgate, who had three goals and 15 assists in his 15 regular-season games with Toronto, brought the big line back to life. The team was playing well going into the post-season.

One of the debates during the 1964 playoffs was about the effectiveness of Imlach's long and tough practices. Mahovlich always felt that Imlach, who was often described as tyrant, worked the players too hard. "I think he over-practiced us," Mahovlich said. "I think he worked us into the ground, really. We left a lot of our games at practice. It was like a horse running three days before the big race and having nothing left."

In the 1964 Stanley Cup final between the Leafs and Detroit, the two teams took quite different approaches to working out. Like the Leafs, the Red Wings were a veteran team with older players such as Gordie Howe, Alex Delvecchio and Bill Gadsby. Their coach, Sid Abel, went easy on them. On off days, they didn't practice. Instead they would go to the track or hang around by the hotel pool. Imlach, on the other hand, felt that hard workouts improved endurance, and he whipped his players, even during the final. This seemed to upset the Red Wings, perhaps worried that their coach might adopt a similar routine. Said Bill Gadsby at the time, "That Imlach must be nuts. Those older guys like Kelly, Stanley and Armstrong can't take it. The business of working out every day, it's killing them."

Events seemed to prove the Red Wings correct when the Leafs fell behind 2-1 in the series and then 3-2. But in the sixth game in Detroit, Bower was magnificent, holding his team close in the first two periods, until Billy Harris tied it near the end of the second period. After a goalless third, the Leafs went into overtime facing elimination. A goal by the Wings would end Toronto's Stanley Cup string at two.

The hero that night was Bobby Baun, whose story will be told for as long as the Maple Leafs are a team. Baun had been helped off the ice with a suspected fracture of his ankle. But the hard-rock defenceman refused to have the injury X-rayed and when overtime started he was on the bench. After the first line change, out he came. Seconds after the puck was dropped, the play moved into the Detroit end and Baun took his position on the right point of the blueline. It was Bob Pulford who was able to control the puck and get it back to Baun. His shot wasn't hard, but as Red Wing goalie Terry Sawchuk positioned himself to stop it, Gadsby moved in. The puck hit Gadsby's foot, changed direction and fell in behind Sawchuk.

Back in Toronto, the Leafs made short work of the Wings, defeating them 4-0, with Andy Bathgate getting the winner.

It was an immensely satisfying Stanley Cup championship for Imlach. Bathgate had made a significant difference in the playoffs. Imlach's theory of working his players hard in practices had been vindicated. And one of Imlach's greatest critics, Gadsby, had turned out to be goat of the series.

At this point, Imlach was at the peak of popularity in Toronto. Despite his unimpressive appearance, there was a charisma about him, a self-confidence and sense of invincibility that drew followers, not only from the sports public, but also from the media. One sports writer titled his notes at the bottom of his stories, Punch Lines. Red Burnett, the beat writer for the Toronto *Star,* was an old friend of Imlach's and almost a father figure, going back to the Thirties when Red coached a minor hockey league that included young George.

One criticism of Imlach was that he was never able to get along with his two most talented young players, Frank Mahovlich and Carl Brewer, although this might be unfair, because Dave Keon was of their skill level and he had a pretty good relationship with Imlach.

Brewer was intense and very much his own man. Red Kelly describes him as "panicky." He was high-strung and easily frustrated. During the season, he would lose a large amount of his hair from the stress of competition. Very often Brewer's conflict with Imlach was over money. As general manager, Imlach negotiated the contracts and he wasn't generous. Mahovlich can remember haggling over $500 after his 48-goal season.

In the early Sixties, Brewer decided to enlist the help of a friend when he needed to negotiate. Brewer had grown up in the west end of Toronto with Bob Pulford and Billy Harris, and one of their pals had been Alan Eagleson, a good lacrosse player who had opted for law. Eagleson was interested in the representing athletes and agreed to act for Brewer. This was something that had rarely been done in the past, and Imlach was violently opposed to it.

When Brewer was chosen as a first-team all-star in 1963, he felt his accomplishments warranted more money than Imlach was willing to pay. When no financial reward was forthcoming from Imlach, Eagleson advised Brewer to retire and enroll in university, which he did at McMaster in Hamilton. When he was photographed in a McMaster football uniform, the Leafs started to worry. Before long, King Clancy, who, by then, was Imlach's assistant, arrived on campus to tell Brewer his demand had been accepted.

A year later, Brewer broke his arm in the playoffs. He felt he should have been compensated for not being able to work that summer, and when the Leafs refused, it was back to school. Not long after, Clancy showed up again and a settlement was reached. This, of course, infuriated Imlach. Later, in 1967, Brewer, Baun, Harris and Pulford assisted Eagleson in establishing the NHL Players' Association, which was more than Imlach could stand. Eagleson would say, "There are two names Imlach can't stand. Mine and Brewer's."

Imlach's policy was to treat everyone on the team the same, and, as Kelly recalls, the laziest, most ineffective players set the tone for the practices. "He tended to take his worst players, ones not in top condition, and drive everyone from that standpoint."

It worked for most of the players, particularly the veterans, who had been around long enough to accept what Imlach was doing. But it didn't work for Brewer and Mahovlich. Baun says, "Punch sort of psyched Carl out. He did much the same thing with Frank Mahovlich. Imlach could be very difficult with the needle and he sort of put everyone in one category. He had the big hammer and he used it in the motivating end. It wasn't really motivation. It was play or else. And that didn't work for a guy like Carl, who was very headstrong."

For Mahovlich it became a tortured existence. Imlach would attempt to motivate him through intimidation but it didn't work. Instead Mahovlich withdrew. He didn't play well and his ice time was decreased. The fans booed him. The stress resulted in his taking two leaves of absence from the team. Finally, he was traded.

"They put me in a hospital for a rest," Mahovlich says. "There were a couple of times it happened. I was just exhausted. And I think the main problem was that I wasn't getting along with Imlach. The outcome of that was they had to get rid of me. I wasn't going to perform up to my ability there. There was the pressure to perform from the fans and here's some guy whipping you."

In 1968, Mahovlich was traded to Detroit; in 1971, the Red Wings moved him to the Canadiens. He had outstanding seasons with both clubs. In his final two years in Toronto he scored 18 and 19 goals respectively, but with the Red Wings and Canadiens his enthusiasm returned. He had 49 goals one year in Detroit and 43 in Montreal a few years later. "As soon as I left Toronto, my production went sky high," he says. "It was as if a piano had been lifted off my back."

The Leafs went into eclipse after the 1964 championship. They failed to get past the first round of the playoffs in either 1965 or 1966. Brewer retired in 1965 at the age of 27. New players came in, such as Jim Pappin, Ron Ellis, Brit Selby and Peter Stemkowski. Dickie Moore, the former Canadiens' star, attempted a comeback with the Leafs.

By the spring of 1967, nobody expected Toronto to be a factor in the playoffs. In a 10-game stretch during the season, they had gone winless and had slipped as far down as fifth. Imlach had been admitted to hospital suffering from exhaustion. But as the season drew to a close, the Leafs improved and finished in third place. Still, they were a very old team. Armstrong was 36, Kelly 39, Horton 37, Stanley 41 and Bower 42. Newspapers called them the "Over the Hill Gang," or the "Old Folks Athletic Club."

There was one other old-timer — Sawchuk, who was picked up by the Leafs in the 1964 waiver draft. Sawchuk had accomplished amazing things in his career, but by 1967 he was 37 years old and considered well past his prime. However, that spring, Sawchuk together with Bower would work a miracle for the Leafs and bring them one more Stanley Cup.

In the semi-finals Toronto faced the Chicago Black Hawks, a team that had dominated the regular season, finishing in first place, 22 points ahead of Montreal. Mikita led the team in points, but Bobby Hull had collected 52 goals playing with a promising young centre, Phil Esposito. The Leaf oldtimers were given little hope of beating them.

Chicago won the first game easily 5-2, and a sweep was predicted by the media. Then, in the early minutes of the second game,

Sawchuk stopped a shot from Hull with his mask and fell to the ice. When the Leaf trainer rushed to his side and asked if he was injured, Sawchuk said, "I stopped it, didn't I? Now let's play hockey."

And play he did. Sawchuk held Chicago to one goal that night and the Leafs won 3-1. With Bower and Sawchuk sharing the goaltending, Chicago was able to score only seven goals against Toronto in the next five games. The two old men turned back wave after wave of Chicago attackers. Up front, a mix of young and old, led by Dave Keon, checked and counterattacked. It was an inspired effort by the oldtimers, most of whom knew this would be their last playoff and, indeed, final games in professional hockey.

In the other semi-final series, the Montreal Canadiens swept the New York Rangers in four games, setting up a Leaf-Canadien final, which was appropriate. For one thing, 1967 marked the end of hockey's six-team era. In the next season, the NHL entered its expansion era, doubling in size from six to 12 teams. The year 1967 also marked Canada's 100th anniversary, and it somehow seemed fitting that the two Canadian teams in the NHL would meet for the country's most famous trophy, the Stanley Cup.

The Leafs weren't given much hope. Nor did it help that Imlach, as he was wont to do, fanned the flames of the famous rivalry by telling Montreal *Star* sports editor Red Fisher that the Leafs had the edge in goaltending, referring to 21-year-old Rogatien Vachon as a "Junior B goaltender." That remark grabbed headlines all over Quebec, but as the series progressed, Imlach revised his assessment, calling Vachon "the best Junior B goaltender in Canada" to finally a "Junior A goaltender."

In the first game, the Canadiens handled the Leafs easily, winning 6-2. Sawchuk left the game in the third period with an injured ankle and was replaced by Bower, who started the second game and was brilliant in a 3-0 shutout. When the Leafs returned home to Toronto for the third and fourth games, they were already being hailed as living, if ancient, marvels. Bower certainly gave the fans no reason to think otherwise, stopping the Canadiens again in the third game for a 3-2 Leaf win.

In the warmup for the fourth game, however, Bower pulled a groin muscle and had to be replaced by Sawchuk, who didn't play well. He let in two goals in the first period, three more in the second and another in the third. The Leafs were trounced 6-2 and the series was tied.

It was at this point that Sawchuk received a telegram from a fan in Newfoundland. The same fan had sent a congratulatory telegram when Sawchuk had earned his 100th career shutout. Earlier in the playoffs, when he had starred in the series against Chicago, winning three games, he had received another telegram from the fan, wishing him well. The third telegram, after Sawchuk's second bad effort against Montreal, simply asked: "How much did you get?" Sawchuk was shocked and deeply hurt. "How can people say those things?" he said later. "I tried just as hard."

Despite Sawchuk's problems in goal, Imlach had no choice but to bring him back for the fifth game at the Forum because of Bower's injury. But this time, the calendar turned back 20 years, and Sawchuk played one of the greatest games of his career. Time after time, he stopped the Canadiens: they came at him in waves. Jean Beliveau, Henri Richard, Bobby Rousseau. But he turned them all away, except for one goal that bounced in off Tim Horton in the first period. The Leafs defeated the Canadiens 4-1 in Montreal and were now one win away from their fourth Cup of the Sixties.

To everyone, even the Toronto fans, the Leafs had not been considered Cup contenders in 1967. But presciently, some of the Leaf oldtimers knew right from the beginning that they could do it one more time. In Bower and Sawchuk, they had two of the game's greatest goaltenders, but there was also the feeling that the Leafs' defensive style of play gave them a big advantage in a seven-game series.

Brian Conacher, Charlie Conacher's nephew, and at 25 years old one of the younger players on the team, can remember George Armstrong telling him near the end of the regular season, "You know, if we get in the playoffs, we can beat anybody. If we play the same team for seven games, we'll win. It's the way we play." Said Conacher, "The older guys really felt that, because Punch made them work so hard, and because they always paid the price and were strong defensively, in a long series, they'd win."

For the sixth game, the Leafs had the opportunity to win the Cup on home ice. As the players dressed for the game, Conacher recalls Imlach walking into the room with a large box of cash, which he threw down in front of the players. "This is what you're playing for," was all that Imlach said.

Conacher says: "What he was telling us was we had to win the Cup that night. In the regular season, we hadn't played well in Montreal. The fact that we had been able to get two wins in the final at the Forum was amazing. I think we all realized, including Imlach, that we wouldn't win a seventh game back in Montreal. We had to do it that night."

From the drop of the puck, Keon, the Leafs' best forward in the playoffs, led the attack. Sawchuk was splendid. He stopped the Canadiens in the first period, and then the Leafs scored two of their own in the second. The Canadiens netted one early in the third and, with the Leafs hanging on to a 2-1 lead, pulled their goalie in the final minute.

For the critical faceoff in the Toronto zone, Imlach elected to send out the men who had been loyal and with him from the beginning; Red Kelly, George Armstrong, Bob Pulford, Allan Stanley and Tim Horton would be on the ice for some of the most important seconds in the club's history.

At that time, the Leaf defence took the faceoffs in their own zone, which meant that Stanley would be up against Beliveau. The Gardens patrons collectively held their breath as the puck was dropped. A columnist reported the next day that the dropping of a pin would have been heard at that moment. Beliveau went for the puck, but Stanley was quicker. He got his blade on it and directed it to Kelly, who took one stride, looked up, and hit Pulford. Frantically the Canadiens swarmed at Pulford, but he was moving ahead, looking for an open man. Suddenly, Pulford saw Armstrong and fed him a perfect pass outside the Leaf blueline. The Leaf captain took off down the ice in his awkward skating style, but staying ahead of faster men. As he crossed the centre red line, he calmly, deliberately measured his target, the open net, and fired from 90 feet. He was dead on, and as the puck slid in, the Gardens exploded.

Almost to a man, the Leafs regard that victory as their most memorable. No one had expected them to win. No one had expected them to be in the final. But backstopped by two old goaltenders, led by their indefatigable centre, Keon, and guided by the discipline and resolve of the old warriors, they had come through with one last Cup. And with an average age of 31, they were the oldest team ever to win an NHL championship.

The 1967 triumph marked the end of an era for the Leafs, as well as the league. That summer, Baun, Armstrong, Horton, Pulford, Stanley, Bower and Kelly all retired or moved to other teams. The team declined rapidly in the late Sixties. Imlach was fired in 1969. Facing charges relating to fraudulent business practices at the Gardens, Stafford Smythe died of a bleeding ulcer in 1971. His partner Harold Ballard was also charged and eventually was found guilty of fraud and theft. Ballard returned from a year in prison to run the Leafs. But with Ballard in control, the team declined steadily until it became the worst in the league. After 1967, there were no more Stanley Cup champions in Toronto, but only the sullied image of a once-great franchise.

6

Montreal's Les Glorieux

*T*he debate started almost immediately after the Montreal Canadiens won their fourth consecutive Stanley Cup in 1979. Which Montreal dynasty was the best: the Canadiens of the Fifties, winners of five consecutive championships; or the dynasty of the Seventies, which won four in a row?

If we are to evaluate a dynastic period in its entirety, the Canadiens of the Seventies must be tied to the Canadiens of the Sixties. From 1965 to 1979, Montreal, in a period of 15 seasons, won 10 Stanley Cups. They were victorious in '65 and '66, '68 and '69, '71, and '73 and then they took four in a row from 1976 to 1979. So, over this period, are we looking at one dynasty or two? When did one end and the other begin?

Arguably, they're one and the same. For 15 seasons, only three teams were able to break the Canadiens' hold on the Cup. The Toronto Maple Leafs, with their upset in 1967, the Boston Bruins in 1970 and 1972, and the Philadelphia Flyers with their two championships in 1974 and 1975.

This period was, without question, the Canadiens' golden era. Players came and went, some of the teams fared better than others.

There was an occasional decline, but they were brief and always followed by long periods of success.

In the early Sixties, which were dominated by the Toronto Maple Leafs, Frank Selke and his assistant Sam Pollock quickly rebuilt the Canadiens. When Montreal reclaimed the Cup in 1965, defeating Chicago in a seven-game series, the only holdovers from the 1956 championship team were Jean Beliveau, then 33 years old, Jean-Guy Talbot and Henri Richard. Doug Harvey had been traded. Bernie Geoffrion and Dickie Moore had retired. In a 1963 blockbuster trade largely engineered by Pollock, Jacques Plante, who had played poorly in 1962-63 and was viewed by the Montreal hierarchy as an eccentric who had lost his confidence, was the principal player in a deal for Rangers' goaltender Gump Worsley.

The young players developed by the Montreal organization more than adequately filled the shoes of the departed stars. They included Yvan Cournoyer, Bobby Rousseau, Claude Larose, Jacques Laperriere, John Ferguson, Gilles Tremblay and J.C. Tremblay. Even without the great Doug Harvey, Montreal's defence was strong. The gangly Laperriere was Harvey's heir apparent and began his NHL career brilliantly, winning the rookie of the year award in 1964 and the Norris Trophy in 1966. But J.C. Tremblay and later Serge Savard were more in the mold of Harvey. They were both gifted puck handlers and a stabilizing presence on the Montreal blueline.

Up front, Cournoyer and Rousseau were little speed merchants whose protection consisted of John Ferguson, the most feared man in the league and fighter without equal. And of course, there was the even-present Beliveau, now into his thirties but still a dominant force. More than any other time, Beliveau showed his mettle in the Sixties by leading a team that lacked the talent of the Fifties' dynasty to four championships. Beliveau, with his graceful strides and dazzling stickhandling, was a tireless worker, who, in the last year of his career in 1970-71, at the age of 40, led his team in scoring with 25 goals and 51 assists in 70 games.

It is often purported that one of the advantages the Canadiens had throughout their history was the first right to the top two junior prospects in Quebec. Pollock debunks this theory, however, calling it "a much maligned myth." Until 1964, the Canadiens recruited players in the same manner as the other five NHL teams. If they found a prospect first, they signed him to a C-form and the player became the club's property for life, unless his rights were traded. The Canadiens had an obvious advantage in Quebec, of course, because they did business in the province and had superior contacts. Every boy who played hockey in Quebec wanted to skate for the legendary *club de hockey*.

In fact, from 1964 to 1969 Montreal,was granted the right to the first two prospects in Quebec. But as it turned out, this advantage didn't amount to much. Pollock noted that the only year the Canadiens cashed in with two good players was 1969, when they picked up Marc Tardif and Rejean Houle. After 1969, the Canadiens competed equally with the other NHL teams for talent — or as equal as it could be for the other teams, considering they were up against the shrewd Pollock.

Pollock was from Montreal, the son of a Montreal storekeeper who made money from real estate investments. In the Forties, Sam worked as a junior clerk for a railway in Montreal, but his great love was sports. He played hockey, baseball and football, and showed early talent as an organizer and manager of sports teams. By the late Forties, he had caught the eye of Selke, who hired him to manage the Canadiens' top development team, the Junior Canadiens. Pollock moved up in the organization during the Fifties to become first in line to succeed Selke.

The succession in 1964 was not without controversy. Selke, 74, wanted to remain as general manager for one more season, but was denied that opportunity by the Molson family, who owned the club. Pollock's team immediately won Stanley Cups in 1965 and 1966 and again in 1968 and 1969. However, by 1970, the club's future as it entered the new decade was not bright. In the new expansionist era, size and a physical style of play, favoured by the Boston Bruins and Philadelphia Flyers, were increasingly important elements of the game. The Canadiens were neither big nor tough, and there was no apparent successor to the great Beliveau.

In the 1970-71 season, Montreal finished a weak third in the Eastern Division. Serge Savard, the young star on the team's defence, had been sidelined for most of the season with a broken leg and would miss the entire playoffs. The goaltending was only average. Worsley had been traded to Minnesota, and his replacements, Rogatien Vachon and Phil Myre, were young and inconsistent.

If that wasn't enough, the coaching situation was unsettled. Claude Ruel had replaced Toe Blake in 1968, but after one full season behind the bench, found the pressure unbearable and suddenly resigned in December, 1970. His interim replacement was Al MacNeil, a former NHL player and a coach in the Montreal system.

The 1970-71 season looked like a loser in every way. But then, near the end of the season, the Canadiens made a move that changed totally the team's outlook and its future. Ken Dryden, a young goaltender from Cornell University, was called up. Dryden had won a handful of college awards for his goaltending in the Eastern collegiate hockey league and was with the Canadiens' minor league affiliate when he was told to report to the big team. In six regular season games with the Canadiens, he impressed both Pollock and MacNeil. At 6-foot-4, 210 pounds, he was an imposing figure and extraordinarily competitive. When the playoffs started, MacNeil decided to stay with Dryden.

Against the Boston Bruins, the defending Cup champions and the best team in the league, few gave Montreal much of a chance, and even less when it was learned they intended to go with a rookie in goal. In Montreal's first game, Dryden played well, but the Habs still lost, 3-1, at the Boston Garden. However, Montreal came back in the second game and took a wild one, 7-5, to tie the series.

Despite Dryden allowing five goals, there was no thought of pulling him. He had played well and, as it turned out, would get better as the series progressed. The Canadiens also improved. The swarming Habs were quicker than their opponents and able to neutralize the mighty Bobby Orr, particularly at the Forum, where Orr was rarely at his best. The Series went to seven games, but on Bruins' ice, the Habs beat them, 4-2, to advance.

After eliminating Minnesota in six games, the Canadiens faced the Black Hawks in the final. When Montreal lost the first two games of the series in Chicago, it appeared the bubble had burst. But, back home, the Canadiens regrouped and tied the series at two.

Dryden had been sharp in the first two playoff series, but against

Chicago he was not only facing some of the most feared shooters in the league — notably Bobby Hull and his brother, Dennis — but he was also competing against a significant opponent at the other end of the rink — the great Tony Esposito, or simply "Tony O." Esposito was the league's new goaltending star and had won the Vezina Trophy the year before. In the fifth game, at the Stadium in Chicago, Tony showed his worth and blanked the Canadiens 2-0 as the Black Hawks took a 3-2 stranglehold in the series.

If that wasn't enough of a problem, there was trouble in the Montreal dressing room. Al MacNeil was a disciplinarian and some of the players, specifically the veterans, disliked him. After he benched Henri Richard in the fifth game, the veteran blew up and denounced MacNeil, telling the reporters he was an incompetent coach.

The remarks were made within the context of a growing nationalism in Quebec, with the *War Measures Act* of 1970 still fresh in everyone's mind. MacNeil was an Anglo and the Canadiens' first non-French coach since Toe Blake. Because of Richard's comments, MacNeil received death threats and coached the sixth game in Montreal with a body guard beside him at the bench.

The Canadiens pushed the Black Hawks to a seventh game and back in Chicago, Richard took a regular shift, scoring twice to lead Montreal to a 3-2 victory and an upset Stanley Cup triumph. This game might be best remembered for Jacques Lemaire's goal that cut the Chicago lead to 2-1. The puck was fired from just a few feet on Chicago's side of centre and somehow eluded Esposito, for whom it was a humiliating defeat. For Dryden, it was the start of a brilliant career. Based on his performance in the three playoff series, particularly against the Boston, he was voted the most valuable player of the playoffs.

In terms of excitement, hockey people almost always point to their first Stanley Cup. But for Sam Pollock, this one — the upset, the two seven-game series — remains a vivid and splendid memory. "It was very satisfying," he said. "We beat Chicago and Boston, both on their own ice."

In the late Sixties, after expansion, Pollock, more than anyone else, recognized the importance of the universal draft. The old protected lists, in which teams could arbitrarily claim youngsters as young as 14 as property, were now relics of the past. All teams had equal access to the juniors and the key was to pick high in the draft and often. In the early Seventies, the Canadiens were able to do both, by dealing off veteran players for draft choices.

Pollock's most celebrated deal was the acquisition of Guy Lafleur, the top junior in Quebec and the projected number one selection in 1971. The Canadiens appeared to have no hope of getting Lafleur, because of the way the draft was structured. The worst team in the league picked first, the second worst team selected second, and so on. In 1971, Montreal was certainly not going be at the bottom of the league. However, a year earlier Pollock had worked a deal with the California Golden Seals, one of the expansion teams, sending the Seals Ernie Hickey, a veteran forward, and a draft choice, for Oakland's first pick in 1971.

Said Pollock, "When we made the deal with Oakland, they were in ninth place overall, and second in their division. We figured that's about where they'd be the following year. We swapped draft choices because we liked what was available in 1971 more than 1970. There was no thought in our mind of getting the first pick overall."

But by the time the 1970-71 season was half over, mismanagement and bad luck had the Seals falling quickly in the standing. The Los Angeles Kings were almost as bad, but if California stayed in last place, the Canadiens would pick first and get Lafleur. In January of 1971, Pollock appeared to up the ante and secure his bet by sending Ralph Backstrom, who wasn't playing much in Montreal, to the Kings. The 34-year-old centre did well in Los Angeles, getting 14 goals in the remaining 33 games. Pollock denies he traded Backstrom to prop up the sagging Kings. Instead, he points to another factor in explaining the last-place finish of the Seals. Mid-way through the season, the Canadiens were in Oakland for a game when Montreal's Frank Mahovlich fell on Carol Vadnais, California's best player. Vadnais was lost for the season with torn ligaments in his knee. Without their top defenceman, the Golden Seals plummeted.

That spring Montreal picked Lafleur first overall and then, in the second round, took Larry Robinson, a tall, skinny defenceman from Kitchener of the Ontario Hockey League. With two picks, the Canadiens had the cornerstones in the reconstruction of their team.

Lafleur would become the dominant player of the Seventies and Robinson, with his size, skill and aggressiveness, would join Serge Savard and Guy Lapointe to anchor perhaps the finest defence corps of all time.

Pollock has said in the past that Lafleur was clearly the player he wanted out of the 1971 draft. But it wasn't an easy choice. Marcel Dionne was also an outstanding prospect and had played in the Ontario junior league, which was perceived to be stronger than the Quebec league. Still, Lafleur's offensive numbers were amazing. In his final year with the Quebec Remparts, he had scored 130 goals, earned 79 assists for 209 points in 62 regular season games.

But Lafleur's NHL career did not immediately take off. Like Beliveau, he was from a small town in Quebec — Thurso, near the Ontario-Quebec border. He had not lived in a city as large as Montreal and felt homesick for Quebec City, where he had resided for six years while playing junior hockey. As well, there was the pressure of dealing with everyone's high expectations. "I was constantly compared to Jean Beliveau," Lafleur said. It was a new league, a new city and a team. All of these things made it difficult."

In Lafleur's first season, he returned to Quebec every chance he could get, making the 300-mile return trip in his off-days, often driving up after a game. "I had all my friends in Quebec and I would head back there constantly. I really missed it. In Montreal I was lost. Even though Quebec was a pretty big place, it was just not Montreal."

On the ice, Lafleur also seemed lost. He was a natural right winger, but when he joined the Canadiens they had an over-abundance of wingers: Yvan Cournoyer, Frank Mahovlich, Claude Larose, Rejean Houle, Marc Tardif, Jim Roberts, Phil Roberto, Chuck Lefley. In addition to Lafleur, there were three other rookie wingers in the organization: Steve Shutt, Yvon Lambert and Murray Wilson. So Lafleur would play centre. That's where the club needed help, and Lafleur had the speed and skills to be a fine centre.

Lafleur did reasonably well in his first season and ended up with 29 goals and 35 assists for 64 points. Still, he had been outclassed by another French Canadian rookie in the NHL, Richard Martin, who had scored 44 goals for the Buffalo Sabres. As well, Marcel Dionne, in his first year with the Detroit Red Wings, outpointed Lafleur. Guy, of course, didn't win the rookie of the year award, as everyone had hoped, but the Calder Trophy did go to a Canadien, Ken Dryden, who had played in his first complete regular season.

When the Bruins won the Stanley Cup in 1972, it appeared that they would dominate the league for several years. But, instead, it was Sam Pollock's Canadiens that would emerge as the team of the Seventies, despite the difficulties of their star. The 1972-73 Montreal team was an impressive mixture of youth and experience. The coaching was strong. Al MacNeil had been replaced by Scotty Bowman, a former protégé of Pollock's who had worked in the Canadiens' organization before joining St. Louis Blues in 1967 as coach. Not long after Bowman took over as general manager of the Blues in 1969, tensions developed between he and the St. Louis owners, the Solomon brothers, so when the opportunity to coach the Canadiens arose in 1971, Bowman jumped at it.

Bowman's team had a splendid campaign in 1972-73, finishing first in the league with 120 points and losing only 10 game. In the playoffs, the Canadiens eliminated the Buffalo Sabres, and then the Philadelphia Flyers before meeting the Chicago Black Hawks in the final. The series turned out to be something less than a Ken Dryden-Tony Esposito duel. Four of the six games were high scoring with Esposito getting the worst of it. The Black Hawks lost games in which they allowed eight, seven, eight and six goals, in losing to the Canadiens in six games.

Montreal's impressive performance convinced many that an interrupted series of championships was underway. But that didn't happen immediately. Lafleur continued to struggle, one of the results of which was the Montreal front office taking a considerable amount of heat for drafting him. Marcel Dionne had developed into a major star by then and had just come off a 40-goal season on a weak Detroit team. In Buffalo, Rick Martin had just completed his first 50-goal season. Guy, meanwhile, was still in the 20-goal-a-season category.

But another more important development put the Montreal dynasty on hold. The Philadelphia Flyers, were busy changing the face of the league, literally, you might say, as well as figuratively. There had been tough teams in the NHL before, but the Flyers took aggressiveness and bullying to new level. Supplementing a small number of highly talented players, such as Bobby Clarke, Reggie Leach, Rick MacLeish and goaltender Bernie Parent, were the Flyer storm troopers — the goons, are they were called. Dave Schultz, Don Saleski and Bob Kelly were ably assisted by other aggressive performers such as Andre Dupont, Gary Dornhoefer and Ed Van Impe.

Out of this mayhem, the Flyers emerged as the league's top team, winning Stanley Cups in 1974 and 1975. In those two years, the Canadiens lost to the Rangers and Buffalo Sabres in the playoffs and were thus spared the experience of meeting up with the feared Broad Street Bullies.

During the Flyers' reign of terror, the Canadiens lacked aggressiveness. But this deficiency was quickly eliminated by Pollock's drafting. In the Seventies, he used his cache of first rounders to acquire players with size and toughness, as well as skill.

Among the new breed, the first was arrive was Bob Gainey, a first-round draft pick in 1973. Gainey, a left winger from the Peterborough Petes, was a strong, defensive-minded player who would become the team's most respected leader, even though he wasn't a goal scorer. The following year, the Canadiens had five picks in the first round. Three of them, Doug Risebrough, Mario Tremblay and Rick Chartraw, would play important roles in shaping the new personality of the team.

Risebrough was a feisty, combative centre, while Tremblay and Chartraw were two genuinely tough players who would fight anybody. By 1975, the rebuilding of the Montreal was almost complete. Centre Doug Jarvis, a defensive specialist, was added. So was defencemen Bill Nyrop and Brian Engblom. At centre there was Peter Mahovlich, Jacques Lemaire, Risebrough and Jarvis. On the wings were the two most robust players, Yvon Lambert and Mario Tremblay, plus Murray Wilson and Bob Gainey, both of whom were good skaters and checkers. In terms of pure talent, the key wingers were Steve Shutt, Yvan Cournoyer and Guy Lafleur.

After three average seasons, Lafleur had finally come into his own. With the influx of young players plus the defections of Frank Mahovlich, Rejean Houle and Marc Tardif to the WHA, Lafleur saw himself as a veteran and team leader. At the start of the 1974-75 season, Guy doffed the helmet and instantly became *le Demon Blond*. In his natural position of right wing and without the hat, Lafleur took off, scoring 53 goals and adding 63 assists for 119 points.

By 1975-76, the Canadiens had more talent than the Philadelphia team and just as much muscle. But the Flyers' space was psychological — they engendered genuine fear in opposing teams and Montreal was no different from the others. However, Scotty Bowman remembers two pre-games in the fall of 1975 that changed the Canadiens' attitude permanently. For an exhibition game at the Forum, the Flyers had loaded up on goons. The Canadiens, with mostly smaller players in the lineup, were beaten up badly.

The next night, the teams played again, at the Spectrum in Philadelphia. For this game, Bowman dressed his toughest players and supplemented them with the nastiest thugs from the Canadiens' farm team at Halifax. Predictably an all-out brawl ensued, but this time with the Canadiens getting the best of it.

"From that point on, we really cleaned up on them," says Bowman. "They knew they couldn't intimidate us. That was the beginning of the end for them."

Mario Tremblay also remembers that exhibition series. "We beat them at their own game," he says. "We knew we had more talent than them, and now we could match them in toughness."

Both Philadelphia and Montreal enjoyed terrific seasons in 1975-76. The Flyers had won the Cup for the past two years and were now recognized as a great team, bullying tactics or not. Through his leadership and intensity, Bobby Clarke had become the most respected player in the league and probably the best all-round player. He had already won two most-valuable-player awards and was on his way to his third, a wonderful achievement for any player in any era. With Bobby Orr's career over because of knee problems, Boston Bruin coach general manager Harry Sinden had no hesitation in calling Clarke "the greatest player in hockey." Sinden said, "They'll follow him anywhere and do anything he wants."

The Flyers won their division easily, losing only 13 of 80 regular season games and finishing 17 points ahead of the second-place Rangers. The Canadiens, too, had dominated their division. They lost only 11 regular season games and ended up with 127 points, tops in the NHL.

The playoffs went pretty much as expected. Montreal swept Chicago in four games and then brushed aside a young New York Islander team in five. The Flyers also made it to the final, but not without a tough battle with a tenacious Toronto Maple Leaf team that pushed them to seven games. The Flyers then trounced the Bruins in five in a series that was rough and sometimes brutal. At one point, Bruin winger Wayne Cashman said of Dave Schultz, the most feared fighter of his day and one of the players for whom the term goon was coined, "Schultz is the only complete goon I've seen in my life. The way he goes around when he's on the ice makes me sick."

Schultz or not, the Flyers' aggressiveness and win-at-all-costs attitude impressed everyone. Tim Burke, a sports columnist with the *Gazette* in Montreal, covered the Boston-Philadelphia series and had come away convinced the Flyers would win their third consecutive Stanley Cup. Below a banner headline in the *Gazette*'s sports section on the eve of the final, Burke predicted a Flyer victory in six games. Much was also made of the fact the Canadiens had not won a game at the Spectrum in Philadelphia in two and a half years.

And so began the Flyers-Canadiens final. Montreal had home ice advantage in the series, but it didn't seem to mean much in the first game when the Flyers jumped into a quick two-goal lead. Montreal fought back to tie it in the second period with goals by Jim Roberts and Larry Robinson. But then the Flyers took the lead again, early in the third, on a goal by Larry Goodenough. The Flyer advantage held until the mid-way point of the period when a harmless backhander by Jacques Lemaire froze the Philadelphia goalie Wayne Stephenson and went in. The defensive battle continued until the 19th minute of the third when Guy Lapointe, joining the attack, fired the winner.

The bristling defensive battle continued in the second game. Scotty Bowman's main concern in the series was the Flyers' big line of Bobby Clarke, Reggie Leach and Bill Barber. Leach, particularly, had enjoyed a phenomenal season in which he had scored 61 goals.

This Flyer line was also strong defensively. In one season, Bowman recalls the trio allowing only 35 goals-against during even-strength play, which was quite amazing. The next closest offensive line in the league would have allowed about twice as many goals-against. Montreal's unit of Peter Mahovlich, Lafleur and Steve Shutt, for example, was about equal to the Clarke line in offensive ability, but wasn't close to being as strong defensively.

The key to the Flyer attack was Clarke. The Philadelphia defencemen were competent, but with the exception of Jimmy Watson and perhaps Larry Goodenough, didn't have the skill needed to carry the puck out of their zone. In their own end, their strategy was to rifle the puck around the boards. The Flyer wingers would station themselves at the boards and hold their position long enough to deflect or pass the puck to Clarke, the open man in the middle of the ice. Clarke then would carry the puck to the centre ice area and lead the attack.

The Canadiens, in the past, had used one centre, Doug Jarvis, to check Clarke. But in this series, Bowman decided to use three — Lemaire, Risebrough and Jarvis. In fact, Bowman can remember using all three in one shift against Clarke. "They each brought something a little different," Bowman said. "Risebrough was the toughest against Clarke. Jarvis was the best checker. And Lemaire had the best offensive skills. As the game progressed, I'd give Lemaire more ice time against Clarke because he was more of a threat to score."

Bowman's strategy worked to perfection in the second game of the series. The Canadien centres, all of whom were strong defensively, wore Clarke down. Jarvis, who took the faceoffs against Clarke, won all but four of the 18. Neither team scored in the first, but late in the second Montreal struck on a goal by Lemaire. Lafleur gave the Canadiens a two-goal cushion in the third. The Flyers attempted to mount a comeback, but a rare goal by Dave Schultz was the best they could do. Montreal, heading to Philly for the next two games, had a commanding two-game lead in the series.

The crucial game, everyone agreed, was the third, at the Spectrum. The unanswered questions included: Would the Canadiens fold under the intense pressure of the Flyer forechecking on home ice? Would they be intimidated?

The Canadiens answered these questions by jumping on the Flyers quickly and taking the lead on a goal by Shutt. It turned into a hard-hitting, bitterly fought game, but there were no brawls and no gooning. Bowman notes that neither team could afford to take bad penalties. "By then the referees were watching the Flyers pretty closely. Both teams played hard and aggressively, but there weren't a lot of cheap shots."

Two goals by Reggie Leach eventually gave the Flyers the lead, but Shutt came back with his second goal to tie it. After that, both teams battled to a standstill until mid-way through the third when Pierre Bouchard, one of the Canadiens' defencemen, got the winner.

Even though Montreal had a 3-0 stranglehold on the series, no one was claiming total victory. The Flyers, a proud team that epitomized the work ethic, never gave up and were in the faces of the Canadiens constantly, with their intense checking and aggressive play.

But Montreal was quickly making believers of everyone. Jean Beliveau, by then an executive in the Canadiens' front office, said at the time, "People always say the Canadiens between 1955 and 1960 were the best, but I'm beginning to believe this one might even be better. We have three defencemen — Savard, Robinson and Lapointe — who are not only all-stars but could win any trophy in hockey."

Jimmy Watson of the Flyers was also impressed. "What's Sam Pollock going to do about Team Canada?" he said, alluding to the first Canada Cup scheduled for a few months ahead in September, 1976. "Now, he'll probably just send the whole Canadiens team and leave it at that."

The Flyers competed gamely in the fourth match of the series, but the pattern had been set, and it followed form for this game as well. The teams played evenly until the third period, when Montreal, with more offensive skill and speed, pulled away. The Cup was clinched with third-period goals by Lafleur and Peter Mahovlich.

The series had been hard-fought and the outcome very much in doubt at the beginning, but the inescapable fact was that Montreal had swept them in four games. In three playoff series, Montreal had lost only one game. In the regular season Montreal had lost only 11 games.

Could it get any better than that? The answer was yes. The following season, the Canadiens were defeated in only eight regular season games, winning 60 and tying 12. No team of the modern era dominated one season so totally, before or since. In the playoffs, it was almost a clean sweep. The St. Louis Blues fell in four. An improving Islander team took two from Montreal before losing. But in the final, the result was the same as the previous spring. This time, it was the Bruins who went out in four.

The next season, 1977-78, the Canadiens continued to run roughshod over the league. This time they lost 11 games, won 59 and tied 10. In the playoffs it was a repeat performance. Detroit was pushed aside in five games. The Toronto Maple Leafs were swept in four. In the final, the feisty Bruins pushed the Canadiens to six games, but the outcome was the same. Montreal won its third straight Cup.

In assessing those three years the salient fact is that in 240 regular-season games the Canadiens lost only 29 times. In three playoff campaigns, there were five Montreal sweeps — two of them in the final. In 42 playoff games, there had been only six losses.

The Canadiens of that era had excellent forwards, but the team was great because of what it had on the blueline and in goal. What impressed Bowman most about Ken Dryden's goaltending was the way he could shut out external complications and pressures and focus on the game at hand. He was the team's resident intellectual and philosopher. But hidden behind the Dryden academia, Bowman notes, was an "ultra-competitor," a man who hated to lose and was always able to bounce back after a bad game.

"The team always felt that he could win them a big game if he had to," Bowman said. "He was the most consistent goaltender I have ever coached and a fierce competitor."

Other teams had great goalies. But what other teams didn't have was Montreal's big three on defence. Serge Savard, Guy Lapointe and Larry Robinson were all-stars. Savard was the best defensive defenceman of his era. Guy Lapointe was among the top two or three offensive defencemen during his career. From 1976 to 1980, Robinson rivalled the New York Islanders' Denis Potvin as the most dominant defenceman in the game. Robinson was a two-time Norris Trophy winner as the league's best defenceman and winner of the Conn Smythe Trophy as the most valuable player in the 1978 playoffs.

Robinson and Savard played together and they were perfectly suited. Savard seldom made a mistake in his end and rarely took a penalty. Robinson could spark an offensive thrust with a pass, had a great shot from the point and was a physical presence. Of the three, Lapointe had the best offensive skills and was most dangerous when he joined the attack, moving into the offensive zone either with the puck or waiting for a pass. Lapointe, in his career, scored so many key goals for the Canadiens, particularly in the playoffs.

The supporting cast on defence was also impressive. As Mario Tremblay points out, the extras would have been first-line defencemen on other teams. Bill Nyrop, Pierre Bouchard, and Rick Chartraw, who could play the wing or defence, were big and talented.

Up front, Bowman had a strong mix of offence, defence and aggressiveness. The big line consisted of Steve Shutt, Guy Lafleur and, in the beginning, Peter Mahovlich, and then Jacques Lemaire at centre. Shutt was often called the line's garbageman, because he would pick up the loose pucks or rebounds and score. But Shutt was the fourth player taken in the 1972 draft and he steadily improved, by fifteens, as Bowman notes. In Shutt's first full season with Montreal he scored 15 goals. He doubled that the next year, added another 15 the following season when he scored 45 goals. And he got 15 more in 1976-77 to hit 60 for the season, tops in the NHL.

Mahovlich was an effectively rangy centre who made it possible for Lafleur and Shutt to develop into all-stars. But when Mahovlich was traded to Pittsburgh in 1977 for Pierre Larouche, Jacques Lemaire stepped in and not only brought his own considerable offensive skills to the line, but also his fine defensive work.

"In our own end, Lemaire would come back deep and almost be a third defenceman," Bowman says. "That allowed Lafleur and Shutt to stay high. Usually they were no deeper than the top of the faceoff circle, and they were so quick they could get their stick on a puck coming out and suddenly create a two on one or a breakaway."

But the key to it all, indeed, the key to the Montreal Canadiens of the Seventies, was Lafleur. By 1976, Lafleur had met all expectations. He was by now the most purely talented player in the league — elegant, clean, master of the right wing and a worthy successor to the great Beliveau. Lafleur, in his career, would win three scoring championships, three MVPs, plus a most valuable player award in the playoffs.

Bowman says, "He played the wing like a centre. He was a great playmaker and an underrated shooter. Dryden used to say that for pure power he had one of the hardest shots in the league."

For five consecutive years, Lafleur scored 50 or more goals a season, with his highest total being 60 in 1977-78. He didn't use a big windup with his shot. Instead it was a short, tight slapper, almost a wrist shot. But its velocity was high and the puck hit like a ton.

Mario Tremblay remembers Lafleur as tremendously motivated, despite the fact he could have looked respectable without a full effort. "He was always the player who tried to go through the top. He didn't like middle performances."

Because of his ability, Lafleur was consistently fouled. Players would slash at him. He was highsticked, elbowed and knocked to the ice. Often stars will complain about this, protest to the referee. But Lafleur never acknowledged a foul, never let on that he might have been hurt. He just continued on, exacting his revenge by playing the game as his top level. Gainey says, "He was above all that (the fouls). At the peak of his career, those kinds of details didn't bother Guy. It didn't come into his mind. He played from inside of himself."

The Lafleur line was the Canadiens' most dangerous, but Bowman felt the scrappy aggressive unit of Risebrough between Tremblay and Lambert set the tone and motivated the other line combinations to produce. "They never took a night off," he said. "Our other lines saw how hard they worked and did the same. They set the trend for the entire team. We were never outworked."

The Canadiens could throw a wall up in front of any team. Gainey's line would shut them down and, if that wasn't enough, Risebrough's unit was there to help. Gainey called it "being in control" and in those years, the Canadiens were always in control. They had the scoring power, they had the size and the aggressiveness, and they had the defence.

The general impression of people close to the team was that the players, to a man, disliked Bowman intensely, found him manipulative, bullying and unpredictable. Bernard Brisset, the sports editor of *Le Journal de Montreal*, covered the team those days as a beat writer for *La Presse*, and says flatly, "The players hated him." A famous quote attributed to Larry Robinson was that Bowman treated everybody equally, "like dirt." Al Strachan, another journalist working in Montreal during that period, has often said that the players hated Bowman 364 days of the year, the one exception being the day they won the Stanley Cup.

More than 15 years after the fact, the players, or at least the ones interviewed for this book, speak well of Scotty. Gainey acknowledges that Bowman had whipping boys, often Steve Shutt, because of his weight problems, and Mario Tremblay, because he responded with fierce aggressiveness to Bowman's criticisms.

One of Bowman's problem players was Peter Mahovlich, a free spirit who refused to conform and for a few weeks matched Bowman headline for headline in a publicized feud until he was traded. Mahovlich told Montreal author Chrys Goyens, "Scotty played his favourites, no doubt about it, and he loved playing one guy against another. The important thing is, Scotty's way worked. His teams might have hated him, but he got them to play to their capabilities and not too many coaches can say that. Agree or disagree, love him or hate him, he won and that's all people remember now."

The players saw Bowman as distant and aloof. He wasn't a so-called "player's coach," but instead a brilliant tactician, a man who knew the game as well as anyone and had excellent instincts.

The result of Bowman's creative motivational techniques and his skilfullness behind the bench was a team that seldom, if ever, underachieved. A rare loss was treated as a major setback. *Les glorieux,* or glory boys, as the Montreal media called them, were a swaggering, supremely confident group of stars who considered failure an embarrassment.

Bernard Brisset can remember riding the team bus from the hotel to the opposing team's arena. Peter Mahovlich would sit at the front of the bus, and after he left, Yvon Lambert. As the bus pulled into the parking lot, the word was always the same, "Let's get two points and f... off." There was no concern over the game at hand at hand. They knew they would win. It was a case of picking up two points with as few complications as possible.

Gainey says, "We had a dominant offence and a dominant defence. All the different positions on our team were filled with the best people. We could have won with a sixty per cent effort, but we didn't. We beat the bad teams badly and the good teams consistently.

We didn't measure ourselves against other teams. We were our own measuring stick."

It seemed, in those days, that the championships in Montreal would never end. The Canadiens who won their third consecutive Cup in 1978 were still a young group. If the team needed upgrading, Sam Pollock, the hockey genius, would be there and would find a way of acquiring the right player. But suddenly, everything changed in 1978 with the sale of the team.

In 1957, the Molson family had bought the Canadiens from Senator Donat Raymond. Then in 1971, they sold the club and Forum to a consortium consisting of Edward and Peter Bronfman, the Bank of Nova Scotia and Baton Broadcasting of Toronto for $15 million. Jacques Courtois, a prominent Montreal lawyer, was named president. To assist in the business side of the operation, the Bronfmans brought in Irving Grundman, who had made money from a chain of bowling alleys in Montreal. Pollock stayed as vice president and general manager, as did Jean Beliveau and Toe Blake in their front office jobs with the Canadiens.

It remained that way until 1977-78, when rumours suggested that the John Labatt Ltd., which just a year earlier had become a major shareholder in Toronto's American League franchise, the Toronto Blue Jays, were angling to buy the Canadiens. Determined to stop the rival brewery from moving into markets in Montreal as well as Toronto, Molson Breweries of Canada Ltd., moved quickly and bought the Canadiens outright for $20 million.

But when the Bronfmans handed over the Canadiens in 1978, they didn't leave the club untouched. They took Pollock, who had an equity position in the Bronfmans' company, Edper Investments. With the departure of Pollock, Bowman had hoped and expected to become the club's general manager, and was stunned when he was passed over for Grundman.

Bowman believes today that the new owners simply wanted him to continue in his job as coach, something he did with considerable effectiveness. So Scotty stayed as coach, and Grundman, who had worked for six years with Pollock, was given the new title of managing director.

It is widely believed that Grundman was Pollock's chosen

successor. In their six years together in the Canadiens' front office they had become close and Pollock had taught him the business. It has also been speculated that Pollock was concerned that Bowman's autocratic management style wouldn't have worked in the Montreal hockey office.

Whatever the reasons and motivations, Bowman was bitterly disappointed. In a meeting that summer he told Grundman bluntly that he would not work for him and would seek employment elsewhere at the end of 1978-79. When the season started, the players immediately noticed a change in Scotty. He was quieter, less involved, almost detached.

Steve Shutt told authors Chrys Goyens and Alan Turowetz, "It wasn't vintage Scotty. It was a strange year. We did all right in the standings, even though we weren't steamrolling teams the way we had in the past. We still would win the big games against most teams, although the Islanders played us very tough. And all through this Scotty was really calm. Like he was somewhere else."

The Canadiens won their division handily, losing only 17 games. But that wasn't good enough for top spot. The young and powerful Islanders had the best record that season with 51 wins, 15 losses and 14 ties.

In the Stanley Cup semi-finals, however, the Islanders were upset by the Rangers in six games. Over in the other semi-final the Canadiens, for the first time in four years, were in a fight for their lives against the Boston Bruins.

The Bruins had changed radically through the Seventies. At the start of the decade they were the league's dominant team led by Bobby Orr and Phil Esposito. But after the 1972 championship, the team declined. Hobbled by knee problems, Orr failed to reach a contract agreement with the Bruins in 1976 and signed with the Chicago Black Hawks. Esposito never regained the magnificent form he showed in the 1972 playoffs and September Summit Series between Canada and the Soviet Union, and, in a blockbuster 1975 trade, was sent to the Rangers, along with defenceman Carol Vadnais and winger Joe Zanussi for centre Jean Ratelle and defenceman Brad Park.

A year earlier, Don Cherry had taken over as coach. Together with general manager Harry Sinden, Cherry remade the Bruins into an aggressive, physical and hardworking unit. They were the grinders, a blue-collar team, Don Cherry's Lunch Bucket Brigade. Skilled players such as Ratelle, Park and Rick Middleton were complemented by a tough but fairly competent group that included Don Marcotte, Wayne Cashman, John Wensink and Al Secord.

In the 1979 semi-final, the Canadiens had their hands full. It started well for Montreal with two wins at the Forum. But in the Boston Garden, the Bruins won the third game and then took the fourth on an overtime winner by Ratelle. Back in Montreal, the Canadiens dominated the Bruins, defeating them 5-1.

Another Montreal team in another year would have finished off the Bruins in Boston. But that didn't happen. Sparked by Cherry's favourite player, a muscular little pit bull called Stan Jonathon, the Bruins defeated the Canadiens 5-2 with Jonathon getting the hat trick. So, for the first time in eight years, the Canadiens found themselves in the seventh game of a Stanley Cup playoff series. A loss meant elimination and the end of the dynasty. And only three of the Canadiens had played in a seventh game — Jacques Lemaire, Serge Savard and Ken Dryden.

The game started poorly for Montreal. The Bruins badly outplayed them in the first two periods and took a 3-1 lead. But early in the third, Montreal fought back. Lafleur, playing as if his life were on the line, set up two goals, one by Mark Napier and another by Guy Lapointe. But then the Bruins regained the lead on a goal by Middleton.

Bowman says this game was the most pressure-filled he had ever coached. "We were facing elimination and we kept getting snake bitten," he said. "We'd catch up and then they'd go back into the lead."

As the seconds and minutes ticked away, the numbing reality of elimination set in. The crowd at the Forum had quieted and the fans awaited a miracle. It came at 17:26 of the third when the Bruins were caught with too many men on the ice. Montreal had the power play and a chance to tie the game. There would be one last gasp.

When all the elements of a crucial game are refined to their essence, when the money is on the line, the best players usually come to the fore. So it wasn't surprising that Guy Lafleur would score the tying goal. It was sudden, dramatic and unexpected. In his effortless skating style, Lafleur crossed the blue line in full flight, received a back pass from Lemaire and in one motion fired from 45 feet. Bruin goalie Gilles Gilbert didn't move. "It was a bullet," says Bowman. "It was low shot that picked the far corner. I'd seen that shot many times before."

Lafleur's goal sent the game into overtime and for more than nine excruciating minutes the play went end to end. Bowman used only three defencemen in overtime, rotating Savard, Robinson and Lapointe. "I figured if we lose, we'll lose with our best. If we win, we'll do it with our best."

It ended at 9:33 of overtime. Doug Risebrough fired on the net. Yvon Lambert, his big winger, was standing to the left of the goal and was able to re-direct the puck past Gilbert.

The final was anti-climactic. The Rangers caught the Canadiens by surprise in the first game, but Montreal won the next four to clinch the Cup.

The dynasty didn't officially come to an end until the following spring when the red-hot Minnesota North Stars upset Montreal on their way to the Cup final against the New York Islanders. But, in real terms, the Canadiens ended it in the summer of 1979. Bowman made good on his promise to leave the organization and joined the Buffalo Sabres as general manager and coach. Lemaire retired, and so did Dryden. The Canadiens still had a fine team, but without Bowman there to drive them and without Dryden to make the game-winning saves, Montreal didn't quite have enough for another Cup.

By 1980, a new era was beginning. The NHL had made peace with the World Hockey Association and four new teams had joined the senior league — Winnipeg, Edmonton, Hartford and Quebec. The New York Islanders were the new power. But already, the brash Edmontonians were boasting that they were the team of the future. For Montreal the dynasties were over. The team would decline in the Eighties, but in 1986 would rise again in an unexpected drive for another Stanley Cup, thus rekindling memories of the way it had been almost every spring for so long.

7

A Suburban Champion

*I*n the early Seventies, the Montreal Canadiens, Boston Bruins and New York Rangers battled fiercely for superiority in the NHL. But on a much larger scale, another hockey rivalry was being played out. The World Hockey Association opened for business in 1972 and battled the NHL for the North American market through most of the decade until peace was finally made in 1979.

One of the byproducts of the WHA-NHL war was the founding of the New York Islanders. To checkmate the WHA in the rich New York market, the NHL, in late 1971, decided to place a team in Long Island, at Uniondale, N.Y., a town of 20,000, 50 kilometres from Manhattan. The Islanders would begin play the following 1972-73 season.

Uniondale's Nassau Coliseum already housed Roy Boe's National Basketball Association New York Nets, and Boe was awarded the Islanders franchise for $3 million. Unlike Madison Square Garden, the home of the Rangers, which sat above Penn Station in downtown Manhattan, the Nassau Coliseum was situated on a wind-swept field not far from where Charles Lindbergh had embarked on his 1927 solo trans-Atlantic flight. Long Island, a region of small towns, villages and resort areas, had undergone phenomenal post-war growth in the Fifties and Sixties. This was now American suburbia and the Islanders were hockey's first suburban team.

Boe's opening move in early 1972 was to hire Bill Torrey as general manager of the expansion franchise. When Torrey left for a 23-day scouting trip in February, the Islanders had neither an office, phones nor secretaries. By the time Torrey returned from his trip, they did have a staff of three scouts: Ed Chadwick, Henry Saraceno and Earl Ingarfield.

Torrey was an experienced hockey man who had grown up in Montreal in the Thirties and Forties. He attended St. Lawrence University in Canton, N.Y., and played for the varsity hockey team. After graduating with a bachelor of science degree, he joined the minor-league Pittsburgh Hornets as a public relations man. He later became business manager. When the NHL doubled its membership in 1967, Torrey took over the expansion California Seals as executive vice-president. In a period of almost three years, Torrey worked for a succession of six club owners, including Charlie Finley, who also owned the Oakland A's of the American League. During those three years, Torrey learned, more than anything, how not to run a hockey franchise.

Said Torrey, "I remember the first thing Finley said to me when he bought the team was, 'We have to find a way to get the team out of here.' He thought we should take it to New Orleans because there were a lot of French people there."

As the 1972 expansion draft approached, Torrey made it clear to his new boss, Boe, that there would be no saviours among the players available. "I told Boe, 'Okay, you're going to go through the expansion draft and get nineteen problem children. Either the guys can't play, they're too old, or they have personal problems. Second, your product is going to be constantly compared to the New York Rangers,' who were then the second-best team in hockey. Also, we were in the East Division with Montreal, Boston, the Rangers and four other established teams. We were guaranteed last place. But there was a ray of hope if we were patient because everyone in hockey knew that the amateur draft for the next few years was loaded. What other choice did we have?"

Of the 19 players the Islanders selected in the expansion draft, several were offered one-year deals. Torrey wasn't impressed with what was available and he decided not to throw a lot of money at them. As a result, eight of the 19 players he selected jumped to the rival WHA, with two of the players signing with the WHA's New York Raiders. Because of this, Torrey was widely criticized in the New York media for a lack of preparation and for being cheap. More remembered from that draft is Torrey's ability to find talent.

In the expansion draft, the Islanders acquired Eddie Westfall of the Stanley Cup champion Boston Bruins and Billy Smith, a 21-year-old goaltender with the Los Angeles Kings. The Islanders also took defenceman Gerry Hart and acquired veteran Arnie Brown through a trade with the Detroit Red Wings.

In the amateur draft, they picked first overall and chose winger Billy Harris of the Toronto Marlboros. In the later rounds, the Isles took forwards Lorne Henning, Bob Nystrom and Garry Howatt, all of whom have their names on the Stanley Cup.

The Islanders' first training camp was in Peterborough, Ont., and Torrey invited 90 players, although, as he told E.M. Swift of *Sports Illustrated,* "We cut two the first night, before we had stepped on the ice. One had a Mohawk haircut and behaved pretty badly at the hotel bar. The other guy brought his wife and wouldn't send her home. Not that I blamed him. We were all sorry to see her leave."

Torrey felt it important to institute discipline, so the players were not allowed to bring their cars. From the Holiday Inn where they stayed they had to walk the half mile to the rink. However, Eddie Westfall and Billy Harris, the baby-bonus rookie, parked their cars a block away from the hotel and secretly sneaked rides back and forth.

"The Bruins were happy if you just showed up for practice," Westfall said. "But when you're going well, you get those fringe benefits. The Islanders had us skate an hour and half twice a day, and they still expected us to walk to and from practice. That almost pushed some of the players over the edge."

Dry-land training was held on the infield of a nearby harness racing track. When one of the drivers complained about the players spooking the horses, Torrey replied, "Dogs do spook horses sometimes."

The Islanders plumbed new depths of ineptitude that year. They won 12 games, lost 60 and tied six, setting an all-time record for losing in the NHL. The team wasn't called the New York Islanders in the media as much as it was referred to as the Hapless Islanders. In Long Island, the Isles also had a major identity problem. Torrey can remember an early exhibition game against the Rangers at Nassau Coliseum. "When the Rangers came out they got a standing ovation. When our team hit the ice there was silence — nothing, just dead silence."

The Rangers, the swaggering Blueshirts of Broadway, were the city team and enthusiastically supported by all New Yorkers. The Islanders, as the poor country cousins, were not only bad but anonymous.

Still, some personalities did liven an otherwise dismal season. Billy Smith earned his reputation for fighting with the opposition more than stopping pucks. The most popular player was probably Brian (Spinner) Spencer who had been picked up in the expansion draft from the Maple Leafs. Spencer had in his contract a bonus clause for the number of hits had made, although more often than not, he missed his target and hit the boards. It was the job of Hawley Chester, the team's first public relations man, to count Spencer's hits. "I used to give him credit for the misses, too. That was all right with Torrey. At least everyone would wake up when Spence hit the boards."

The first victim of the team's bad play was coach Phil Goyette. He quietly suffered through a period in which the Isles went 1-24-3 at one point and then lost 12 in a row. After one loss, he made the players skate in practice for 30 minutes going in one direction and then made them turn around and go in the other direction for 30 minutes. "That's what you have to do in a game," he told them, "skate 60 minutes." After a loss, Goyette invariably told the media, "I can't skate for them," which infuriated the players.

Goyette, a proud veteran of some great Montreal and New York Ranger teams, couldn't cope with the consistent losing. At the end of January, Torrey ended the ordeal and fired him.

For the remainder of the season, scout Earl Ingarfield ran the team. But the following year, Torrey had his sights set on Al Arbour, who had been dismissed early in the 1972-73 season as coach of the St. Louis Blues. Arbour had been a journeyman defenceman in the Fifties and Sixties before ending his career with the Blues in 1971. Perhaps best remembered as one of the few players who wore eye glasses during games, Arbour had impressed Torrey with his diligence and determination.

"I had a tremendous amount of respect for him as a player," Torrey said. "He was limited, but he was tenacious and studious. He learned everything about the game. I felt, 'Here's a guy who can relate and teach young players.'"

Arbour initially turned down Torrey, mainly because Al, who was from Northern Ontario, and his wife did not want to live in New York. A chance meeting with friends in Florida during a vacation changed the Arbours' mind when they were told that Long Island had large rural, residential areas that were quiet and beautiful.

So Arbour took the job and became one of the finest coaches ever to work in the NHL. And in the years to come, the Islanders, despite their woeful start, would present a textbook case on how to build an expansion team into a winner. The Islanders, in fact, would become the most successful expansion franchise in any sport, winning three Stanley Cups in the first 10 years of operation. No other team had done that, not even the Dallas Cowboys, America's Team of the Seventies.

One of Torrey's self-imposed rules was to build from the draft. He would not trade high draft choices. He also wanted to concentrate first on strengthening the team's back end. Goaltending and defence were priorities.

At the 1973 amateur draft Torrey's vow never to trade a first rounder was severely tested. By virtue of finishing last, the Islanders again picked first and this time the best player in the draft was Denis Potvin, a young defenceman with the Ottawa 67s of the Ontario Hockey League. In those days, the draft age was 20, but even at the age of 18 Potvin had possessed enough size and talent to play in the NHL. He was a huge talent, the best junior defenceman since Bobby Orr and a man around whom a pro franchise was built.

In the months leading up to the draft, Torrey received several interesting offers for his first-round pick. The most persistent caller was Montreal Canadiens' general manager, Sam Pollock, who just a few years earlier had acquired Guy Lafleur by dealing off veterans for a first round selection. Torrey remembers vividly the morning of the draft in Montreal. When he came down for breakfast, Pollock was in the lobby waiting for him. "Let's go for a walk," Pollock said.

They walked around the Mount Royal Hotel three times as Pollock made offers. When their stroll ended, Torrey looked at Pollock and said, "No."

"Let's go around one more time," said Pollock.

But Torrey wouldn't budge. He kept his pick and the Islanders drafted Potvin. The Islanders bolstered their defence even more by taking Dave Lewis in the third round and then picking veteran Bert Marshall in the intra-league draft of established players. Potvin's older brother Jean was also added to the defence corps.

Almost overnight, the Islanders had put together a competent defence, despite the inexperience of Denis Potvin and Lewis. Very quickly, it became apparent that Arbour's team would stress defensive play. Arbour was from the old school and had played for two coaches, Scotty Bowman in St. Louis and Punch Imlach in Toronto, neither of whom would tolerate sloppiness or poor checking.

In 1973-74, the Islanders won only seven more games than in the previous year, but they lost 19 fewer games, because of so many tied games (18). Most important, they established their defensive play, knocking exactly 100 goals off their goals-against total of 1972-73.

With a realignment of the NHL into four divisions, the Islanders played the 1974-75 season in the Patrick Division with the Rangers, Flyers and Atlanta Flames, and had their first winning season, 33-25-22. In the playoffs, the surprising Isles knocked off the favoured Rangers two games to one. Potvin calls that victory the result of an "imbalance of attitudes." He says, "We came in as the scrappers. We knew what we had to do. The Rangers were a veteran team caught by surprise. Before they could recover, the series was over."

In the next round, the Islanders played the Pittsburgh Penguins and promptly lost the first three games. Arbour had missed some of the games because of a back problem, but for the practice before the fourth game, he was on the ice.

Arbour remembers taking the players to a corner of the rink and telling them they would still come back and win. "I had my doubts," he says. "But I told them that anybody who didn't think we still had a chance should leave the ice and take off their equipment. And furthermore, they could forget about ever playing for the Islanders again."

Curiously, that wasn't the part of the speech Potvin and others remembered. "The first thing he did was apologize to us for not being behind the bench," Denis said. "Naturally, we were expecting him to say something else. He said he blamed himself for not fighting through the pain. He said he felt that he had deserted us. And then he told us how proud he had been of what we had done that year. That, by itself, caught our attention. It inspired us and we felt, if we could just get the next win . . ."

The Islanders did win the fourth game, and the next two, to tie the series. At that point Potvin saw a change in the Pittsburgh players. "All of a sudden a look in their eye changed from confidence to a quizzical look. We knew we had them."

In the seventh and deciding game, the two teams battled to a scoreless tie until 14:42 of the third when Eddie Westfall gave New York a 1-0 lead. For the remaining 5:18 minutes, the Islanders shut down the Penguins, not allowing a shot on goal. With the victory, the Isles became the second team in Stanley Cup history to rebound from a 3-0 deficit and win a series.

Now, the Islanders, an expansion team in only its third season, were in the Stanley Cup semi-finals against the Philadelphia Flyers, the defending champions. The Flyers, of course, were intimidators without equal. But not to the Islanders. They were probably the first team in the league to stand up to Philadelphia — to give back as much or more than was handed out.

This first occurred in the fall of 1973 during the pre-season. It was Potvin's first training camp and although a rookie, he was 20 years old and already an important member of the team. One day, Arbour showed Potvin a video tape of a game between Islanders and Philadelphia played the previous year, before the tougher players such as Bob Nystrom and Garry Howatt had joined the team. What Potvin saw made him sick.

"It was an embarrassment," he says. "Two or three of the Flyers were skating around at will, taking punches at Islander players. Nobody was doing anything to stop them. I had fought a lot in junior hockey and I said to Al, 'That will never happen again.' "

It so happened that the Flyers and Islanders met a few days later. There were two major brawls in the game and the Islanders bettered the Flyers in both. Potvin fought with Don Saleski. Howatt, a short but strong man and a fierce fighter, tangled with Dave Schultz. Nystrom, who was among the toughest players in the league, beat up Andre (Moose) Dupont. "We got the best of them," Potvin said. "Man for man, we were a much stronger team. They had some little guys who didn't fight much, like Orest Kindrachuk and Bobby Clarke, and we just had them beaten in size and toughness."

The 1975 semi-final wasn't about intimidation. It was about hard, tough hockey, which was the Flyers' bread and butter. In the first game, they decisively beat the Islanders 4-0. In the second game, Philadelphia outlasted New York, winning in overtime. The Flyers took the third game, this time 1-0.

But once again, the Islanders mounted a comeback. At Long Island, they won in overtime. Then they went back to Philadelphia and won again, 5-1. A 2-1 victory at home by the Isles locked the series at three and forced a seventh and deciding game.

At the Spectrum in Philadelphia, the Flyers brought in their good luck charm, singer Kate Smith, to perform her famous rendition of "God Bless America." With appropriate fanfare, the Flyers threw down the carpet just a few feet from the Islander goal where goaltender Chico Resch stood, and amid the swaying spot lights and strobes, out came Smith. The crowd exploded in cheering and Smith sang her song. Resch, a few feet away, took it all in.

Bill Torrey thinks the spectacle unnerved Resch, who was not in top form that night. After playing extraordinarily well for the Islanders in the playoffs, he allowed three goals inside of the first eight minutes. The Flyers went on to win 4-1 and take the series, and eventually their second consecutive Cup.

In the next four years, the Montreal Canadiens supplanted Philadelphia as the league's top team. The Islanders, meanwhile, matured and evolved. In the front office, a key addition was Jimmy

Devellano, a young man from Toronto who had worked as a part-time scout for the St. Louis Blues. When the Blues decided not to retain Devellano, he approached Torrey in 1973 about a job. Devellano rose quickly in the Islander organization, from scout to director of player personnel and finally assistant general manager.

During this period, Devellano played an important role in the Islander scouting apparatus. In 1974, picking fourth overall, they took Clark Gillies, a 6-foot-3, 215-pound left winger who would become the best player at his position and, for a few years, the most physically dominating winger in the NHL. In the same draft, the Islanders selected Bryan Trottier, a centre from the Swift Current Broncos, in the second round.

That year, NHL teams were allowed to pick 18-year-olds in an attempt to counteract the raiding of the top juniors by the WHA. The best 20-year-olds went first, which in part is why Trottier, at age 18, was still available at the 22nd pick.

It turned out to be one of the great steals of any draft. Trottier developed into the best all-round centre in the game and the man who would spearhead the Islanders' attack for 15 years. But the Islanders didn't stop there. With their sixth pick they took defenceman Dave Langevin, who became one of the finest defensive defencemen in the league. And with pick number 13 they selected a Swede, Stefan Persson, a skilled defenceman who became a key part of the Islander power play.

In his book, Wayne Gretzky writes about the excellent draft of the Oilers in 1980 when they took Paul Coffey, Jari Kurri and Andy Moog. (Gretzky also included Glenn Anderson, but he was picked in 1979.) But who would you take if you were starting a team? The three Oilers — Coffey, Kurri and Moog? Or Bryan Trottier, Clark Gillies, Dave Langevin and Stefan Persson? Gretzky called the 1980 Oiler draft "maybe the best . . . in the history of the league." Others would suggest that standing belongs to the Islander draft of 1974.

The next important year for Torrey and his scouting staff was 1977. By now the Islanders were among the best teams in the league and were no longer picking high. The team had all the components of a winner, except one — they did not have a natural goal scorer. Not that many teams did, other than Montreal who had Guy Lafleur,

Buffalo with Rick Martin, Los Angeles who had Marcel Dionne, and Toronto, with Lanny McDonald.

In four seasons with Laval of the Quebec junior league, Mike Bossy, a right winger, had produced consecutive 70, 84, 79 and 75 goal seasons. Despite these numbers, most NHL teams did not rank Bossy highly in the 1977 NHL draft. He did not play physically, did not check, was an average skater and compiled his numbers in a league that was perceived to be the weakest of the three major Canadian junior leagues.

A scout for the Montreal Canadiens advised against taking Bossy because he said he had not played well in Sherbrooke, Quebec, where the coach was often quoted as saying his players intended to inflict harm on Bossy. Still, Henry Saraceno, who scouted the Quebec league for the Islanders, liked what he saw, and was one of the few to recognize Bossy's talent and potential.

In the draft, Bossy was passed over by the first 14 teams. When it came the Islanders' turn, they called a timeout. A major disagreement developed over who should be taken. Saraceno argued strongly for Bossy. But other scouts wanted Dwight Foster, a centre with Kitchener of the Ontario Hockey Association. Foster had led the OHA in points with 143 and had scored 60 goals. Furthermore, he was a rugged, defensive-minded player — an Islander type.

Finally Torrey announced on the floor of the draft his choice: Mike Bossy of Laval. It was that decision, as much as any other, that would make the Islanders into champions, because Bossy would become the most prolific goal-scoring right winger in the history of the league.

But he was more than a gunner. He passed well, understood systems and had a fine sense of the game. He wasn't a tough player, but he accepted punishment to accomplish his goals. Like all great players, he was competitive and he had a significant ego.

Says Arbour, "Bossy was a very proud individual who wanted to prove to everybody that he was a complete player. He worked very hard to become a complete player and, of course, he was a brilliant scorer. There may have been other players over the years who could score like him, but nobody did it with as much flare and grace."

Earlier in his rookie season, Bossy was placed on a line with

Bryan Trottier and Clark Gillies. This threesome quickly became the league's dominant unit. In the 1977-78 season, Bossy scored 53 goals to win the rookie of year award and a second-team all-star berth. Trottier led the league in assists with 77 and picked up 46 goals, good enough for a spot on the first all-star team. And Gillies had 35 goals plus 50 assists, which won him a spot on the first team.

The Islanders, as a team, won their division handily and finished third over all in points, behind Montreal and Boston. But that year, the Isles' run at the Stanley Cup ended abruptly in the quarterfinals when they were defeated by the Toronto Maple Leafs. Roger Neilson, in his first year behind the bench for the Maple Leafs, had built the Toronto club into a tough defensive-minded team. Keying on the Islanders' big line, the Leafs shut down the Islander attack. Led by Darryl Sittler and Lanny McDonald, and backed by Mike Palmateer's strong goaltending, the Leafs upset the Islanders in seven games.

It was a stunning loss for Islanders and one that would be repeated the following spring when they would fall to the Rangers in the semi-final after a brilliant regular season in which they led the league in points with 116 (51 wins, 15 losses and 14 ties). It has been speculated that the Islanders could have ended Montreal's Cup reign at three had the two teams met in the playoffs. The Islanders always played well against Montreal and had won their series of games during the regular season.

Looking back to the 1979 series, Bossy blames himself, in part, for the loss to Rangers. The series was wildly hyped in the media as "the Battle of New York." As the favourite, the Islander team felt the pressure, and no one more than Bossy. He was using a new brand of hockey stick, which wasn't working for him, consistently breaking and feeling wrong in his hands. The Ranger line of Steve Vickers, Walt Tkaczuk and Anders Hedberg effectively checked the Isles' big line and Bossy, particularly, could do nothing. As the pressure built, he stopped talking to the media. Spooked, after losing the first two games of the series at home, the Islanders fell in six.

Bossy and Potvin feel immaturity was the main reason for the 1978 and 1979 upsets. The Islanders had not yet learned how to handle pressure. They had been world-beaters in earlier years when the other teams were the favourites. But when the burden of high expectations shifted to them, they had trouble. Given the highs and lows, it was easy, also, to forget the Islanders had been in the league only seven years. And the key players were still young. Goaltender Billy Smith was 28, Clark Gillies and Denis Potvin were 25. Bossy and Trottier were only 22. For these players and the others, the spring of 1979 marked a coming of age.

Says Bossy, "The two big setbacks before the Stanley Cups served as a lesson. We realized that if we wanted to keep going, if we wanted to keep the same guys together, we had to get down to business and do the job. It became a quest for us, to win the Stanley Cup. We felt it was just a matter of facing up to the challenge."

Torrey did not intend a major shakeup. With age catching up to the Montreal defence, the Islanders now had the best blueline in the league. In goal, Billy Smith was a scrapper and second only to Ken Dryden in ability. The Islanders' big line of Trottier, Bossy and Gillies was without equal. And there were some fine wingers such as Bob Nystrom, Anders Kallur, Bob Bourne and a young John Tonelli. But what the team lacked was a second offensive centre, someone to lead a strong number two line, someone to take the pressure off Trottier.

During the 1979-80 season, Torrey talked to the Maple Leafs about Darryl Sittler, who was feuding with general manager Punch Imlach, but Torrey finally decided Imlach was asking for too much. Torrey was looking for more than a performer. He wanted a certain personality and Sittler didn't fit the bill.

"We had a great bunch of guys. It was a dedicated and hard working team," Torrey says. "But it was also a quiet, introverted team. I wanted somebody who had a swagger about him, who could walk into the dressing room and just take over."

That player turned out to be Butch Goring, a 30-year-old centre with the Los Angeles Kings. There was nothing fancy or stylish about Goring. He wore a battered old helmet that had gone out of style years before and he skated bow-legged. But he had speed and was an excellent forechecker, as well as a top-notch penalty killer. To get Goring at the trading deadline in March, 1980, Torrey had to pay a heavy price, sending two players younger than Goring to the Kings, Billy Harris and Dave Lewis.

It turned out to be an excellent trade for New York. With Goring in the lineup, Arbour was able to balance his attack. He took Gillies off the big line and put him with Butch and Duane Sutter, a tough winger. That was the Islanders' new grinding line, but it could also produce goals. Bourne, one of the best skaters in the league, was moved into Gillies' spot and suddenly the big line had more speed.

The first challenge came in the playoffs, after the Islanders had eliminated the Kings. The opposition was Boston, a big aggressive team that included Terry O'Reilly, Al Secord, Wayne Cashman and Stan Jonathon. Torrey remembers it as the "toughest, most physical series we had ever been in." The Bruins adhered to the theory that the Islanders, specifically Trottier and Bossy, could be battered into submission. The Leafs had done it in 1978 and so they would do it, too.

"It was a big series for me," said Billy Smith, the Islanders' goaltender, who played in 20 of the team's 21 games, winning 15. "But I've always said that us winning came down to one thing: we stood up for ourselves. We had Clark Gillies to thank for that."

Gillies remembers arriving in Boston the day before the series started and watching the news that evening with his roommate Nystrom. "The sportscaster came on and said the Bruins would win the series in five games, mainly because they would intimidate us. I thought Bobby was going to climb through the TV. We both looked at each other and said, 'Uh, uh.'"

Four times during the series, Gillies fought the Bruins' toughest player, Terry O'Reilly, and won. In the second game, Nystrom gave John Wensink a terrible beating. Howatt bettered O'Reilly in another fight. The rest of the team rallied behind them and in five games the series was over. "It wasn't hockey," Gillies says. "It was a circus. It was obvious they wanted to intimidate us, like other teams had. We knew we couldn't back down and we didn't."

There remained now one last hurdle. The Philadelphia Flyers had been the class of the league in the regular season. They had finished first overall with 48 wins, 12 losses and 20 ties for 116 points, which was 25 points ahead of Islanders who had gone through a very average season. Many of the Flyer veterans of the Stanley Cup championship years of 1974 and 1975 were still with the team. They included Bill Barber who had scored 40 goals in 1979-80 and Reggie

Leach would had hit 50. They were ably supported by a new breed of aggressive players that included Ken Linseman, Paul Holmgren and Behn Wilson.

To grab the ring, the Islanders had to oust the Flyers and, if the series went the distance, they would have to do it on Philadelphia ice. The first game, at the Spectrum, went into overtime with Potvin getting the winner with a power-play goal. He was a tower of strength in the game, scoring twice in the 4-3 victory. Philadelphia won the next game 8-3. But at home for the next two games the Islanders were confident they could take both.

One of the reasons for the optimism was the Islander power play — the best in the league with a success rate of close to 30 per cent. That, in itself, was quite remarkable. The average power-play effectiveness of teams today is 20 per cent.

Trottier was the playmaker, Bossy the sniper. Gillies, with his strength and size, worked the corners and the front of the net. On the points were Potvin and Stefan Persson, an underrated offensive defenceman. Because of Persson's skills, opposing teams could not focus solely on Potvin. And all Potvin needed was a split-second to make a play.

The Edmonton Oilers' power-play unit, with Wayne Gretzky, Mark Messier and Jari Kurri, might have been on a par, but their success rate was never as high. The Oilers perhaps exceeded the Islanders in pure offensive talent and flare, but Potvin and company played with discipline. They were more patient and deliberate.

"We were a perfect fit," Bossy said. "We had great anticipation and we never panicked."

On the Island, Potvin played another terrific game, scoring twice and picking up two assists in a 6-2 Islander victory. The Isles followed that up with another win at home. They were now one game away from the Stanley Cup.

But in Philadelphia, the Flyers kept the series alive, winning 6-3 and forcing a sixth game back at the Nassau Coliseum. Suddenly the pressure was squarely on New York. Would they fold again? Bossy felt they had to win Game Six at Long Island. The chances of prevailing in a seventh game at the Spectrum were not good.

The game, which was played on a Saturday afternoon, turned into a thriller. The Flyers took the lead in the eighth minute. But four minutes later Potvin tied it. Before the first period was over, the grinders had given New York the lead — Sutter from Gillies and Goring. But then Brian Propp tied it for Philadelphia.

In the second, the Islanders jumped into a two-goal lead on markers from Bossy and Nystrom. But Philadelphia gamely fought back, scoring twice early in the third period to knot the game at four. For the remainder of the period, the Flyers and Islanders fought to standstill. It would take overtime to decide the winner.

Back and forth the play went until eight minutes into the overtime period, when Lorne Henning broke up a play at centre ice. In a quick move, he sent the puck over to John Tonelli. Suddenly the Islanders had a two-on-one break. As Tonelli crossed the blueline he threw the puck over to Nystrom, who could do little but jab at it with his stick and hope it went in the direction of the net. It did, over and behind a sprawling Pete Peeters.

As the Islanders leapt over the bench, a thunderous ovation rained down on them. Long Island had its first major-league championship team, but not its last. The Islanders' hold on the Cup would last four seasons, and before it was over they would be hailed as one of the finest champions of all time.

In Potvin, they had the top defenceman of that era. He was superior to any of the three stars on the Canadiens — Robinson, Lapointe and Savard — simply because he could do more. He was brilliant offensively, a fine playmaker and goalscorer. In his 11-year career, he had three 30-or-more goal seasons. Only three times did he miss scoring 20 or more. In 1978-79, he had a 101-point season, with 31 goals and 70 assists. At the time of his retirement, he held the record for points and assists for defencemen, and was only second only to Bobby Orr in goals. (Red Kelly also had more goals than Potvin, but he played the last seven years of his career as a forward.) Potvin won the Norris Trophy as the league's top defenceman three times and was a first-team all-star five times.

Arbour says, "Potvin could hurt you in so many ways. He could hurt with a defensive play, or a pass, or a goal from the point. He also had a mean streak, so he could hurt with his stick, or just physically, with his body."

Potvin almost ended the career of Bill Derlago, a rookie centre with Vancouver, when he caught him low with a check that tore up the ligaments in his knee. In the 1976 Canada Cup spectators close to ice level in Toronto saw Potvin take a Czechoslovak into the corner and pin him up against the glass, face first. Both had their sticks up, but Potvin's was in his opponent's face and cut him.

Trottier, too, was tough and sometimes dirty. But at his peak, he was also the best centre in the league. Even after Wayne Gretzky came along, many felt Trottier was a better all-round performer. He wasn't exceptionally talented in any particular area. Others skated better. There were superior goalscorers and playmakers. But when all of Trottier's abilities were added up — his defensive work, his leadership — he came out ahead of everybody, the one exception being perhaps Gretzky.

For his part, Bossy had the misfortune of being overshadowed early in his career by Guy Lafleur and later in his career by Gretzky. On his own team, Trottier was generally considered to be the key forward, not his high-scoring right winger. But Bossy ranks beside Gordie Howe, Maurice Richard and Lafleur among the best right wingers in the game. As a pure goal scorer he has no equal.

He became the first man to match Maurice (Rocket) Richard's 50 goals in 50 games. And in the nine full seasons Bossy played in the NHL, beginning in his rookie season, he never dipped below 50 goals. Nobody before or since has had nine consecutive 50-goal seasons. Amazingly, there were five seasons in which Bossy had 60 or more goals. Only in his last year did he fall under the 50-goal mark, scoring 38; but he scored those in only 63 games, while playing with the constant pain of a back problem that finally forced him into an early retirement.

Because of the brilliance of the big three, the Islander supporting players were often overlooked. Gillies was an all-star, Goring a fine number-two centre. Winger Anders Kallur provided excellent penalty killing and had offensive skills. In terms of tough, all-purpose wingers, Nystrom and Duane Sutter fit the bill. John Tonelli was so talented that as a teenager he had jumped from the Toronto Marlboros to the World Hockey Association. He emerged from the WHA a strong, power winger, a bull of a man who was unequalled in determination along the boards.

In the 1980 draft, the Islanders further strengthened their team by acquiring Brent Sutter, Duane's brother, in the first round. Six Sutter brothers would end up playing in the NHL, but of them all, Brent, a centre, was the most talented. Another addition in late 1980, was defenceman Ken Morrow, who joined the team from the gold-medal winning U.S. Olympic team.

The consistency of the Islanders was the product of Al Arbour's coaching philosophy. He was not a ranter or a bully, but a stern father figure who had the players' respect and attention, always. Bossy says he notices players today on the bench looking over their shoulder to the coach, as if to say "Get me on the ice." Bossy says, "You would never do that with Al. He was completely in control and you could not challenge his system."

The Islanders, under Arbour's system, were sometimes described as a old-style hockey team, not unlike Hap Day's defensive teams in Toronto during the Forties. Occasionally Arbour was criticized for being predictable and under-using his best players. In Edmonton, Wayne Gretzky and Jari Kurri would sometimes play 35 minutes a game. But in Long Island, Bossy got his 22 minutes and very little more.

But it worked because of the team's depth and because of the emphasis on defence. Over and over, Arbour would drill the players on positional play. "He'd drive you and drive you," Potvin says. "He'd do things that were repetitive, over and over, repetitive to the point that it was a bore, and then he'd watch you make a mistake in practice and he'd stop the play and yell at you. But it became so automatic, the things he taught, that I'd turn around and make a pass and it would land on somebody's stick. It made me look great, but really here's my teammate knowing exactly what I'm going to do by repetition."

Not that the Islanders were boring and repetitive on the ice. They could play the game any way the opponents wanted. They could match Montreal's offence. They could out-hit the Bruins and out-fight the Flyers.

Potvin says, "We had the wonderful ability to expand into any game you wanted. If one of them wasn't working, we could always go back to what made us — solid defence."

The Islanders might have lacked flash, but in their deliberate and businesslike way they were devastatingly effective. On the eve of the

Islanders' 1981 Cup championship, *The Globe and Mail*'s Neil Campbell wrote, "New York should be dressed in grey flannel instead of blue and orange. They've become so routinely awesome that they're almost reminiscent of the baseball's great New York Yankee teams of the Fifties. Remember when somebody wrote that rooting for those Yankee teams was like rooting for General Motors? The Islanders are making victory look just as inevitable as those Yankee teams did, and they're having a lot better year than General Motors."

The corporate image of the Islanders was appropriate. This was a mature group that took a no-nonsense approach to the game. Egos, some of which were considerable, were left at the door of the dressing room door. "There were no superstars in the dressing room," Potvin said, "just twenty guys working together equally. Our theory was that if the team wins everybody benefits."

A player's character was important in the Islanders' scheme of things. In 1982, for example, Bill Torrey took defenceman Paul Boutilier in the first round, partly because Boutilier came from an achieving family. His father, Ernie Boutilier, was the president of the Sydney Steel Corporation in Nova Scotia. Unfortunately Boutilier turned out to be below-average player who was eventually traded to Boston.

Another player who didn't quite fit in was Pat Price, who had been a star defenceman in the Western Hockey League and the Islanders' first pick in 1975. Bossy, in his biography, tells a story about Arbour and Price which occurred in 1978-79. After a loss, Arbour came into the dressing room, steaming, and said, "You guys played like a bunch of pansies. If I put an egg in each of your pants before the game, none of you would have broken any."

At practice the next day, he came into the room with a basket of eggs and started handing them out. Bossy almost started to laugh, but Arbour was deadly serious, so Bossy and the others looked the other way. Suddenly, Arbour exploded. As Bossy looked over, he saw Price pinned into his stall by Arbour who was screaming, "If it was up to me you'd be gone tomorrow!"

What Price had done was take his egg and break it over Arbour's head. Arbour had egg shells on his head and yoke dripping all over him. Bossy wrote, "Do you know how painful it is not to laugh at the sight of your coach looking so angry and so foolish at the same time? My eyes were watering. I didn't know whether to run out of the room so I could crack up or hang around to see what happened next."

As for Price, he was traded to Edmonton two days later.

If character and chemistry were important, so too was preparation. Arbour says he would start preparing for the playoffs in February, more than two months before they started. The practices would take on more of an edge. The conditioning programs were stepped up. The players were told to forget about first place overall. The Cup was what counted.

For two years, the Islanders dominated totally — regular season and playoffs — as few teams ever have. They finished first in the 1980-81 regular season with 48 wins, 18 losses and 14 ties and then followed up with another league-leading performance in 1981-82, this time earning 54 victories, losing 16 and tying 10.

In the 1981 playoffs, they swept the Rangers in the semi-finals and then took five games to defeat the Minnesota North Stars in the final. In the 1982 playoffs, they became the first team since the Canadiens of 1959-60 to sweep both the semi-finals and the final, knocking off Quebec in the semis and then Vancouver in the final. The next year, they blanked the Oilers in the final, 4-0 to win their fourth straight Stanley Cup.

The Islanders grew stronger and gained confidence as the playoffs progressed. The only time they were vulnerable was in the early rounds. The biggest scare they received was in the first round of the 1982 playoffs against Pittsburgh. The best-of-five series started off routinely, with New York taking the first two games at home. Pittsburgh owner Edward J. DeBartolo Sr. was so upset by his team's performance that he refused to attend games four and five in Pittsburgh and offered a refund to any fan who was embarrassed by the team's performance.

Perhaps motivated by this, Pittsburgh won the third game on an overtime goal by Rick Kehoe and then whipped the Islanders 5-2 in the fourth. Suddenly, the future of the Islander dynasty hinged on one game. It was played in the Nassau Coliseum, but that didn't seem to help. After two periods, the Islanders were behind 3-1.

Bossy remembers panic starting to set in as the players waited for the third period to begin. Bossy asked himself, "What are we going to say after the game if we lose? What's the reason for us losing?"

One of the reasons was Pittsburgh goaltender Michel Dion, who had been almost unbeatable. His mastery of the Islanders continued in the third period. After 10 minutes there had been no scoring. Pittsburgh still led 3-1, the Penguins were checking tenaciously and New York could generate nothing. Bossy recalls the players becoming "desperate and afraid." Then, in the 13th minute, the Penguins took a penalty. Arbour immediately called a timeout and changed goalies. In those days, a replacement goaltender was allowed a warmup. Arbour wanted to use that time to cool off the Penguins and get his team focused.

His strategy worked brilliantly. On the power play, the Islanders' Mike McEwen knocked in a rebound make it 3-2 with 5:27 remaining. Frantically, the Islanders stormed into the Pittsburgh zone to get the equalizer, but Dion held them back. Then, with 2:27 remaining, Tonelli picked up a loose puck in front of Dion and fired quickly. The game was tied.

The drama continued in overtime. Potvin remembers one heart-stopping play early in the overtime period. He was on the ice when Rick Kehoe hit Mike Bullard with a cross-ice pass that sent Bullard in on a breakaway.

Potvin says, "Bullard made a move to his right then dragged the puck back to the left. All I could see was six feet of open net. I thought it was all over. Then, out of nowhere, I saw this big pad come shooting out. I don't know how Smith did it, but he got enough of the puck to stop it. Then, on the next shift, Tonelli got the winner."

Two big goals by Tonelli had saved the day and kept the Islanders alive. They would win the Cup easily that year, defeating Vancouver in four to make it three championships in a row. And they would sweep in 1983 as well, defeating the Edmonton Oilers in four games. Still, there was a foreboding element to the Oiler series. It was obvious Edmonton was on the verge of becoming the new league power. The Islanders knew they would face them again, which they did, the following spring in 1984.

This was the Islanders' Drive for Five, their bid to become only the second team to win five straight Stanley Cups. It did not start well.

In the first round, the Rangers pushed them to a fifth and deciding game. In the conference final, the Isles found themselves down 2-0 to the Canadiens, before rallying to win the next four.

Over in the other conference final, Edmonton made short work of Minnesota, which meant the Oilers had a nine-day wait before meeting the Islanders in the final. They used the time to study videotapes of the Islander team and devise ways of capitalizing on their weaknesses. What the Oilers saw was a team that had grown old and had serious injuries.

On videotape, the Oilers watched the series between the Islanders and the Canadiens and came to the conclusion that Montreal had them on the ropes, but then made the mistake of playing cautiously and allowing the Islanders to come back. Edmonton would not do that. The swift Oiler forwards would attack ferociously and they would not let up.

Nobody knew what to make of the series. Edmonton hadn't won a game against the Islanders in 10 previous meetings and, psychologically at least, had been intimidated by the Isles. Arbour says, "When we beat them in 1983, we were playing perfect hockey. They were a hell of a hockey team, but down deep they really didn't believe they could beat us. Whether they felt they could do it the following year was the unanswered question."

Any confidence the Oilers needed was supplied by the Islander injury report. Bossy had tonsillitis, Trottier was playing with two broken ribs. Ken Morrow had a bad knee. Potvin was suffering from lower back problems that caused him so much pain in his legs that he could barely walk. Persson, Langevin and Nystrom were out of the lineup with shoulder injuries. If that wasn't enough, Langevin's father died of a heart attack during the series, while watching a game on television.

The first game at Uniondale was a defensive battle, featuring wonderful goaltending by Smith and Grant Fuhr. The third period turned in Edmonton's favour when Brent Sutter allowed Kevin McClelland, a checker, to get a shot from a sharp angle on Billy Smith. It was perfect, catching Smith by surprise on the short side.

The Oilers' 1-0 lead held up, but the Islanders won the next game, 6-1, to tie the series. Still, New York felt Edmonton had the edge.

Because of a new format in the final, the next three games, instead of the usual two, would be played in Edmonton. This change was brought in to cut down on air travel. A sixth and seventh game, if needed, would be played back in Long Island. The two-three-two system was universally disliked and lasted only two years, but in 1984 the Islanders had to live with it. They had to win at least one game in Edmonton to stay alive.

When they arrived in the West, they also found that they had to practice at odd hours, which did nothing to allay an already chilly relationship between the two teams. The hard feelings had their roots in 1981, when Wayne Gretzky had told the New York press, after Edmonton had upset the Canadiens, that the Oilers had defeated "the best team in hockey." The Islanders, at the time, were the Stanley Cup defending champions, and the players resented Gretzky's remark.

Dave Anderson of the New York *Times* wrote: "For all his precocious genius on the ice, Wayne Gretzky is indisputably 20 years old in coping with the psychology of playoff diplomacy. By complimenting the Canadiens he unthinkingly had insulted the Islanders."

The Oiler coach, Glen Sather, by himself, angered opposing teams with his annoying cockiness and habit of yapping at players during games. The attitude of some in the Edmon-ton media didn't help either. In the first Cup final between the Oilers and Islanders, for example, the Edmonton *Journal* published a silly editorial that referred to the Islanders as "the bozos from New York," a light-hearted, but also light-headed attempt at partisanship.

Before the first game in Edmonton, Bill Torrey used his speech at the annual Stanley Cup luncheon to complain about the practice time allotted to the Islanders the day before (2 p.m. to 4 p.m.). Sarcastically, Torrey told the guests at the luncheon, "I'd like to thank the people of Edmonton for their hospitality, for the warm weather (it was cool and raining) and for their warm greetings. We're having one helluva time." Later, he said, "Next year, you'll have our ice from 6 a.m. to 8 a.m."

When it was Sather's turn to speak, he parried, "Before last year's luncheon on Long Island, we had to practice at 9 a.m. and we didn't complain. I think it rained that day, too, and we didn't complain about that. We didn't complain, either, about the bad hospitality."

Torrey sat through this, unsmiling, staring straight ahead, perhaps wondering if time really had run out, wondering if his team had anything left — hoping, by some miracle, they could turn back the Oilers one more time.

Bossy says the Islanders approached the games in Edmonton with a simple objective. "We kept telling ourselves we just had to win one game in their building. One win and we would return to Long Island for a sixth game. We knew we wouldn't lose at home. One win in Edmonton, we kept telling ourselves, and we get our fifth Stanley Cup."

It didn't happen; but, early in the first game in Edmonton, the Islanders appeared to be in control. They had a 2-1 lead and were defending well, when suddenly Mark Messier changed the momentum of the game and the series. His victim was rookie defenceman Gord Dineen, who was activated because of the injuries on the Islander blueline. Messier, in the words of Arbour, turned Dineen "inside out," drove in on Billy Smith and rammed the puck past him.

That, by all accounts, was the turning point in the game. With that goal, the Oilers took over. The decimated Islander defence could no long withstand the Oiler attack. Unprotected, Billy Smith's magic disappeared and so too did New York's hope for a fifth Cup.

The game ended 7-2, and two days later the series concluded with a 5-2 Edmonton triumph. Oiler defenceman Kevin Lowe wrote in his biography, "A year earlier we had been the vanquished shaking the hands of the victors. This time it was reversed. I'll never forget the emotion in the faces of the Sutter brothers, Duane and Brent. Both were crying. Potvin was like a soldier, like a general of an army in battle, admitting defeat in his intelligent, straightforward way. I could see that in his face. Clark Gillies' face told me, 'It's been a great career for me, and we've had our day.' I felt genuinely sorry for them."

Sympathy, yes. But no pity. This was a special group, a team blessed with talent and ambition. They won 19 consecutive playoff series, which is a record. They were consummate professionals, a dynasty remembered for its dignity and class.

8

How the West Won
the Stanley Cup

*E*dmonton's quest for the Stanley Cup started long before the birth of the Oilers and, in fact, preceded the formation of the National Hockey League.

In 1908 and 1910, a strong Cup challenge from Edmonton was organized by Fred Whitcroft, who is now a member of the Hockey Hall of Fame and is best known as one of the stars of the illustrious Renfrew Millionaires of 1910.

In both series, Edmonton lost. The Montreal Wanderers defeated them in a two-game total-point series in 1908, even though the Westerners won the second game. And in 1910, the Ottawa Senators eliminated the Edmontonians before falling themselves to the Wanderers.

Hockey thrived in Edmonton before and after these two Cup challenges. The city had a franchise in the Pacific Coast Hockey League and later competed in the Western Canada League, another strong professional loop. But when the NHL strengthened its hold on pro hockey by expanding into the United States in 1926-27, the WCL died, and with it, big league hockey in Edmonton.

Then, suddenly, in 1972, pro hockey returned. It was the World

Hockey Association, a league organized by California promoters Gary Davidson and Dennis Murphy to compete directly with the rival NHL. In Western Canada, the WHA's point man was Bill Hunter, an entrepreneur, huckster and former junior hockey operator. Bill Hunter placed a team in Edmonton and named it the Alberta Oilers. A year later, Hunter's team became the city's own, Edmonton Oilers.

The Oilers were a mediocre team and despite the efforts of the blustery Wild Bill, almost went out of business several times. Then, in 1976, Hunter was pushed out as owner by Nelson Skalbania, a Vancouver real estate tycoon. Skalbania's partner was of the Western nouveau riche, Peter Pocklington, who within months, gained full control of the Oilers — with the blessing of his friend, Skalbania, who decided to focus his attention on his other WHA team, the struggling Indianapolis Racers.

Peter Puck, as Pocklington was called, was a self-made man, the son of an insurance company branch manager in London, Ont. As a child, Pocklington once pilfered his neighbour's cherries, mixed them with water and sold them as preserves. Some would argue that Peter's ethical standards changed very little after childhood.

A high-school dropout, Pocklington bought and sold cars as a teenager and renovated houses. He became a car salesman at Ford dealership in London Ont., and eventually bought Maple City Ford in Chatham, Ont. He sold that business in 1971 and headed west to make his fortune in the Alberta oil boom.

In Edmonton he bought a dealership in Edmonton, which he renamed Westown Ford. In the next 10 years, he added a Toronto car dealership; a soccer team; Gainers Inc., a meat-packing company; Fidelity Trust; Patrician Land, a development company; the Edmonton Trappers, a Triple A baseball team; an oil drilling company; and, of course, the Oilers.

Pocklington's investment in the Oilers in 1976 coincided with the arrival of Glen Sather, a veteran winger who would rise quickly to become the most important man in the Oiler organization. As coach and general manager, he would lead the team to glory in the Eighties and play a key role in the building of the team.

By the time Sather joined the Oilers he was 33 and on the last legs of an unremarkable NHL career. Slats, which was a nickname given to Sather by his friend Eddie Johnston and a reference to his time spent on the bench (the wooden slats of a bench), had been a journeyman player. He was a checker and had never scored more than 15 goals in an NHL season over a career that included stops in Boston, Pittsburgh, New York with the Rangers, St. Louis, Montreal and Minnesota. Sather was only 5-foot-8, 185 pounds, but tough. Broadcaster Bill Mazer once noted that he had never seen the scrappy Slats lose a fight.

A Westerner, Sather was born in High River, Alta., but as a child, lived for a while in the farming town of Viking, Alta., where his mother owned and operated a beauty salon. I once had occasion to interview some of the farmers in Viking, including Louis Sutter, the father of the six NHL Sutter brothers, who told me they remembered Sather as a "snotty little kid," who needed "a licking every noon hour just to keep him from getting too cocky."

Whether that actually happened, is open to debate. Sather told me it wasn't true. What is inarguable is that Sather grew up to be a supremely self-confident young man. He was also bright, resourceful and, above all, ambitious.

Before Sather's first season with the Oilers had ended, Bep Guidolin had been fired as coach and Sather had replaced him. It was speculated that Guidolin had been undermined by Sather, who quickly developed a close friendship with Pocklington. Still, under Guidolin, the team had a losing record. With Sather behind the bench, the Oilers won nine, lost seven and tied two.

Sather's powerbase was soon solidified with his appointment to the position of general manager as well as coach. Still, the Oilers didn't experience any real success until the WHA's final year of operation, when they finished first and went to the championship final, losing to Winnipeg. The improvement of the Oilers in 1978-79 had something to do with a rookie teenager from Brantford, Ont., by the name of Wayne Gretzky.

Today, Gretzky is generally acknowledged to be the greatest hockey player ever to lace on a pair of skates. But back then, there were doubters, including Nelson Skalbania, who was the first owner to sign the Great One to a professional contract.

All through minor hockey, Gretzky had been a phenomenon. He

scored more goals than anyone before him. He had dominated at every level. In his first year of major junior hockey, with the Ontario Hockey League's Sault Ste. Marie Greyhounds, as a 16-year-old, he had smashed the OHA's scoring record. Still, there were sceptics.

For starters, he wasn't a strong skater. Bent over, his head out in front of his body, and with his elbows flapping, he looked more like a bird trying frantically to lift off than a star hockey player in full flight down the ice. And he was small, about 5-foot-10 and as a teenager not much more than 150 pounds.

Still, the WHA needed a marquee player and Gretzky filled the bill. Gus Badali, who was Gretzky's agent at the time, says there were basically three reasons for him advising his client to jump to the WHA. The first was money. Skalbania was offering $825,000 over four years, which was a record contract for a rookie, even in the inflationary period of the WHA-NHL wars of the Seventies. The second was Wayne's coach at the Soo, Paul Theriault, who had joined the Greyhounds midway through the season. Theriault tried to change Gretzky's style of play, which seemed illogical to Wayne since his present system of play had served him quite well, thank you very much. Gretzky once summed up his feelings on Theriault, by saying, "I hated him."

Badali's main concern wasn't Theriault, but the OHA itself. In the middle to late Seventies, it was a violent league. The goons had started focusing on Gretzky near the end of his season, but Wayne, the dipsy doodler, had avoided a serious hit. Still, Badali was worried that Gretzky could suffer a career-ending injury if he stayed in the OHA and felt he would be safer in pro hockey where the players paid a little more attention to the game at hand than beating up or maiming opposing players.

Negotiations became serious when Skalbania flew Wayne, his parents and Badali to his home in Vancouver. Gretzky notes in his autobiography that the engine in Skalbania's Rolls Royce smoked all the way from the airport to his house. In his driveway was another Rolls, but it didn't work either. This, Gretzky thought, could be an omen.

When it came time to sign the $825,000 contract, Skalbania looked up at the skinny kid sitting across from him and asked, "Are you sure you can play?"

"Yes sir," said the 17-year-old. "I can play."

What Gretzky could not do is save the Indianapolis franchise. Eight games into the season, Skalbania peddled Gretzky's rights to Pocklington in Edmonton. Seven games later, Skalbania folded his team.

In Edmonton, Gretzky's relationship began with the Oilers and Glen Sather. Sather, who exuded a casual, self-assurance, and always dressed well, impressed the young Gretzky, who thought he was "cool." When Wayne first arrived in Edmonton, he stayed with Glen and his family until he got a place of his own. One of the first things Sather said to Gretzky was, "One day we're going to be in the NHL and one day you're going to be captain of this hockey team. Remember that."

Other than this prediction, Sather did not put pressure on Gretzky to perform. He just let him play, which was fine with the new Oiler, who found the WHA faster and cleaner than junior hockey. But in a game against Cincinnati, the realities of pro hockey hit home to Gretzky, when he was benched by Sather for a defensive blunder that gave the Stingers the lead. Gretzky, who had never been benched in his life, was stunned and also furious. When Sather let him back on the ice in the third period, Wayne played with a vengeance and, to "show Sather," scored a hat trick.

To Sather, Gretzky's fury was the mark of a true competitor and seasoned pro. "You could have pouted and sulked," he said to Gretzky later. "But instead you came back."

Sather told Oiler defenceman Kevin Lowe years after the fact that the benching in Cincinnati and Gretzky's positive response was the turning point in Wayne's career. "Not just anyone could keep the motivation with a contract like his. But he wants to be the best."

Gretzky, with his aw-shucks modesty, has attempted to hide or at least disguise his considerable hubris. He even had the gall to say on a television documentary produced by Bob McKeown that he wasn't competitive. That, of course, was the farthest thing from the truth. Scotty Bowman's description of Ken Dryden as an "ultra-competitor" applied in double, or perhaps triple, to Gretzky. Teammates noticed that when Gretzky became extraordinarily motivated on the ice, his face would start to redden, with "little red splotches" appearing. And when that happened, look out.

Kevin Lowe remembered goaltender Jim Craig, the hero of the U.S. gold-medal 1980 Olympic team, snapping at Gretzky during a game between the Oilers and Atlanta Flames, shortly after Craig joined the Flames. Atlanta turned out to be Craig's first but not last team in a short and unimpressive NHL career. On that night, the Oilers were two goals behind and Gretzky wasn't playing well. At one point, Craig, in a mocking tone of voice, said, "Gretzky, just who do you think you are, anyway?" Gretzky burned, but didn't say a word. In the next 30 minutes he put three goals past Craig, who wasn't heard to say a word for the rest of the game.

After Gretzky's first WHA season, he still had his doubters, but there were fewer of them when Wayne's goals and assists were tallied. On two WHA teams, the Racers and Oilers, and playing as a 17-year-old who turned 18 near mid-season, Gretzky had scored 46 goals and earned 64 assists for 110 points in 60 games. That tied him for third over all in goal scoring with Peter Sullivan of Winnipeg, behind Real Cloutier of Quebec and Morris Lukowich of Winnipeg. In assists, he was fifth, behind Robbie Ftorek, Kent Nilsson, Terry Ruskowski and Mark Howe. In total points, he was third, behind Cloutier, Ftorek, but ahead of Mark Howe and Nilsson.

That summer, a merger agreement between the NHL and WHA resulted in the WHA folding and four surviving teams, Quebec, Edmonton, Hartford and Winnipeg, joining the senior league. Almost immediately, Sather began telling people that his team would win the Stanley Cup in five years. As it turned out, he was dead on, but what made his brash prediction come true was his young star. Wayne Gretzky was on his way to becoming the most dominant player in the history of the NHL.

Still, the supporting cast had yet to be picked. That would be done by chief scout, Barry Fraser, a former Ontario Hydro employee from Kitchener, Ont., who scouted for junior teams as well as pro clubs before joining the Oilers. Fraser, from his selections in the late Seventies and early Eighties, earned the right to be called the best scout in the business. His now-famous Player Evaluation Report contained 15 categories and 72 lesser sections that rated everything in skating from change of pace, speed, balance, pace, posture, lateral movement to the right and left, turning right and left, and cutting right and left.

To Fraser, the sum of the parts, or categories, was more important than what a player had done in a particular game or even over a season. If the skills added up, it was worth the gamble of the draft. It was this new, organized, systematic approach to assessing players that led to the Oilers acquiring Mark Messier.

As a 16-year-old, Messier had played Tier 2 hockey in his home town of Edmonton. At the end of the season, Portland, of the Western Hockey League, had called him up for the playoffs. In seven games, Messier scored four goals. The following season, Nelson Skalbania brought Messier to Indianapolis, using some of the money he acquired from Edmonton for Gretzky to sign Mark. When the Racers folded a few weeks later, he was peddled to Cincinnati where he played the rest of the season, anonymously, getting one goal and 10 assists in 47 games. In the NHL's entry draft that June, Messier was an unknown and unwanted quantity — but not so to the Oilers.

When Fraser added up all the points on his evaluation report, Messier scored well. He was big, 6-foot-1, over 200 pounds, aggressive, a terrific skater, and he came from a hockey family. His father, Doug, had played in the minor leagues. Where Messier fell short was in playmaking, a scoring touch, and thinking the game. The Oilers were hoping those things would be learned. They drafted him in the second round, 48th overall.

At training camp that fall, Gretzky saw Messier flying down the ice and said to himself, "My God, how did we get this guy with the 48th pick?" The players called him "Moose," but it could just as easily have been the "Edmonton Express," the nickname of Eddie Shore, a tough, brutal Boston Bruin star of the Twenties and Thirties. The Oilers soon saw how aggressive Messier could be after he received a cheap shot from Calgary's Jamie Macoun. Later in the game, Messier slammed Macoun to the ice with a vicious check and then pummelled him, breaking his jaw and putting him out of the lineup for a month. It took a few years for Messier to develop his skills, but he would emerge as the most important player on the team after Gretzky. He was a superstar in his own right, a strong leader, and Sather's favourite player.

With or without Messier, the Oilers' drafting had been brilliant in 1979. First they took defenceman Kevin Lowe, 21st overall, then

Messier, and in the third round, winger Glenn Anderson, who was from Vancouver and had played college hockey at the University of Denver. In 1979-80 he played for the Canadian Olympic team, and then joined the Oilers the following year. He was big, a speedster and a goal scorer. Like Messier and Lowe, he became part of the Oilers' core of star players.

The next year, 1980, the Oilers continued to cash in at the draft. They used their first pick (sixth overall) to take defenceman Paul Coffey, who would become one of most skilled performers ever to play the game and the finest offensive defenceman since Bobby Orr. In the third round, there was right winger Jari Kurri, a Finn, and the product of Fraser's decision to concentrate the Oilers' scouting efforts in Finland rather than spread the club's scouting resources more thinly throughout Europe. Kurri would become Gretzky's trigger man on the big Oiler line, an all-star, and one of the finest two or three Europeans to play in the NHL.

The final piece to the puzzle was Grant Fuhr, a goaltender with Victoria, of the Western Hockey League, whom the Oilers drafted sixth overall in 1981. Drafting a goaltender that high is risky, because there are so many uncertainties associated with the development of goaltenders in the intense environment of the NHL. But Fuhr was the real thing and became the premier NHL goaltender of the Eighties.

To this core of five or six stars, Sather, through trades and drafting, added a fine supporting cast. On defence, Charlie Huddy and Randy Gregg ably assisted Lowe, and Coffey, and the veteran team captain Lee Fogolin. Up front, Dave Lumley and Dave Hunter provided toughness and checking. Dave Semenko was the enforcer, and for a few years the heavyweight champion of the league.

It was now a matter of waiting until the young team matured. Huge strides were made quickly. Gretzky, almost immediately, started tearing up the NHL, setting scoring records never before imagined, let alone approached by other players. In the Oilers' first taste of Stanley Cup playoff competition in 1980, they faced the Philadelphia Flyers, the best team in the league that season. Edmonton lost the series in three straight games, but two of them had gone into overtime.

It was an impressive playoff debut. The Oilers, an expansion team made up of a bunch of youngsters, had given the Flyers a significant test. Great things were predicted and, indeed, the following year the Oilers skyrocketed to national attention.

After finishing with a losing record in its first NHL season, Edmonton only marginally improved in its second year. They still hadn't reached the .500 mark in a season and were given next to no hope of upsetting the Montreal Canadiens in the first round of the 1981 playoffs. Montreal was in decline, but still had most of stars from the glory years of the Seventies. Before the series, the Canadiens' goaltender Richard Sevigny told the Montreal press that Guy Lafleur would put Gretzky "in his back pocket," which of course was the wrong thing to say within earshot of Gretzky.

In the first game at the Forum, Gretzky went out and set an NHL playoff record, earning five assists in a 6-3 victory. After Edmonton's sixth goal, he skated pass Sevigny and patted his back pocket. In Game Two at the Forum, the Oilers, backed by the strong goaltending of Andy Moog, a 21-year-old who had been drafted the previous year, Edmonton won again, 3-1.

At that time, the preliminary round of the playoffs was a best-of-three affair, so Edmonton needed only one more victory for the upset. Again it was Gretzky in another fine performance, scoring three goals and adding an assist to lead the Oilers to a 6-2 win.

It was during these playoffs that the personality of the Oilers took shape, or at least the public perception of the Oilers. The Edmonton persona seemed a combination of Western arrogance and child-like wonderment. They were a group young athletes who were winning and in the process thumbing their noses at the NHL's establishment. Winning teams were supposed to play tight defensive hockey. The Oilers did not. They played a wild, wide-open, fire-wagon style that was popular in the Thirties.

NHL teams were supposed to be respectful of their opponents. The Oilers weren't. Sather, from behind the bench, would ridicule the other players and literally applaud his own.

After upsetting the Canadiens, the Oilers played the Cup champion Islanders. It was in that series the Edmonton players started singing on the bench. The "Here we go Oy-lers, here we go!" incensed the Islander players. Even after New York defeated the

Oilers in six games, what lingered was an intense dislike of the cocky Westerners.

In his autobiography, Gretzky attempted to explain the Oilers' mindset during that series. "Were we scared? Petrified. Were we going to show it? No chance. That was the series where we even sang on the bench. The entire team kept chanting 'Here we go Oy-lers, here we go!' Sure, it was high-schoolish, but we were barely out of high school. Six of us could still have been playing junior hockey! We didn't know yet how to be cool, unflappable, unemotional professionals. We were still nervous, thrilled, jacked up. Singing just felt right. And every time we'd get in trouble, we'd sing."

If the Oilers were nervous pretenders in the spring of 1981, they quickly became heirs apparent in 1981-82. It was a marvelous season for the team. Gretzky and the Oilers had become, almost overnight, the league's top attraction. In every city, the swaggering Oilers attracted media throngs. The star of the show, of course, was Wayne, the Great One, whose accomplishments were mind boggling. Not only was on his way to surpassing Phil Esposito's record for goals scored in a season (76), but he was about to break the 200-point barrier, something nobody had come close to doing. He ended up with 92 goals and 120 assists for 212 points in 80 games.

The team won the Smythe Division by 34 points, with 48 wins, 17 losses and 15 ties, which was the second-best record in the NHL, behind the Islanders. The Oilers were expected to again challenge the Islanders, this time in the final.

It didn't happen that way. Instead, Edmonton fell in the first round of the playoffs to the Los Angeles Kings, a team that had slept through the regular season, compiling a losing record. It was a spectacular defeat. In looking back to that series, Paul Coffey notes that Edmonton underestimated a good veteran team that included Marcel Dionne, Dave Taylor, Charlie Simmer and Bernie Nichols. "We were a talented team, but we really didn't have that much experience and it showed," Coffey said.

Nor did the Oilers have much respect for the Kings. In the first game, they had the Kings down 4-1, but, by totally disregarding defensive play, lost 10-8. The Oilers won the next game and in Game Three had a 5-0 lead. Billy Harris, who was an assistant coach with the team, vividly remembers what happened then. The Kings had the power play, but couldn't move the puck out of their end, let alone generate an attack. The fans at the Forum in Inglewood, California, started booing lustily and then, suddenly, from the Oiler bench, the Edmonton players and even Sather started booing the Kings.

It was an incredibly arrogant gesture that backfired. Infuriated by the ridiculing, the Kings fought back to win the game and eventually the series. Afterward, Harris told the Edmonton media that the team had been "antagonistic toward opponents, officials and referees" and that their behaviour was a "reflection of Glen Sather's personality." Harris didn't need to be diplomatic because Sather did not intend to renew his contract.

The Edmonton media also unloaded on the Oilers, particularly Terry Jones of the Edmonton *Sun*, who wrote that the defeat was the biggest choke in Cup history and the Oilers were "weak kneed wimps." Rather than weak kneed, Harris felt the Oilers were immature. "I felt the players weren't going to mature until the guy running the team matured," Harris said. Gretzky tended to agree. He describes the team at that particular time as "young and obnoxious."

Over the next two years, the Oilers did mature. Harris, who blamed Sather for the playoff loss to the Kings, credits Sather with having the foresight to allow the Oilers to become the most powerful offensive machine to play in the NHL. Because of the skill of Gretzky, Mark Messier, Glenn Anderson, Jari Kurri and Paul Coffey, Sather and Harris had decided at the beginning to allow them to improvise. There had been few constraints. "We turned them loose offensively," Harris said. "We encouraged them to be creative offensively. There were no restrictions."

Gretzky feels this freedom made it possible for him to reach his full potential. With another coach in another more conventional system, he would have been stifled.

One of Sather's great strengths was his flexibility, his readiness to borrow ideas from other sources. He had played only one season in Montreal, but he came away with a deep respect for the tradition of the Canadiens. In Montreal, the work ethic was of paramount import-ance. It was the team that counted, not the individual, and it was essential the players had pride in their team.

Jean Beliveau had long retired before Slats joined the Canadiens. But Sather would tell his Oilers about a young player in the Montreal dressing room angrily throwing his sweater on the floor after a game. Beliveau went over and picked it up and handed it back to the player. "You see this sweater?" he said. "From now on, this sweater never touches the floor."

Kevin Lowe, in his book on the Oilers, tells the story of Bobby Schmautz who played briefly Edmonton after several years with the Boston Bruins. Schmautz talked incessantly about how great it had been in Boston and what a terrific coach Don Cherry had been. When the Oilers visited Denver to play Cherry's Colorado Rockies, Schmautz, as a joke, put on a Rockies' sweater after practice. Sather wasn't amused. A few weeks later, he traded Schmautz to Colorado to be with his friend Cherry.

Years later, when Dave Semenko played in Toronto, which was a perennial loser, the players noticed him in the dressing room, going around and picking up sweaters off the floor. Semenko's career was almost over, but he knew how winning teams conducted themselves.

Day after day, year after year, Sather emphasized pride in the team and the uniform the players wore. He had few rules and regulations, but the one that had to be obeyed was: "Don't at any time embarrass me or the team."

From the Winnipeg Jets, Sather borrowed the free-flow European style of hockey of quick transitions, skating to the open ice and pin-point passing. The Jets had been the best team in the WHA, largely because of the talented Swedes who had played with Bobby Hull. That was the kind of team Sather wanted — players with speed, skill and creativity. With the help of Barry Fraser, Sather built that team.

In the Seventies, Sather saw the Soviet Union national squad practicing and was dazzled by the pace and creativity of the workouts. He borrowed that, too. The Edmonton practices were short, but hard and fast.

It cannot be said the players liked Sather. Paul Coffey describes him as "very tough," but says now that Sather's demanding nature made him a better player and person. Semenko called Sather, "The Sneer," because of the withering look of sarcastic contempt Sather would direct at somebody who was not towing the line. But the players respected him. "Slats directed the mood of the team," Coffey says. "If he came into the dressing room upset, we'd get upset. But in the most important games he was always very confident and never showed any signs of pressure."

As with all the great dynasties, there was a remarkable degree of camaraderie. But Edmonton was unique for several other reasons. On other great teams, there had been a mix of young and old, veterans and rookies. The Oilers, almost to a man, started off as a group of young players, many of them teenagers. On some dynasties, the team had previously enjoyed a degree of success before reaching the top. But in the case of the Oilers, the team and players had struggled together and had experienced the transformation of going from the bottom to the top.

"We were a bunch of kids who grew up together," Coffey said. "It was incredible, really, the closeness. We all matured together and then enjoyed some amazing success." Mark Messier says, "There was so much good feeling and we cared for each other so much. We had all the stars, but there was never a hint of jealousy. We all supported each other in everything and were more than happy when somebody was recognized."

One year after their nightmarish defeat to the Kings, the Oilers were back in the playoffs, and this time, they were in the final. In the 1982-83 season, the Oilers had dominated the Smythe Division. Gretzky led the league in scoring, Messier was seventh, Glenn Anderson ninth and Kurri eleventh. Gretkzy and Messier were first-team all-stars, Paul Coffey made the second team.

Without much trouble, Edmonton advanced to the final, sweeping Winnipeg and Chicago and eliminating Calgary in five games. The New York Islanders had more difficulty, needing six games to knock off both Boston and the Rangers.

But in the final, the Islanders borrowed from the playbook of the Kings and played physically against Gretzky, who, with no goals and four assists, wasn't a factor in the series. Overall, New York's strong defensive play neutralized Edmonton's full-steam-ahead offensive hockey. It wasn't even close. New York swept the Oilers in four games to win their fourth consecutive Cup.

During this period, there was a spirited debate in hockey over which NHL centre was really the greatest — Gretzky or Bryan Trottier, the fine two-way performer and leader of the Islanders. Trottier was better defensively than Gretzky and also stronger and tougher. He was no slouch offensively, either. He had led the league in assists twice, in scoring once. He had scored 40 or more goals five times and had recorded one 50-goal season. In 1979, he had won the Hart Trophy, as the league's most valuable player.

Over his career, Gretzky would prove to have no equal, but in the early Eighties, Trottier was a force to be reckoned with. Because of this, Sather decided at the beginning of the 1983-84 season to move Messier from left wing to centre. If the Oilers met the Islanders against in the playoffs, Trottier would have to be stopped. Who better than Messier?

In 1983-84, Gretkzy won his fourth consecutive scoring title. For the second time, he exceeded the 200-point barrier, with 205 points. Coffey, in a remarkable season, scored 40 goals and added 86 assists for 126 points, the most for any defenceman except Bobby Orr. And the Oilers dominated, accumulating 119 points in the regular season — the highest in the league, with the next closest team, Boston, 15 points behind.

In the playoffs, Edmonton swept Winnipeg, but found themselves locked in tough battle with their Alberta rival. It took the Oilers seven games to eliminate the Calgary Flames, but the conference championship was no contest. Edmonton swept Minnesota in four.

Meanwhile, the Islanders' drive for five consecutive Stanley Cups had slowed to a crawl with long and difficult series against the Rangers and Canadiens. Edmonton ended up with a nine-day wait before meeting the Islanders, who had several key injuries, in the final.

The first game turned into a goaltending dual between Grant Fuhr and Billy Smith. But in the third period, the Oilers took the lead on a goal by Kevin McCelland and were able to hold on to win. After the victory, Kevin Lowe remembers Sather closing the door to the dressing room and telling the players, "What did I tell you guys? You proved to yourselves that you could do it."

Sather then reminded the players that they were now a humble group, at least, before the public. "Let's remember when we're talking to reporters that we're just happy we won a hockey game against the mighty New York Islanders. *We* know we're going to win the Stanley Cup now, but don't you tell anyone that. You tell them that we're just lucky to win a game and we're just happy to be playing in the same rink as them."

The Islanders won the next game 6-1, but back in Edmonton, the momentum changed. During the playoffs, Mark Messier had been the Oilers' best player and in the final he continued to lead. In the first game in Edmonton, the Islanders were ahead 2-1 when Messier made the most important play of the series. After accepting a pass from Lee Fogolin, he broke away from his check, into the Islander zone, where he found himself one-on-one with defenceman Gord Dineen. Messier faked one way, went the other and, before the Dineen could blink, Messier was past him and in alone on Billy Smith.

It's all quite hazy now in Messier's mind, but he remembers what was happening before he scored on Smith and what occurred after. "They had put a defensive wall up and we hadn't been able to get through. When I was able to break in on Smith and get the puck past him, it seemed to give us confidence and we never looked back."

Denis Potvin says, "Messier's goal changed the flow of the series. After he scored, the Oilers completely took over. You could see it in their eyes. They were hungry and they knew they could beat us."

The Oilers won the next two games in Edmonton, 7-2 and 5-2, to capture their first Cup. On that day in May, 1984, many anticipated the reign of the Oilers would be long and uninterrupted. They were the class of the league and were led by group of young superstars. The Oilers could be, the experts thought, the best of them all.

Indeed, the dynasty got off to a good start. In the next season, 1984-85, they didn't skip a beat. Gretzky stayed above the 200-point mark (208 points this time). Kurri finished second in scoring with 71 goals and 64 assists. Coffey was fifth. All three were voted to the first all-star team.

But in that season, the Oilers shared the spotlight with the Philadelphia Flyers, a youthful group that included the best goaltender in the league, Pelle Lindberg; a strong defence led by the underrated Mark Howe, Gordie's son; and a handful of young Turks up front. So impressive were the Flyers that they finished first overall.

Edmonton was second.

In the playoffs, both teams marched toward the final for a showdown between the two best in the league. But in the end, it wasn't that close. Edmonton eliminated the Flyers in five games. What was more interesting were the dymanics at work, particularly between Sather and the Flyer coach Mike Keenan. Keenan, a young man in his mid-30s, was much like Sather — ambitious, driven, tough and with a considerable ego. Keenan was also a brilliant coach and particularly effective at psychological one-upsmanship.

As far as Keenan was concerned, any edge could make a difference, whether it was intimidation or baiting a referee. The Flyers attempted to rough up the Oilers — Ed Hospodar, for example, smashed the Oilers' Mark Napier in the mouth with his stick, knocking out one tooth.

After the third game of the series, in which Edmonton scored all four of its goals on four-on-four situations, Keenan suggested the Oilers were trying to get the officials to call coincidental minors, so Edmonton could play Flyers four-on-four. "If you had the best five players in the world, wouldn't you?" Keenan asked. Sather ridiculed the idea. "That's flattering. If he thinks we can manipulate the referees, that's great."

Late in the fifth and final game, with the Oilers in control and leading 8-3, Keenan sent out his goon Dave Brown. Brown performed his duty which was to harass the Edmonton players and finally got into a fight with defenceman Don Jackson. This incensed Sather who yelled at Keenan from the bench. Words were exchanged, but nothing more developed except a mutual contempt.

Later, the Flyers were gracious in their praise. Captain Dave Poulin said, "The Oilers' offensive talent was awesome. Especially Gretzky and Coffey. I think they tried to outgun each other." In had been, indeed, an amazing performance by Gretzky and Coffey, the Oilers' top gun on defence. Gretzky was the playoff leader in points and assists and short-handed goals. But Coffey had been second in scoring and led everyone in game winners, with four. Gretzky was awarded the Conn Smythe Trophy as the most valuable player in the playoffs, but many, including Wayne himself, felt Coffey should have won it.

At that point, it seemed unthinkable that the Oilers' string of Cups would end at two. They were still very young, most under the age of 25, and they had not reached their potential.

Still, there were lingering doubts about Edmonton's long-term success. Their style of play went against every accepted standard set for Cup champions. Winners played with discipline. They were strong defensively. The Oilers were singularly undisciplined, but had so much talent they could win without a strong defence or adherence to game plan.

Sometimes, this lack of discipline spilled over into their personal lives. Before the start of 1985-86 season, Mark Messier was in the news after smashing up his Porsche in a parking lot. About the same time, Dave Hunter, an Oiler forward, had been charged for third time for drinking and driving. In one of the driving incidents, Hunter had been found in the front seat with a woman who was not his wife. A divorce followed.

The Oilers, as a group, were perceived to be wild, unruly and enthusiastic partiers. After one prominent Toronto sports columnist covered a Eastern road trip by the Oilers, he described the players to friends in Toronto as "a bunch of young drunks."

In the regular season, there was no sign of decline. The Oilers finished first overall, with Gretzky setting a record for points and assists (smashing his own marks). In 80 games, he scored 52 goals and earned 163 assists for 215 points.

But the other NHL team in Alberta had also done well. The Calgary Flames, were a solid team that included the veteran Lanny McDonald and a couple of future stars in defencemen Gary Suter and Al MacInnis, as well as Brett Hull, who would develop into a superstar with the St. Louis Blues. At the trading deadline, the Flames' general manager Cliff Fletcher made a key deal with Bill Torrey that upset Sather. From the Islanders, the Flames acquired winger John Tonelli, a veteran of the four Cup championship teams and a talented and aggressive winger, who in the previous year had scored 40 goals.

Sather felt Torrey had been overly generous in sending help to Calgary and suggested Torrey was motivated by the prospect of seeing the Flames upset the Oilers. By this point, the rivalry between Calgary and Edmonton had become something more than intense.

The teams hated each other. The games had become wars and often there were casualties.

During the regular season, Edmonton had defeated Calgary in their first six meetings, 5-3, 6-4, 5-3, 4-3, 6-3 and 7-4. A 4-4 tie followed, and then in their last game of the regular season, there was an important Calgary victory, 9-3. The Flames entered their series with Edmonton confident and well prepared. It also helped that there was no pressure on the Flames. They were expected to lose.

One of Calgary's strengths was its coach, the late Bob Johnson, who in 1991 took the Pittsburgh Penguins to a Cup championship. In 1986, Johnson devised a Calgary game plan that was simple but effective. For starters, he wanted the Oilers to be the bad guys. If there were altercations, the Flames were to back off in the hope Edmonton would receive the extra penalty. Colin Patterson, one of the best checkers in the league, would shadow Jari Kurri. Joel Otto, a tall, imposing centre, would go head to head against Messier. Putting a blanket on Gretzky and Coffey was a team project. Neither Johnson nor Sather had control over the goaltending. Fuhr would be in net for Edmonton. Johnson opted for his rookie, Mike Vernon.

That the Oilers were in for a rough ride was evident almost from the drop of the puck in the first game. Calgary took the play to the Oilers immediately and didn't relent. When it was over, the Flames had a 4-1 victory on Oiler ice. Verdon had been outstanding, which was more bad news for Edmonton. The Oilers came back to win the second game, but they needed overtime to do it.

In Calgary, the Flames won Game Three. From then on, the series went back and forth, with Edmonton either down or even with the Flames. Never ahead. It was a fiercely played, full-speed ahead thriller — the most exciting playoff in years, according to those who were there. Johnson's game plan was working well, but even he hadn't counted on Vernon's spectacular performance in goal.

After five games, Edmonton found itself behind 3-2 in the series, with the sixth game in Calgary. That night the Oilers came up with their finest game, winning 5-2, and forcing a seventh and deciding match in Edmonton. The momentum appeared to have finally shifted north.

It didn't happen that way. The Flames jumped into a 2-0 lead, forcing the Oilers to scratch and claw their way back to a tie in the second period. That set up a third period, which is remembered solely for the mistake made by Oiler defenceman Steve Smith. A few minutes into the period, he took the puck in the Oiler corner and attempted to make a pass through the crease. But the puck didn't make it. It hit the skate of Grant Fuhr and bounded into the net behind him.

Smith was devastated and broke into tears on the Oiler bench. As the minutes on the clock disappeared, Edmonton tried desperately to come back, but there was nothing left. The game ended 3-2 and the Oilers' string of championships ended at two.

Afterwards, Sather chose not to support his players. He blamed them for the loss and said they had not followed the coaches' game plan. Calgary had defended them much the way the Islanders had in 1983, by taking away the slot and gobbling up passes in the Oilers' attacking zone. Just as in 1983, Edmonton had failed to mount a strong forechecking game. Their offence had let them down and their defence wasn't good enough.

Many of the Oilers resented Sather's remarks. Gretzky felt he had kicked them when they were down. "Slats was always a lousy loser," he said, "so rather than accept the loss he bought out of it all together."

But the humiliation and criticism didn't end with the Oilers' elimination. A few days later, *Sports Illustrated,* in an exclusive investigative piece, reported that there were five cocaine users on the team. Sather immediately denounced the story, but Kevin Lowe notes in his book that when Gretzky was asked to make a statement, he told Lowe, "I don't want to touch that one with a ten-foot pole." That remark can be construed as Gretzky not wanting to give any kind credence to the *Sports Illustrated* story, or choosing not to comment on a sensitive subject. For the record, Gretzky claimed in his biography to have no knowledge of drug use among the Oilers.

Others weren't as sure. Several years later, Fuhr, who was one of the five players *Sports Illustrated* was referring to, admitted to a cocaine problem and underwent rehabilitation. It bothered many that, because *Sports Illustrated* had not named the five alleged users, it cast aspersions on everyone. (From the people I knew at *Sports Illustrated,* I learned the names of the other four suspected Oilers.

For the most part, they were not front-line players and they did not include Gretzky, Messier, Kurri or Coffey.)

In looking at the dynastic years of the Oilers, the spring and summer of 1986 can be correctly identified as the turning point. These months marked a period of soul-searching and maturation. Kevin Lowe notes that what the players came to realize was that it took more than talent to win a championship. Dedication, discipline and the work ethic were equally important. The Oilers were determined to restore their reputation and reclaim the Cup.

By the late spring of the following year, one team stood in their way. Like the Oilers, the Philadelphia Flyers had also matured, after suffering the tragic loss of Pelle Lindberg, who had died in a car accident. Lindberg's replacement was Ron Hextall, a tall (6-foot-3), aggressive goaltender whose NHL debut was the most spectacular of any goalie since Ken Dryden 15 years earlier. Hextall had an amazing season, winning the Vezina Trophy in his rookie year and earning a spot on the NHL's first all-star team. Hextall's magic continued into the playoffs as his team moved closer and closer to the final and a rematch with the Oilers.

Edmonton appeared to have the series well in hand after winning the first two games at home. Back in Philadelphia, the teams split the two games, which meant the Oilers were returning to Edmonton up 3-1, with the opportunity of winning the Cup at home.

But it wasn't to be. A gutsy effort by Philadelphia extended the series and, back in Philadelphia, the Flyers won again. Suddenly, the Oilers, who seemed to have the series under control just a few days earlier, found themselves in a seventh and deciding game in the Cup final — the first time since 1971 that this had happened. All of the old questions and insecurities returned. Would the Oilers choke? Had they already choked?

Paul Coffey remembers the tension in the dressing room before the game. He was not normally a vocal presence in the room. Nor was Gretzky. Superstars rarely are. Messier wasn't a rah-rah type either, although he exerted a tremendous amount of pressure on teammates to play up to their ability. He would, for example, confront somebody after a poor effort and say, "Come on, pick it up!" That night, Coffey, a quiet and somewhat introverted young man, stood up said, "Listen, I think we should forget all about those two losses. We're in the seventh game of a Stanley Cup final. If somebody had told me that when I was a kid that I was in the seventh game of the Stanley Cup final, I would have said, 'I can't think of anything better.' Now we're in it, so let's take it to them."

That night, the Oilers went out and played what some say was the best all-round game in their history. It wasn't a blowout. No scoring records were set. But what the spectators at the Northlands Coliseum saw was a team at its peak, playing with confidence and in full control. The power, the speed, the talent and the discipline was there for everyone to see. They outchecked the Flyers, they beat them in the corners and they flew by them in open ice. Hextall did his best to hold Philadelphia in the game and the Flyers actually held a 1-0 lead for a while. But gradually the Oilers took over. Messier rammed in Edmonton's first goal. In the second, Kurri gave them the lead.

Then, in the third, the Oilers closed it down. Philadelphia could manage only two shots on goal in 20 minutes. When Glenn Anderson got Edmonton's third goal, the game was locked up. The Stanley Cup again rested in Edmonton. After the game, Mike Keenan, the Flyer coach, said, "The Oilers played a fabulous game."

If the Oilers were awesome in 1987, they were unbeatable in the spring of 1988. In reaching the Cup final, they had trounced Winnipeg and Detroit, losing only one game to each team, and they had swept Calgary. The Boston Bruins were never really in the final. They went out in four straight.

Maturity and experience had made the Oilers a devastatingly powerful team. They had won four Stanley Cups in five years. A conservative prediction would have had them winning at least two more consecutively, perhaps three. Unfortunately we did not get to see how great this team would be. In August, 1988, Pocklington traded the team's heart and soul and greatest player to Los Angeles for draft choices and players and $15 million (U.S.).

To understand the impact of the Wayne Gretzky trade on the players, the team's psyche must be understood. From the earliest days, Sather drilled into the players the importance or pride and loyalty. They were told that the Oilers operated on the same principle as the Canadiens. The work ethic was all important. If you paid your dues and played with pride, you would eventually be rewarded.

But it didn't work that way. What they did learn was that Pocklington wasn't to be trusted, that loyalty and the concept of a "team" didn't mean much to him. In Gretzky's first season, he recalled Pocklington announcing near the end of the season that each player would receive a round-trip vacation to any Club Med resort in the world if they advanced to the WHA final. Before the sixth game of the final, with the Oilers down 3-2 to Winnipeg, Pocklington visited the players in the dressing room carrying a box. "Great," thought the players, "the tickets."

But no. Instead Pocklington brought out men's bikini swim suits, waved it in front of them, and then handed one to each player, as well as a bottle of Coppertone. Gretzky wrote in his autobiography, "We were sort of blank-faced. I guess that was his idea of an inspiration to win the game, a reminder of the Club Med vacation. When he left, we all laughed so hard our guts hurt. We were so dumbfounded by this man that we went out and played the worst game of the year. Winnipeg scored on their first four shots and we were out of it. . . . Naturally we never got the tickets."

Even when the players were rewarded with a gift, there seemed to be strings attached. Coffey remembers everybody receiving a set of golf clubs one year for winning the Cup, but with the clubs came a $1,500 income-tax responsibility. The most outrageous fraud was the phoney Stanley Cup diamond rings. After the Oilers won their first championship, Pocklington gave rings to everyone, but the size of the diamond depended on how Pocklington judged the player's contribution to the team. The trainers and equipment men received tiny diamonds, those given to journeymen were a little bigger, and, so on, up to Gretzky who got the biggest.

Gretzky didn't know anything about the diminishing diamonds until then-assistant coach John Muckler told him that the hand on the diamond meter had gone the wrong way when he had his ring appraised. Muckler, assistant coach Ted Green, and all the training staff were given fake diamonds.

"Here we'd spent the last five years trying to bang through everybody's skull that we were a team . . . and Peter goes and ranks us all by carat," said Gretzky. "I was so embarrassed I took all the trainers' rings and had them done properly."

When it came to paying the players, Pocklington and Sather were tough negotiators. For years, Gretzky, the acknowledged king of the game, had a base salary considerably less than that of several players in the league, despite the Oilers consistently claiming he was making $1 million annually. Paul Coffey, whose contract dispute with Sather eventually led to his trade in November, 1987, says that the Oilers' facade of generosity quickly disappeared when a player asked for a raise. "The Oilers tried to make it look like they were treating you like kings. They gave you the best weight training equipment, you stayed at the best hotels, you had the best of everything. Except they wouldn't pay you."

When Coffey refused to report to the training camp in the fall of 1987, he was portrayed as a greedy, selfish, immature ingrate. Pocklington told the media Coffey didn't deserve the money he was seeking, because he lacked courage as a player. Alluding to a conversation with Coffey's agent, Badali, Pocklington said, "Gus asked me why I wouldn't give Paul the $800,000 a year he wants and I said he hadn't played well enough last year to deserve that kind of money. I said, that many times, he appeared to lack intestinal fortitude in games and didn't seem to have the balls to go into the corner for the puck. I realize he had a bad back and perhaps that was the reason."

The remarks infuriated Coffey, who vowed never to return to Edmonton, regardless of how much he was offered. Coffey viewed loyalty on the Oilers as a one-way street. Neither he nor Gretzky saw much of it from Pocklington or Sather. Gretzky recalled the Oilers' team captain Ron Chipperfield being traded to Quebec in March, 1980, at the NHL trading deadline while Chipperfield was away from the team visiting his terminally ill mother.

Lee Fogolin, who succeeded Chipperfield as captain, was perhaps the best-liked member of the team, a determined competitor on the ice, but a quiet, gentle man, of whom Coffey says, "He was just a good guy and a good role model for the younger players."

In 1983, Fogolin decided to pass the "C" on to Gretzky, saying, "I want the younger players to know that the veterans believe in you." In 1986-87, Fogolin made it known that would be his last season. He intended to retire, but wanted to play out the final months of his career in Edmonton. But at the trading deadline in March, Sather sent him to Buffalo along with Mark Napier for a couple of players, one of whom, Wayne Van Dorpe, played three games for Edmonton. The other, Normand Lacombe, was a fringe player. Says Coffey "I remembered seeing Lee in the dressing room the day he was traded. There were tears in his eyes. He was trying not to show it, but he was upset. I said to myself, 'This guy doesn't deserve this.'"

Coffey's relationship with Sather had deteriorated by the time of his trade. The same was true for Gretzky. For whatever reason, Gretzky and Coffey had become Sather's whipping boys. Gretzky figures it was Sather's way of showing the players that nobody was above criticism.

Still, Gretzky wasn't traded because of Sather. In was a bottom-line made by decision by Pocklington, who was fond of describing Gretzky as "a diminishing asset," because he was growing older.

Despite rumours in hockey circles, there was no real evidence that Pocklington was cash strapped in the summer of 1988 and needed the money from the Gretzky deal. During the recession of the early Eighties, Pocklington's business empire had collapsed. He had won and lost a fortune in land speculation. His trust company, Fidelity Trust, had been one of the largest in Canada, but when it went under, a federal agency, Canada Deposit Insurance Corp., was left holding a $200-million bag. The other losers were people who had owned what became worthless preferred shares of the trust company.

When his financial troubles started making headlines in 1983, Pocklington shifted his major companies from federal to Alberta registration, thereby escaping any obligation to disclose financial information.

This, coupled with Pocklington's close ties with the ruling Progressive Conservative party in Alberta, improved his business prospects. Huge provincial loans were issued to Pocklington's companies and any move against them by the government would have threatened hundreds of jobs and further embarrassed the Tories, who were already under fire for failing to protect investors in the ill-fated Principal Group Ltd. By the time of the Gretzky trade, Pocklington's empire had largely recovered. Loan payments were being honoured and further acquisitions planned. The Gretzky trade was not a move made in panic by an owner who needed quick capital. It was a cold-blooded business decision.

Nobody could have predicted the extreme reaction to the trade. A country — indeed, the entire hockey world — was stunned. Commentators decried the trade as the loss of a "national treasure." Pocklington was reviled and Gretzky's teammates were shocked. There was talk of an Oilers' strike, of the players refusing to report to training camp. Sather did his best to defuse the situation by saying the team had to put behind them their "emotions," and concentrate on the business at hand, the 1988-89 season. Nevertheless, the players started the season still numb from the events of that summer.

Craig Simpson, who was acquired from Pittsburgh in the Paul Coffey trade, says the veterans were particularly affected by the Gretzky deal. "For the older guys there was a sense of bitterness and betrayal," he said. "The team was also undergoing growing pains. Young players were being worked into the lineup and it was a difficult time."

For all intents and purposes, the Gretzky trade marked the end of the dynasty. The Oilers stayed barely above .500 in the season that followed, winning 38, losing 34 and tying eight. They finished third in their division, behind Calgary and Gretzky's team, the Kings. And in the playoffs, they departed in the first round, losing to the Kings in seven games. There would be no Cup continuum for Edmonton, no third in a row.

It was this sense of hopelessness that made the events of the following spring quite amazing. It was tantamount to a rising up from the grave, if you will, or perhaps, a last hurrah. With the departure of Gretzky, Mark Messier had assumed the leadership of the team, although many doubted he would be effective in that role. He had thrived as the Oilers' number-two man, comfortably in the shadow of the Great One, who was his best friend. How would be react to the pressure of being No. 1?

As it turned out, just fine. A year removed from the loss of Wayne, Messier was fresh and inspired. Almost by himself, he picked up the Oilers and carried them back to respectability. They finished second in the Smythe Division and Messier ended up second in the scoring race behind Gretzky.

Simpson says, "I don't think we could have pulled it out without

Mark. He held us all together. The team also came to the realization that 'Wayne's gone and there's nothing we can do about it and we had to make our own destiny.' Any time we fell back, Mark picked us up and got us back on track.

"We developed our own confidence and identity, and we grew as a team. To me, the 1989 playoffs, in which the Kings beat us, really accomplished a lot for us. We realized Wayne wasn't sitting around moping about the trade. He was leading the Kings to victories against us. So it was time for us to stop feeling sorry for ourselves."

Despite the Oilers' new sense of identity and Messier's wonderful play, few gave Edmonton much hope in the playoffs. First, they had to get out of their division, which would be difficult. After that it just got harder. And they would be without Grant Fuhr. Injuries had kept Fuhr out of the Oiler lineup for most of the year. In the playoffs they would use 23-year-old Bill Ranford.

It didn't start well for Edmonton. A surprisingly strong Winnipeg team pushed the Oilers to seven games. Next were Gretzky's Kings, who had been impressive in knocking off the Calgary Flames in six games.

But that's when it all came together for Edmonton. Ranford started playing as he never had before. In the first game, he blanked the Kings. In the second, he allowed just one goal. With a 2-0 lead in the series, the Oilers hit full stride and took the final two games from the Kings in Los Angeles. Suddenly, and most unexpectedly, the Oilers were back.

The Chicago Blackhawks presented a more difficult challenge. With Mike Keenan's move from Philadelphia to Chicago, the Blackhawks were a typical Keenan team, tough and gritty, with a combination of skilled veterans such as Denis Savard and Steve Larmer, and talented younger players, the most impressive of whom was Jeremy Roenick.

The teams split the first two games in Edmonton. Then in Chicago, the Blackhawks won to take a 2-1 lead in the series. It was in fourth game that Messier played what many believed to be the finest game of his career. In a 4-2 victory, he scored two goals of his own and assisted on the other two. He physically intimidated the Blackhawks, killed penalties and played a strong defensive game. Afterwards, the Oilers' Adam Graves said, "He took the bull by the horns. He had one of the best games I've ever seen a player have. Aside from the two goals and two assists, he must have had ten or twelve hard hits. He blocked shots, killed penalties, worked on the power play. He was unbelievable."

Messier's spectacular performance marked the turning point of the series. The Oilers won the next game in Edmonton and then returned to Chicago to trounce the Blackhawks 8-4. The Oilers were back in the final, against an old rival, Boston. As it turned out, it wasn't close. Edmonton's defensive play combined with Ranford's heroics in goal allowed the Bruins only one win. In five games, Boston could score only eight goals. On May 24, 1990, the Cup returned to the Oilers.

The afternoon of the final game, Kevin Lowe remembers he and Messier lying on their beds in Boston resting. At one point, Messier looked over and said, "Let's win this one for the G-man."

And, of course, they did. That fifth and last Cup was for the man who wasn't there. Of Gretzky, Lowe said, "He was so great, we were able to follow on his coattails for years. He took a lot of pressure off us. He showed us how to win. In our hearts, he's still part of this." During the Oiler celebration, a camera from the SportsChannel America network zoomed in on a jubilant Messier, who said, "Wayne, this one's for you."

Today, only the memories remain for most of the Oiler stars. A year later, Messier was traded to the New York Rangers. By then, Kurri had been gone for a year, first to Europe and then back to the NHL with the Kings. Glenn Anderson and Grant Fuhr were sent to the Toronto Maple Leafs. The dynasty was over and rebuilding was underway.

The players of that era have fond memories, but those memories are tinged with regret. Not for what was, but for what might have been. For those who remain, there is the loyalty and pride that Sather wanted so badly to instill in his players. But it is loyalty toward each other and for those who have left. Pocklington could not destroy what Gretzky, Coffey, Messier and the others spent almost 10 years to build. Simpson says, "I look around the dressing room and I see the stalls where those future Hall of Famers sat, and I realize it's our responsibility to carry on their tradition."

9

The Right Stuff

*T*he trail of the Stanley Cup is littered with coulda-been's, woulda-been's and never-were's. Great teams have failed to become dynasties and some wonderful players have never sipped champagne from the Cup.

For the purposes of this book, a dynasty has been defined as a team able to hold the Cup for at least three consecutive years over a period of time in which more championships may have been won. We made exceptions for two teams — the Detroit Red Wings of the Fifties and the Edmonton Oilers of the Eighties. Neither had three uninter-rupted championship years. Still, the Wings won four Stanley Cups in six years; the Oilers took home five Cups in seven years. Both were brilliant offensive machines led by a handful of superstars, but both were lacking in defensive skills and perhaps luck.

If the journey to the Stanley Cup has taught us anything, it is that a team needs more than talent to win a title. Mark Messier, who played on all five Oiler championship teams, lists four required elements: hot goaltending, team chemistry, confidence and good fortune. Denis Potvin of the New York Islanders, who won four Cups, includes on his list, discipline, the ability to play well defensively and strong special teams (the power-play unit and penalty killing).

History shows that assembling a squad of stars isn't enough. Hockey's first all-star team was probably the Renfrew Creamery Kings, or Millionaires as they were also called. They were bankrolled in 1909 by Canadian railroad and mining multi-millionaire Michael John O'Brien, who lived in the small town of Renfrew, in the Ottawa Valley. The seven-man team his son, John Ambrose, put together in 1910 was a high-priced who's who of hockey — Lester and Frank Patrick, Fred (Cyclone) Taylor, Newsy Lalonde, and Fred Whitcroft. All of these players are in the Hockey Hall of Fame along with John Ambrose as a builder. But even with that lineup, the Millionaires finished third in the newly formed National Hockey Association and never got a chance to play for the Stanley Cup.

The Toronto Maple Leafs won the Cup in 1932 and had the best record in their division for four of the next six years. In the decade of the Thirties, they went to the final seven times, more often than any other team. But they didn't win another championship until 1942. A lack of leadership from the top players, as well as Dick Irvin's coaching, has been blamed. Before his death, Ace Bailey, one of the stars of the Leafs in the early Thirties said, "We had some tremendous goal scorers and we were the finest group of players in the league. But we never played as a team well enough after 1932 to win it all. The boys forgot about their defensive responsibilities and we were out to get goals."

In the Forties, the Montreal Canadiens were the class of the NHL in terms of talent, but not when it came to success. The over-achieving Maple Leafs of that decade outplayed the Canadiens to become the NHL's first dynasty. Why? The Canadiens did not play as well defensively as Toronto, nor were they as tough as the Leafs or the Detroit Red Wings. Again, the coaching of Dick Irvin, by then with Montreal, was questioned.

At the conclusion of the 1960-61 season, the team of the future, and present, appeared to be the Chicago Black Hawks. Their starting lineup couldn't be matched by any team in the league. Glenn Hall in goal, Pierre Pilote on defence, Bobby Hull on left wing, Stan Mikita at centre and Kenny Wharram on right wing were either all-stars or future all-stars. All but Wharram are in the Hall of Fame.

But after their 1961 championship season, the Black Hawks never won again. Mikita thinks the team did not place enough emphasis on defence and lacked the depth of the Maple Leafs and the Canadiens of the Sixties.

Bobby Hull is critical of the Chicago coaching staff. He notes that he and Mikita, who were the two best forwards, never played together, which Hull thinks was a mistake. He also feels the Hawks had more than their share of bad luck, citing the seventh game of final against Montreal in 1971, when Tony Esposito let in a slapshot from Jacques Lemaire almost from centre ice. Chicago was leading 2-0 at the time, but the fluke goal motivated the Habs and they went on to win 3-2.

Another team that shoulda-been but never-was, was the Boston Bruins of the late Sixties and early Seventies. The Bruins, led by Bobby Orr and Phil Esposito, won two Stanley Cups, in 1970 and 1972, but they should have had more. Why didn't they? Esposito says he never rebounded from the emotional 1972 Summit Series with the Soviet Union. Although he had some fine seasons after 1971-1972, he could not reach the same level of intensity. For his part, Orr had trouble playing in the Montreal Forum, which was critical to the success of any team during that era. Although Orr was easily the greatest player of his time, possibly of all time, he was too often only good, instead of great, against the Canadiens. So it was Montreal, not Boston, that won championships in 1968, 1969, 1971 and 1973.

There were other reasons, of course. Outside the core group of stars, the talent on the Bruins dropped off quickly. They lost key players such as Derek Sanderson, Johnny McKenzie and goalie Gerry Cheevers to the World Hockey Association. And when it came to defence, well, they weren't really very interested. The rebuilt Boston team of the mid-to-late Seventies was competitive, but never quite good enough to go all the way.

On the flip side, there have been teams that played up to their potential, often overachieving, but just falling short of winning the magical three Stanley Cups in a row. The Ottawa Senators doubled in 1920 and 1921 and finished first in the NHL in the 1921-22 season. In a two-game series against Toronto, the Senators outplayed the St. Pats. But they couldn't beat Toronto goalie John Ross Roach and ended up losing the total-goal series, 5-4 and 0-0.

The Canadiens of the early Thirties, which included Howie Morenz and Aurel Joliat, won championships in 1930 and 1931. By 1932, however, time had run out. The New York Rangers defeated the Habs three games to one in the playoffs, and then a strong Maple Leaf team eliminated the Rangers in three straight to win the Cup.

Jack Adams' Red Wings of the Thirties flirted with greatness, winning in 1936 and 1937. But in 1937-38, they dropped to last place in the NHL's American Division and failed to even qualify for the playoffs.

In the mid-Seventies, the Philadelphia Flyers won the right to be called the NHL's finest team. Although remembered more for their gang fights and wolf packs, the Broad Street Bullies were also disciplined and defensively sound. They were led by the best goaltender in those years, Bernie Parent, as well as a handful of star players that included Bobby Clarke, Bill Barber, Reggie Leach and Rick MacLeish. The Flyers won the Stanley Cup in 1974 and 1975, and were threatening to make it three in a row. Perhaps in another time, they would have won their third Cup. But in 1976 they had the misfortune of going up against one of the great teams of any era, the Canadiens, with Guy Lafleur, Larry Robinson and Ken Dryden. In the Stanley Cup final, the Flyers fell in four. But all of the games were close. It wasn't an easy victory for the Canadiens.

Since the Forties, dynasties have dominated the NHL. First there were the Leafs, then the Red Wings in the first half of the Fifties, followed by the Canadiens in the latter half of the same decade. In the Sixties it was the Leafs again and then in the Sixties and Seventies the Canadiens. Montreal was followed in the Eighties by the New York Islanders and the Edmonton Oilers. In the pre-NHL years, hockey's finest dynasty was the Ottawa Hockey Club, better known as the Silver Seven.

Which one was the greatest?

We will start at the bottom and work our way up. The Detroit Red Wings won Cups in 1950, '52, '54, and '55. They accomplished this against some extraordinary competition — the strong Leaf teams of the early Fifties and the emerging Montreal powerhouse. During the Red Wings' dynasty, they did some amazing things. They finished first in the regular season for seven consecutive years, from 1948-49 to 1954-55, which is an NHL record. They were the first team to sweep the playoffs, the semi-finals and final, defeating Toronto and Montreal in 1952 in the minimum number of eight games. During the 1952 playoffs, the opposition failed to score a goal at the Olympia in Detroit, where Sawchuk recorded four shutouts.

But when the Red Wings stand beside the other dynasties, they fail to measure up. Although they won four Stanley Cups in six years, they could not get three in a row.

It's hard to know where to rank the Silver Seven. They played in another era and under different rules. Still, the Ottawa Hockey Club was a proud and determined team that was the first to hold the Cup for three consecutive years, four actually, if you count their challenge victories in February 1906, before they finally lost to the Montreal Wanderers in March, 1906. We rank them ahead of Detroit but behind the others.

The Maple Leafs of the Sixties are remembered fondly in Toronto for winning three straight championships from 1962 to 1964 and then coming back for a last hurrah in 1967. These triumphs did not come easily. The Leafs finished first in the regular season only once during their dynasty, in 1962-63. The following season, manager/coach Punch Imlach had to make a key trade, acquiring veterans Don McKenney and Andy Bathgate for younger players, to put the Leafs over the top in 1964. The 1967 championship was an upset, won by players with an average age of 31. Still, the Leafs won and these four Cups are significant achievements, enough to make them the best team of the Sixties. Their triple beats Montreal's twin doubles in 1965 and '66, and 1968 and '69.

One of the most colourful dynasties and, in some ways, the most tragic is the Edmonton Oilers. If the Oilers had not been dismantled by owner Peter Pocklington; that is, if the best players had not been sold for millions of dollars, they quite likely have would become the greatest team of any era. At the time of Wayne Gretzky's trade in 1988, Edmonton was at its peak. The players were mature, dedicated and by far the most talented of any group in the league. It's almost a given that they would have repeated as Cup winners in 1989. Even without Gretzky, they won in 1990. That would have given them four consecutive Cups or six in seven years. It's quite possible they would have won again in 1991, giving them five straight or seven in eight years.

But these are if's and woulda's, the stuff of late-night hot-stove discussions, because the Gretzky sale for $15 million (U.S.) ended any hope of Edmonton becoming the greatest of all the dynasties. Pocklington eventually peddled or traded his other stars. Jari Kurri fetched $1 million from Los Angeles Kings owner Bruce McNall. Mark Messier was sold to the Rangers' owner, Paramount Communications, for an amount estimated between $3 million and $5 million. Glenn Anderson and Grant Fuhr, and their considerable contracts, were traded to the Leafs. Today, despite a fine rebuilding job by Glen Sather, the Oilers are simply another good young team that may someday win another Cup.

For the title of the greatest dynasty of all time, we are left with the Leafs of the Forties, the Canadiens of the Fifties, the Canadiens of the Sixties and Seventies, and the New York Islanders.

Anybody who loves the game admires what the Leafs of the Forties accomplished. In the 1942 final against Detroit, they lost the first three games of the series, but then roared back to become the first and only team in NHL history to win the Cup final after dropping the first three games. (The Islanders also came back for a 3-0 disadvantage in 1975, but it was a quarterfinal series.)

In 1945, the Leafs weren't supposed to win against Montreal, "the greatest hockey team in history," according to the Canadiens' colourful and controversial coach Dick Irvin. Most of the Leafs' best players were away fighting in the Second World War, so coach Hap Day used, basically, two forward lines and four defencemen. Led by a young Ted Kennedy and Frank (Ulcers) McCool in goal, Toronto upset Montreal in six games.

After a surprising collapse in 1945-46, a hastily rebuilt Leaf team won three Stanley Cups in a row, and then, rebounded after an upset loss in 1950 to win one more time in 1951. In all, the team had six Stanley Cup triumphs in 10 years. They were the first in the NHL to win three consecutive Cups and the league's first dynasty. Ted Kennedy believes his team would have won five in a row, were it not for the controversial accident in the 1950 semi-final against Detroit that put Gordie Howe in the hospital. Kennedy was blamed for

Howe's injury and the attention the incident received threw the Leafs off their game, according to Kennedy. Toronto ended up losing in seven games, the deciding game of which went into overtime.

The Canadiens of the Fifties are the only team to win five straight Cups. But the Fifties dynasty must also include the 1953 team. In eight years, Montreal actually won six Cups. They were a spectacular offensive machine with a power play so devastating that a rule change was instituted in 1956-57 to allow the penalized player to return to the ice after a power-play goal was scored during a minor penalty. This was to stop the Canadiens from running up the score with the man advantage. During their reign as Cup champions from 1956 to 1960, the Habs finished first in the league four out of five times and capped their dynasty with a playoff sweep in 1960, defeating Chicago and Toronto in four games each. The Canadiens so dominated that in the five years they held the Cup, they finished each season with the highest number of goals scored and the lowest number of goals against. I rank them second among the dynasties.

The best?

The Montreal Canadiens from 1965 to 1979. In a period of 15 years, the Canadiens won 10 Stanley Cups, which is an accomplishment that compares favourably with the dynasty of any other North American professional team, from the Yankees of the Forties, Fifties and Sixties, who won 15 American League pennants and nine World Series in 18 years, to the Boston Celtics of the National Basketball Association who won 11 National Basketball Association titles in 13 years.

The Canadiens constantly evolved during their 15-year dynastic period. The character, personality and style of the team changed, as players retired or were traded, and new people took their place. But the team never became less than what it had been. Indeed, it continued to strengthen, with the best left for last — four consecutive championships from 1976 to 1979.

But this dynasty's total is more impressive than its parts. As suggested earlier, Montreal's twin doubles in the Sixties don't rank with Toronto's three straight. It should also be noted that the Canadiens of the Seventies dominated during the period when the NHL was weakened by the on-going competition for players from the rival WHA.

Of all the teams with uninterrupted championship years, we would rank the Islanders rank first. They played in a more competitive era and, when the Isles won four consecutive Stanley Cups from 1980 to 1983, they accomplished something the other dynasties did not. They won 19 consecutive playoff series. The Canadiens of the Fifties won only eight consecutive playoff series. The Canadiens of the Seventies won 13. In the pressure of playoff competition, New York made consistency its trademark.

The complete dynasties:

1. **Montreal Canadiens, 1965 to 1979. Ten Stanley Cups in 15 years, an uninterrupted string of four (1976-79).**
2. **Montreal Canadiens, 1953 to 1960. Six Stanley Cups in eight years, an uninterrupted string of five (1956-60).**
3. **New York Islanders, 1980 to 1983. Four consecutive Stanley Cups.**
4. **Toronto Maple Leafs, 1942 to 1951. Six Stanley Cups in 10 years, an uninterrupted string of three (1947-1949).**
5. **Edmonton Oilers, 1984 to 1990. Five Stanley Cups in seven years. Back-to-back championships in 1984-85 and 1987-88.**
6. **Toronto Maple Leafs, 1962 to 1967. Four Stanley Cups in six years, uninterrupted string of three (1962-64).**
7. **Ottawa Silver Seven, 1903 to 1906. Held the Stanley Cup for three years as well as two months of 1906. A total of 10 triumphs in Cup challenge series.**
8. **Detroit Red Wings, 1950 to 1955. Four Stanley Cups in six years. Back-to-back championships in 1954-55.**

A shared characteristic of all these teams is an intensely close relationship among the players. On each dynasty, friendships thrived and the players often socialized outside the workplace. In his book of sports sociology, *The Soccer Tribe,* anthropologist Desmond Morris wrote that when players become close friends, passes are more accurate and frequent. Even at the professional level, players who are friends will be more productive than players who are not.

In 1990, *Globe and Mail* columnist Al Strachan suggested that closeness on the Oilers, a team for which Strachan has shown a considerable amount of admiration, wasn't simply encouraged by management; it was demanded. He wrote: "A player joining the Oilers is expected to conform and to become a part of the crowd. He is expected to socialize with teammates off the ice, interact with teammates during the game's preparatory stages and, in general, become part of the Oiler 'family.'"

It takes more than a family, of course, to win the Cup. Messier points to luck, which can mean avoiding injuries or having the puck bounce the right way. In the seventh and deciding game of the Oilers' 1986 series against Calgary, the puck went the wrong way when Oiler defenceman Steve Smith banked a pass off Grant Fuhr's skate into the net behind him.

Still, in that game, the Oilers had plenty of time remaining in the third period to tie it, but could not. The Islanders, faced with a more daunting comeback in 1982 in the deciding game of their series against Pittsburgh, scored twice; late in the third period to tie the game, and then got the winner in overtime. If luck is about preparation meeting opportunity, then the Islanders were perhaps better prepared, and tougher mentally, for pressure situations than the Oilers.

Defence and goaltending should not be underestimated. Every Cup dynasty has had one or both elements. The Red Wings of the Fifties were not strong defensively, but, in Terry Sawchuk, they had the best goaltender in the league. Defence wasn't a priority of the Oilers either, but, like Detroit, they had the league's top stopper in Grant Fuhr.

Over the years, the Canadiens were famous for their "fire-wagon hockey," which was about speed and a smothering offensive attack. What is forgotten is that Montreal, during its glory years of the Fifties and Seventies, also had the best defence in the league and allowed the fewest number of goals against. For the Leafs of the Forties and Sixties, and the Islanders of the Eighties, defence was paramount.

But more than systems and strategies, it is the men on the ice who win the Stanley Cup. Some terrific players such as Marcel Dionne, Gilbert Perreault, Darryl Sittler, Brad Park and Norm Ullman never played on Cup winners. For others, such as Henri Richard, who holds the record for playing on 11 championship teams during his 20 years in the league, sipping champagne from the Cup was almost an annual rite of spring.

Just as some players tasted victory more than others, some were more responsible than others for bringing championships to their teams. Usually the best players make the difference. So in picking the all time Stanley Cup all-star team we are forced to choose between many of the greatest players.

At centre, the choices come down to Wayne Gretzky, Mark Messier, Jean Beliveau, Bryan Trottier and Ted Kennedy, who was not a prolific scorer, but an outstanding faceoff man and Toronto's leader during the Forties.

Gretzky is the most phenomenal scorer in the history of the league. He holds the record for most points in the playoffs, most goals in the playoffs, most assists in the playoffs, and the most points in one playoff year. He is the two-time winner of the Conn Smythe Trophy which is given to the most valuable player in the playoffs. All of this makes Gretzky a cinch for the first-team all star-spot, yes? No.

Gretzky played on four Cup teams in Edmonton. In the Oilers' first championship, he was not the key player. It was Mark Messier who was dominant throughout. He scored the most important goal of the final against the Islanders and was voted the playoff MVP. Again in 1990, Messier led the Oilers to the championship. The Conn Smythe that year went to goalie Bill Ranford, who was outstanding, but it just as easily could have been awarded to Messier.

One way of evaluating a player's performance in the playoffs is to compare his post-season productivity to his regular-season productivity. Murray Townsend did this in the April 3, 1992, edition of *The Hockey News* and discovered that Messier, over his career, has thrived under the pressure of playoff competition. Gretzky has not, at least not compared to his regular-season output.

The methodology is simple: Taking the statistics up to and including the 1990-91 NHL season and the 1991 playoffs, a player's points-per-game average in the regular season is determined and then compared with his point-per-game average in the post season. Messier, for example, averaged 1.22 points per game in the regular season. But in the playoffs his average jumped to 1.30 points, which is a difference of plus .08.

Gretzky, on the other hand, averaged 2.32 points during the regular season. But in the playoffs his average dropped to 1.99, for a difference of minus .33.

Like Gretzky, Trottier's effectiveness diminishes in the playoffs. In the regular season he averages 1.18 points per game. In the playoffs .89 points per game. Trottier has been in more playoff games than anyone except Larry Robinson, but he trails Gretzky and Messier in career points, goals and assists in the playoffs.

Beliveau played on 10 Stanley Cup championship teams in 17 years. He was the first player to win the Conn Smythe Trophy in 1965. Had the Smythe award been in existence earlier, he most certainly would have won it in 1956. That spring, he led the Canadiens to the first of their five consecutive championships. In those playoffs he ranked first in goals (12 in 10 games) and points (19). In Montreal's final game he scored the first goal and assisted on the other two as the Canadiens defeated Boston 3-1. Over his career, he had two Cup-winning goals, which ties him with six other players.

Beliveau's value to the Canadiens increased even more in the Sixties, when the Montreal teams weren't as strong. In 1965, at the age of 34, he almost singlehandedly led them to their first championship in five years. In his final year, 1970-71, he again was a tower of strength in the playoffs. He finished first in playoff assists, with 14 in 20 games, and fourth in points. In comparing Beliveau's career points production in the regular season to the playoffs, it's almost a dead heat. In the regular season, Beliveau averaged 1.08 points per game. In the playoffs he averaged 1.09 points per game, for a plus .01 ranking.

Beliveau is our choice at centre, but we want Messier, too, so he plays left wing.

On the right side, the best in the post season have been Maurice (Rocket) Richard, Gordie Howe, Jari Kurri, Guy Lafleur and Mike Bossy.

Howe set a record for points in the 1955 playoffs with 20 (nine goals and 11 assists). Twelve of those points came in the final against Montreal when he scored five goals and earned seven assists. Howe's 12 points are good for second place overall for points in Stanley Cup final, behind Gretzky who had 13 points in the 1988 final.

Kurri, Bossy and Lafleur also have posted impressive playoff numbers, but Richard, during his career, was an incredible clutch performer. In 15 years, he played on eight Stanley Cup champions. He still holds the record for the most overtime goals in the playoffs (six). He is tied with Mel (Sudden Death) Hill for the most overtime goals in one playoff year (three in 1951). He is tied with Gretzky for the most game-winning goals in the playoffs (18). Although Richard played in the tight-checking era of the Forties and Fifties, he still ranks in the top five among the all-time playoff goal scorers with 82 goals in 133 games. His points per game average is about the same in the playoffs as it is in the regular season. Howe's ratio is about equal as well.

It's a close one, but we'll take Richard over Howe for the all-star right wing position. Richard scored more important and decisive goals, and he played on eight championship teams.

On defence, the candidates are Doug Harvey, Red Kelly, Bobby Orr, Larry Robinson, Denis Potvin and Paul Coffey.

When Boston won championships in 1970 and 1972, Orr scored both Cup winners and was selected the Conn Smythe winner each year. But the Bruins underachieved in the late Sixties and early Seventies, and Orr did not skate on enough championship teams to make him our all-star. Like Orr, Doug Harvey was the best defenceman of his era and an important element of the Canadiens' success in Fifties. But Harvey did not have the impact of the high-scoring defenceman of the Seventies and Eighties.

Red Kelly was an offensive defenceman during the Fifties with the Red Wings, but his offensive production dipped considerably in the playoffs. In the regular season during Kelly's Detroit years, he averaged .56 points per game. In the playoffs it was .39 points per game.

Potvin's record speaks for itself. He was the Islanders' captain and arguably the team's best player during the New York dynasty in the Eighties. In his prime, he was the league's most dominant defenceman both offensively and as a physical presence. In all-time playoff scoring, he ranks seventh with 56 goals and 108 assists for 164 points in 185 games. That places him first among defencemen. He also leads defencemen in playoff goals and is second to Robinson, who has played six more years, in playoff assists. At the end of 1991, Robinson had 116 assists to Potvin's 108.

Potvin earns a place on defence. The other spot is between Coffey and Robinson. Coffey holds several playoff records for defencemen, including the most goals by a defenceman in one playoff year (12) and most assists (25). Both those records were set in 1985, when Coffey and Gretzky led the Oilers to their second Stanley Cup. Gretzky ended up winning the Conn Smythe Trophy that year, but many, including Gretzky, thought it should have gone to Coffey.

Robinson has enjoyed a terrific career and some of his best hockey has been played in the post-season. In 1978, he led the Canadiens to their third straight Cup with four goals and 17 assists for 21 points in 15 games. The 17 assists and 21 points were tops among all players that year, and he won the Conn Smythe Trophy. Robinson has been a better defensive player than Coffey. He further enhanced his position when he anchored the Montreal defence in their upset 1986 Cup triumph. Robinson joins Potvin on the all-star blueline.

In goal, the standouts over the years have included Turk Broda, Terry Sawchuk, Jacques Plante, Johnny Bower, Bernie Parent, Ken Dryden and Billy Smith. Any one of them is a worthy selection, but what Turk Broda of the Leafs accomplished in the Forties and early Fifties was quite remarkable. Broda looked nothing like an athlete. He had a round face and a constant weight problem. During the regular season, he was criticized for being inconsistent. But in the playoffs, the Toronto dough-boy was a rock. He was in goal for five of the Leafs six championships, the one exception being 1945, when he served in the Second World War. During the Leafs' dynasty, he led in playoff victories four times. His goals-against average was tops on five different occasions. His career average over 102 playoff games is 1.98, compared with a 2.53 during the regular season. None of the other goaltenders can match those numbers, which is why Broda is our goalie on the all-star team.

But we're not finished. This all-star team has seven players. Until 1911-12, hockey teams had a seventh man called a rover who played forward and defence. The greatest rover of them all was Frank McGee of the Silver Seven, although he also played centre. McGee set a handful of pre-NHL playoff records — most goals, 63 in 22 games, most goals in one playoff series, 15 in two games and most goals in one playoff game, 14. That's good enough for us. McGee makes the team.

The coach? Hap Day of the Leafs, whose playoff winning percentage (.613) is second only to Toe Blake (.689). Blake coached teams that were far superior in talent to the Leafs of the Forties. More than any other coach, Day got the most from his men.

The all-star team would have co-managers, Frank Selke and Sam Pollock of the Canadiens. It was Selke who built the Canadiens dynasty of the Fifties and laid the foundation for the Montreal dynasty of the Sixties and Seventies. It was Pollock's trading and drafting that made the team great.

STANLEY CUP ALL-STAR TEAM

MARK MESSIER	JEAN BELIVEAU	MAURICE RICHARD
Left wing	Centre	Right Wing

FRANK McGEE
Rover

LARRY ROBINSON	DENIS POTVIN
Defence	Defence

TURK BRODA
Goal

HAP DAY, coach
FRANK SELKE, SAM POLLOCK, managers

Six dynasties are represented on this all-star team. If these seven players could get together, Denis Potvin would find himself playing on the same team as his childhood hero Jean Beliveau. Beliveau and Rocket Richard would be reunited. Larry Robinson and Mark Messier might reminisce about the playoff battles between Montreal and Edmonton in the early Eighties. Turk Broda could rib Richard, gently, about a save he made against him in the 1947 final. Hap Day would begin teaching his style of defensive hockey. McGee would need some clarification of the rules. When he played there was no forward passing and each game was divided into two halves. But before long, this squad would be playing as a team. There would be camaraderie, dedication and pride. That's what makes a Stanley Cup champion and it is champions who build dynasties.

By the spring of 1992, many felt the NHL's dynastic period was over. In three years, three different teams had won the Stanley Cup. The defending champion Pittsburgh Penguins had been inconsistent during the 1991-92 regular season and had finished only third in the Patrick Division. By April 25, they were on the verge of elimination from the playoffs, down three games to one to the Washington Capitals.

But the Penguins, led by superstar Mario Lemieux, 20-year-old phenomenon, Jaromir Jagr, and goaltender Tom Barrasso, mounted a remarkable comeback. They won three in a row against Washington and then eliminated the favoured New York Rangers in six games. They were not to be stopped. In the minimum number of eight games, the Penguins defeated the Boston Bruins and Chicago Blackhawks to become only the fourth team in history to sweep the Stanley Cup semi-finals and final. Detroit had done it in 1952, Montreal in 1960 and the New York Islanders in 1982.

A third championship in 1993 would establish the Penguins as hockey's ninth dynasty. But will others follow? Many are skeptical. With the success of the entry draft, parity has arrived in all its egalitarian blandness. Moreover, the cost of salaries discourages the recruiting and re-signing of high-priced stars needed to build a dominant team. But whatever develops, the glory of winning the Stanley Cup will not diminish. Children will still dream of hoisting the trophy over their heads. And players will strive to reach the summit.

The End

Stanley Cup Timeline

1892

Lord Stanley of Preston, Canada's Governor General, awards a trophy for "the leading" hockey team in Canada. The Stanley Cup is designated as a challenge trophy, to be contested by any team deemed worthy by the Cup's trustees.

March, 1893

The Cup is first awarded to the Montreal Amateur Athletic Association (AAA), even though a playoff is never played.

March 22, 1894

The Montreal AAA defeats Ottawa 3-1 to win the Cup in the first challenge match.

March 14, 1903

The dynasty of the Ottawa Silver Seven begins with a challenge match victory over Rat Portage.

December 19, 1904

The Dawson City team begins a 23-day trek from the Yukon to Ottawa to challenge for the Stanley Cup.

January 16, 1905

Frank McGee scores 14 goals as the Ottawa Silver Seven defeat Dawson City 23-2 to retain the Stanley Cup. McGee sets a record for most goals scored in a playoff series (15 goals in two games).

March 17, 1906

The dynasty of the Silver Seven ends when they lose a two-game total-goal series to the Montreal Wanderers.

January, 1907

The executive of the Kenora Thistles, upset by two players on the Montreal Wanderers they deem ineligible, threatens to throw the Stanley Cup into the Lake of the Woods. Peace is restored and the Thistles win the Cup.

February, 1907

Owen McCourt, a player with Cornwall, is killed during a stick fight between players on Ottawa and Cornwall. Charges are laid, but it can't be proved who wielded the death blow, so there is no conviction. Cornwall resigns from the league and Ottawa is awarded the championship.

March 25, 1917

The Seattle Metropolitans become the first U.S. based team to win the Stanley Cup, six months prior to the formation of the National Hockey League.

March, 1918

The Toronto Arenas defeat Montreal Canadiens in the NHL's first Stanley Cup playoffs. It was a two-game total goal series. Rink rental cost $600 per game and travel expenses ran to $300 per team. The gate receipts from the home-and-home series were divided equally between the NHL's three teams: Montreal, Toronto and Ottawa (the fourth team, the Montreal Wanderers, dropped out after their arena was destroyed in a fire). The Ottawa club was entitled to verify the gate receipts from the two-game series. The Arenas went on to defeat Vancouver in a Cup challenge to become the first NHL team to win the Cup.

March, 1919

An influenza epidemic halts the final Cup series between Seattle and Montreal Canadiens. Several players become ill, including one of

Montreal's star players, Joe Hall. A few days later, Hall dies in a Seattle hospital. No championship is awarded in 1919.

March, 1925
Players for the Hamilton tigers, the top team in the NHL, demand $200 each to play in the Cup playoffs. The league suspends the players and the playoff series is awarded to the Montreal Canadiens.

April, 1926
The last Cup challenge takes place between the defending champion Victoria Cougars of the Western Hockey League and the Montreal Maroons of the NHL. Montreal wins the series and from then on, the Cup is the domain of the NHL.

April 7, 1928
When the starting goaltender for the New York Rangers gets hurt in a playoff game against the Montreal Maroons, the Maroons refuse to allow the Rangers to use a substitute. As a result, Ranger coach Lester Patrick, 44, straps on the pads and leads his team to an overtime win. The Rangers go on to win the Stanley Cup. As well, Ranger forward Frank Boucher sets a scoring record for the playoffs, with seven goals and three assists for 10 points in nine games.

November, 1928
The NHL's board of governors empowers league president Frank Calder to loan a spare goaltender from another team in the event of an injury. The club is required to compensate the team lending the goaltender $200 per game, plus travel expenses.

April 3, 1933
The second-longest game in Cup history is played between the Toronto Maple Leafs and Boston Bruins, with Kenny Doraty scoring at 4:46 of the sixth overtime period to win the game for Toronto. Overtime lasted a total of 104 minutes 16 seconds.

March 24, 1936
The longest overtime game in Cup history is played between the

Montreal Maroons and Detroit Red Wings. At 16:30 of the sixth overtime period, Modere (Mud) Bruneteau scores for Detroit. Overtime lasted a total of 116:30

April, 1936
The NHL decides that each member of the Stanley Cup winning team will receive a medal from the league. This tradition is later replaced with the presentation of a miniature version of the Stanley Cup to each member of the championship team.

1938-39
NHL increases the length of the playoff series from best of five to best of seven.

March, April, 1939
Boston's Mel (Sudden Death) Hill scores the overtime winner in three games of the Bruins' series against New York Rangers, including the seventh-game winner.

April, 1942
The Toronto Maple Leafs become the first and only team to lose the first three games of the final and then win the next four, defeating the Detroit Red Wings in seven games. This marks the beginning of the Leaf dynasty of the Forties.

March, April, 1944
Toe Blake leads the Canadiens to the Stanley Cup and sets an NHL record for points in the playoff with seven goals and 11 assists in nine games. On March 23, 1944, Maurice Richard scores all five goals for Montreal as the Canadiens defeat the Leafs 5-1. Richard shares the record for most goals in one game with Newsy Lalonde of the Canadiens (1919), Darryl Sittler of the Toronto Maple Leafs (1976), Reggie Leach of the Philadelphia Flyers (1976), and Mario Lemieux (1989).

1946-47
The NHL is given formal responsibility as trustee of the Stanley Cup.

April 16, 1949
The Leafs win their third consecutive Stanley Cup, defeating Detroit in four games.

April 23, 1950
The Detroit Red Wing dynasty begins with a final series victory over the Rangers in seven games.

April, 1952
The Detroit Red Wings become the first team to sweep the Cup semi-finals and final. Red Wing goalie Terry Sawchuk blanks the opposition on Detroit ice, registering four shutouts at the Olympia.

April, 1953
The Cleveland Barons of the American Hockey League issue a Stanley Cup challenge, but are turned down by the NHL's board of governors.

April, 1955
Gordie Howe leads the Red Wings past the Montreal Canadiens in a seven-game series and sets a record for points in the playoffs with 20 (nine goals and 11 assists) in 11 games. Detroit's victory marks their fourth Cup in six years.

April 10, 1956
The dynasty of the Montreal Canadiens begins with a victory over Detroit in the Cup final. After a record five consecutive Stanley Cups, the dynasty ends in March, 1961, when Chicago Black Hawks eliminate the Canadiens in the semi-finals.

April 22, 1962
The Toronto Maple Leaf dynasty begins with a victory over Chicago in the sixth game of the final. The Leafs win three consecutive Cups and a fourth in 1967, before the dynasty ends. In April, 1962, Chicago's Stan Mikita sets a playoff record for points with six goals and 15 assists for 21 points in 12 games.

April, 1965
Jean Beliveau is the first recipient of the Conn Smythe Trophy, which is awarded to the most valuable player of the playoffs. Until 1971, voting for the award was conducted by the NHL's board of governors. Since that time, members of the Professional Hockey Writers Association have handled the balloting.

April, 1968
With the NHL expanding to 12 teams, the playoffs now consist of a quarter-final series, as well as semi-finals and final.

May 4, 1969
The Canadiens win their fourth Cup in five years and another dynasty is underway.

April, May, 1970
Boston's Phil Espositio sets a playoff record for points with 13 goals and 14 assists for 27 points in 14 games.

May 19, 1974
The Philadelphia Flyers become the first expansion team in the league's modern era to win the Stanley Cup.

April, 1975
When the league expands to 18 teams, a preliminary round is added to the playoffs, allowing 16 teams to compete in the post-season.

May 16, 1976
The Canadiens win their first of four consecutive Stanley Cups. The dynasty ends in the 1980 quarterfinals when Minnesota defeats Montreal.

January, 1977
Before 1976-77, only those players who compete in the Stanley Cup playoffs are eligible to have their names engraved on the Cup. In January, 1977, however, the NHL changes the criteria to allow

players competing in 40 regular season games or one final series game to have their names on the Cup.

May 24, 1980

The dynasty of the New York Islanders begins with a victory in the Cup final over Philadelphia. The Islanders become the second team to win four straight championships. The dynasty ends in May, 1984. Also in 1980, the Islanders' Bryan Trottier sets a record for points in the playoffs with 12 goals and 17 assists for 29 points in 21 games.

April, May, 1981

Mike Bossy of the Islanders sets a record for points in the playoffs with 17 goals and 18 assists for 35 points in 18 games.

April, May, 1983

Wayne Gretzky of the Oilers sets a record for points in the playoffs with 12 goals and 26 assists for 38 points in 16 games. Gretzky currently holds the record (16 goals and 28 assists for 44 points in 23 games).

May 19, 1984

The dynasty of the Edmonton Oilers begins with a final series victory over the Islanders in five games. The Oilers will win back-to-back championships in 1984-85 and 1987-88.

May 6, 1988

New Jersey Devils coach Jim Schoenfeld confronts referee Don Koharski after a loss to Boston in the NHL Conference final and says, "Have another doughnut you fat pig," the result of which is a one-game suspension to Schoenfeld. On the day of the next game, the Devils obtain a court injunction blocking the suspension. Because of the injunction, NHL linesmen and referees refuse to work the game. The league is forced to use amateur officials. The dispute is resolved before the next game when Schoenfeld agrees to serve the one-game suspension.

May 24, 1988
The fourth game of the Cup final between Edmonton and Boston is halted because of a power failure at the Boston Garden. The game is replayed two days later in Edmonton.

May 26, 1990
The Oilers win their fifth Cup in seven years, defeating the Boston Bruins in four games.

April, 1992
Stanley Cup playoffs are delayed by almost two weeks because of the player's strike. The late start means the playoffs will not conclude until mid-June.

June 1, 1992
Because of the players' strike in April, the Stanley Cup playoffs conclude on the latest date in history. The Pittsburgh Penguins win their second consecutive championship and become only the fourth team to sweep the semi-finals and final, defeating Boston Bruins and Chicago Blackhawks in eight games. The Penguins also tie the league record with 11 consecutive wins, set earlier in the playoffs by Chicago.

Stanley Cup Champions

1893 Montreal Amateur Athletic Association

1894 Montreal Amateur Athletic Association

1895 Montreal Victorias (no challenger)

1896 Winnipeg Victorias (February)

1896 Montreal Victorias (December)

1897 Montreal Victorias

1898 Montreal Victorias

1899 Montreal Shamrocks

1900 Montreal Shamrocks

1901 Winnipeg Victorias

1902 Winnipeg Victorias (January)

1902 Montreal Amateur Athletic Association (March)

1903 Montreal Amateur Athletic Association (February)

1903 Ottawa Silver Seven (March)

1904 Ottawa Silver Seven

1905 Ottawa Silver Seven

1906 Ottawa Silver Seven (February)

1906 Montreal Wanderers (March)

1907 Kenora Thistles (January)

1907 Montreal Wanderers (March)

1908 Montreal Wanderers	1934 Chicago Black Hawks
1909 Ottawa Senators	1935 Montreal Maroons
1910 Montreal Wanderers	1936 Detroit Red Wings
1911 Ottawa Senators	1937 Detroit Red Wings
1912 Quebec Bulldogs	1938 Chicago Black Hawks
1913 Quebec Bulldogs	1939 Boston Bruins
1914 Toronto Blueshirts	1940 New York Rangers
1915 Vancouver Millionaires	1941 Boston Bruins
1916 Montreal Canadiens	1942 Toronto Maple Leafs
1917 Seattle Metropolitans	1943 Detroit Red Wings
1918 Toronto Arenas	1944 Montreal Canadiens
1919 No decision	1945 Toronto Maple Leafs
1920 Ottawa Senators	1946 Montreal Canadiens
1921 Ottawa Senators	1947 Toronto Maple Leafs
1922 Toronto St. Pats	1948 Toronto Maple Leafs
1923 Ottawa Senators	1949 Toronto Maple Leafs
1924 Montreal Canadiens	1950 Detroit Red Wings
1925 Victoria Cougars	1951 Toronto Maple Leafs
1926 Montreal Maroons	1952 Detroit Red Wings
1927 Ottawa Senators	1953 Montreal Canadiens
1928 New York Rangers	1954 Detroit Red Wings
1929 Boston Bruins	1955 Detroit Red Wings
1930 Montreal Canadiens	1956 Montreal Canadiens
1931 Montreal Canadiens	1957 Montreal Canadiens
1932 Toronto Maple Leafs	1958 Montreal Canadiens
1933 New York Rangers	1959 Montreal Canadiens

STANLEY CUP CHAMPIONS

1960	Montreal Canadiens	1986	Montreal Canadiens
1961	Chicago Black Hawks	1987	Edmonton Oilers
1962	Toronto Maple Leafs	1988	Edmonton Oilers
1963	Toronto Maple Leafs	1989	Calgary Flames
1964	Toronto Maple Leafs	1990	Edmonton Oilers
1965	Montreal Canadiens	1991	Pittsburgh Penguins
1966	Montreal Canadiens	1992	Pittsburgh Penguins
1967	Toronto Maple Leafs		
1968	Montreal Canadiens		
1969	Montreal Canadiens		
1970	Boston Bruins		
1971	Montreal Canadiens		
1972	Boston Bruins		
1973	Montreal Canadiens		
1974	Philadelphia Flyers		
1975	Philadelphia Flyers		
1976	Montreal Canadiens		
1977	Montreal Canadiens		
1978	Montreal Canadiens		
1979	Montreal Canadiens		
1980	New York Islanders		
1981	New York Islanders		
1982	New York Islanders		
1983	New York Islanders		
1984	Edmonton Oilers		
1985	Edmonton Oilers		

BIBLIOGRAPHY

Bossy, Mike, and Barry Meisel. *Boss: The Mike Bossy Story*. Toronto: McGraw-Hill Ryerson, 1988.

Coleman, Charles L. *The Trail of the Stanley Cup*. Toronto: National Hockey League. Vol. 1 (1966), Vol. 2 (1969), Vol. 3 (1976).

Cosentino, Frank. *The Renfrew Millionaires*. Burnstown, Ontario: General Store Publishing House Inc., 1990.

Cruise, David, and Allison Griffiths. *Net Worth*. Toronto: Viking, 1991.

Devaney, John, and Burt Goldblatt. *The Stanley Cup*. Chicago: Rand McNally & Company, 1975.

Duplacey, James, and Joseph Romain. *The Stanley Cup*. Toronto: W.H. Smith Publishers, 1989.

Duplacey, James, and Joseph Romain. *Toronto Maple Leafs: Images of Glory*. Toronto: McGraw-Hill Ryerson, 1990.

Fischler, Stan. *Rivalry: Canadiens vs. Leafs*. Toronto: McGraw-Hill Ryerson, 1991.

Fischler, Stan, and Maurice Richard. *The Flying Frenchmen*. New York: Prentice-Hall, 1971.

Fischler, Stan, and Shirley Fischler. *The Hockey Encyclopedia*. New York: MacMillan, 1983.

Fitkin, Ed. *Detroit's Big Three: Gordie Howe, Ted Lindsay, Sid Abel.* Toronto: Baxter Publishing Co., 1963.

Goyens, Chrys, and Allan Turowetz. *The Lions of Winter.* Toronto: Prentice-Hall, 1986.

Green, Gordon, and Frank Selke Sr. *Behind the Cheering.* Toronto: McClelland and Stewart, 1962.

Gretzky, Wayne, and Rick Reilly. *Gretzky.* Toronto: HarperCollins, 1991.

Houston, William. *Inside Maple Leaf Gardens: The Rise and Fall of the Toronto Maple Leafs.* Toronto: McGraw-Hill Ryerson, 1989.

Imlach, Punch, and Scott Young. *Hockey Is a Battle.* Toronto: MacMillan, 1969.

Lowe, Kevin, Stan Fischler and Shirley Fischler. *Champions.* Toronto: Prentice-Hall, 1988.

McDonald, Lanny, and Steve Simmons. *Lanny.* Toronto: McGraw-Hill Ryerson, 1987.

McFarlane, Brian. *The Story of the Stanley Cup.* Toronto: Pagurian Press, 1971.

Melady, John. *Overtime, Overdue: The Bill Barilko Story.* Trenton, Ontario: City Print, 1988.

Mouton, Claude. *The Montreal Canadiens.* Toronto: Van Nostrand Reinhold Ltd., 1980.

Orr, Frank. *The Stanley Cup: The World Series of Hockey.* Toronto: Longman Canada, 1976.

Roxborough, Henry. *The Stanley Cup Story.* Toronto: McGraw-Hill Ryerson, 1971.

Smythe, Conn, and Scott Young. *Conn Smythe.* Toronto: McClelland and Stewart, 1981.

BIBLIOGRAPHY

Vipond, Jim. *Gordie How, No. 9.* Toronto: Ryerson Press, 1968.

Young, Scott. *Hello Canada! The Life and Times of Foster Hewitt.* Toronto: Seal Books, 1985.

Young, Scott, and Astrid Young. *O'Brien: From Water Boy to One Million a Year.* Burnstown, Ontario: General Store Publishing House Inc., 1967.